Diplomatic Theory

Diplomatic Theory

A Focused Comparison Approach

Barry H. Steiner

ROWMAN & LITTLEFIELD
Lanham • Boulder • New York • London

Executive Editor: Dhara Snowden
Associate Editor: Rebecca Anastasi

Credits and acknowledgments for material borrowed from other sources, and reproduced with permission, appear on the appropriate page within the text.

Published by Rowman & Littlefield
A wholly owned subsidary of The Rowman & Littlefield Publishing Group, Inc.
4501 Forbes Boulevard, Suite 200, Lanham, Maryland 20706
www.rowman.com

Unit A, Whitacre Mews, 26-34 Stannary Street, London SE11 4AB, United Kingdom

British Library Cataloguing in Publication Information Available

Library of Congress Cataloging-in-Publication Data

Names: Steiner, Barry H. (Barry Howard), 1942- author.
Title: Diplomatic theory / Barry H. Steiner, Emeritus Professor of Political Science, California State University, Long Beach.
Description: Lanham, Maryland : Rowman & Littlefield, [2018] | Includes bibliographical references and index.
Identifiers: LCCN 2017054319 (print) | LCCN 2018002885 (ebook) | ISBN 9781442239074 (Electronic) | ISBN 9781442239050 (cloth : alk. paper) | ISBN 9781442239067 (pbk. : alk. paper)
Subjects: LCSH: Diplomatic negotiations in international disputes. | Diplomacy. | Interpersonal relations. | Conflict management.
Classification: LCC JZ6045 (ebook) | LCC JZ6045 .S744 2018 (print) | DDC 327.1/ 7—dc23
LC record available at https://lccn.loc.gov/2017054319

♾ ™ The paper used in this publication meets the minimum requirements of American National Standard for Information Sciences—Permanence of Paper for Printed Library Materials, ANSI/NISO Z39.48-1992.

Printed in the United States of America

Contents

Preface

This study, supported by more than twenty-five years of largely independent work, presents a novel understanding of diplomatic statecraft. It outlines and advocates for empirically based generalizations generated through inductive case comparisons. Though still in a preliminary stage, with a relatively modest yield, the research is presented in the hope that others will build on it.

The impetus for a diplomatic theory-building project came in 1988 from Sasson Sofer. In "Debate Revisited: Practice over Theory," Sofer wrote, "The discussion of diplomacy is somewhat marginal in international relations theory. Diplomacy 'exists' within international theory, but is rarely analyzed or extensively explored."[1] Sofer's observation, which I accepted as a challenge, prompted me to ask whether diplomacy had to remain in this "marginal" position and, if not, what could be done to provide it with theoretical respectability.

I am indebted to Alexander L. George, Hans J. Morgenthau, Thomas C. Schelling, Martin Wight, and I. William Zartman for ideas shaping this study. They would not agree with everything that is found here, however.

I have avoided identifying with any one individual or paradigm, no matter the debt I have incurred from them. The point is most vividly made in connection to Morgenthau, whose writings I first read as an undergraduate student of the late Ross N. Berkes at the University of Southern California. Professor Berkes, who taught a popular upper-division international politics course centered around Morgenthau's *Politics among Nations*, had mixed feelings when I ventured to criticize Morgenthau's assumptions. As a committed political realist, as well as a fine teacher, he was not accustomed to being challenged by his students, yet he acquiesced to my questioning. This

vii

volume's restlessness in sorting out paradigmatic thinking is rooted in my fortunate interaction with Ross Berkes.

The focused comparison method has proven an ideal vehicle for seeking diplomatic theory. Apart from what the method has yielded in the particular exercises in these pages, it has demonstrated the value of taking apart the constituent elements of diplomatic conflict management, thereby clarifying them individually and in their interrelationships. It has also lessened (though not eliminated) theorists' subjectivity, calling for case material to be examined as much as possible on its own terms.

Two chapters of this book appeared earlier in somewhat different form. Chapter 6 appeared in *International Negotiation* 14 (2009): 7–40 (published by Koninklijke Brill NV); and chapter 7 appeared in *Contemporary Security Policy* 31 (December 2010): 379–405 (published by Taylor & Francis).

Nancy St. Martin assisted at the beginning of this project by preparing my manuscripts in typed form before she insisted that I could do just as well on my own personal computer. My students and longtime teaching mission at California State University, Long Beach, helped define puzzles and provisional answers. And my development editors at Rowman & Littlefield, Marie-Claire Antoine and Dhara Snowden, provided just the right encouragement.

The Public Affairs office of the U.S. Department of State has kindly furnished for the cover of this book a photograph of American secretary of state John Kerry and Iranian foreign minister Mohammad Zarif during negotiations of the 2015 Joint Comprehensive Plan of Action on the Iran nuclear program.

Finally, my wife, JoAnn, and my twin children, Mitzi and Benjamin, were present during the creation of this text. This work is dedicated to them.

NOTE

1. Sasson Sofer, "Debate Revisited: Practice Over Theory?," *Review of International Studies* 14 (July 1988): 195–208.

List of Cases

Tables

1

Introduction

Diplomacy is standard in the practice and teaching of international relations and foreign policy. Diplomatic agents have generally been the means by which governments communicate with each other about their objectives. They have also been tasked with negotiating when governments seek agreement. These functions, as Paul Sharp has noted, have been long-lasting because they usually take place when separated groups interact. "The social character of all but the most brutal and simple of relations between groups very quickly brings diplomacy, if not diplomats, into existence," he argues. "It is diplomacy which constitutes, and diplomats . . . who produce, the international societies which put relations between separate groups on a more stable and peaceful footing than they otherwise would be."[1]

Diplomacy is also widely accepted as centrally important for how states relate to each other. "One hundred years ago," Sharp reminds us, "it was possible to maintain that diplomacy and international relations were synonymous. . . . If you understood the rules of diplomacy, both formal and tacit, then you would understand what was important to know to make sense of international relations. Those who studied international relations agreed."[2] Following the Second World War, the pioneer political realist Hans Morgenthau maintained that diplomacy was essential for "establishing the preconditions for permanent peace we call peace through accommodation."[3] Martin Wight argues that "the diplomatic system is the master-institution of international relations."[4]

Despite diplomacy's ubiquity and significance, however, the study of diplomacy has lagged in theoretical insights relative to other elements of international relations (IR). First, students of diplomacy have been much less

1

accepting of theory than have students of IR. IR textbooks routinely depend on theory as a learning and explanatory device, building on insights from such fields such as economics and psychology. One text explains that "a *theory* is a set of propositions and concepts that seeks to explain phenomena by specifying the relationships among the concepts; theory's ultimate purpose is to predict phenomena. Good theory generates groups of testable *hypotheses*: specific statements positing a particular relationship among two or more variables. By testing groups of interrelated hypotheses, theory is supported and refined, and new relationships are found that demand subsequent testing."[5] Another text accentuates the convenience rather than the logical consistency of theory, viewing it as "a kind of simplifying device that allows you to decide which facts matter and which do not. . . . Like pairs of sunglasses that can block different amounts of sunlight, a theory can limit what we see or, like magnifying glasses, help us to see things better."[6]

Students of diplomatic practice, on the other hand, are skeptical about using theory. Jean-Robert Leguey-Feilleux writes in a diplomacy text, "Despite the considerable advances made by the social sciences and by political science in particular, there is no general theory of diplomacy or theoretical framework to facilitate systematic analysis. The significant changes taking place in contemporary diplomatic practice are probably making the development of a general theory more difficult."[7] Another diplomacy text, which aims to "help students grapple with the 'diplomacy puzzle,'" only seems to add to the mystery. "There are complex empirical and intellectual developments in world politics that are challenging our understandings of diplomacy," it observes. "*Globalization* processes, including revolutionary means of communication and accessing information, are generating debate about the nature of contemporary diplomacy and whether or not traditional understandings and practices still work for managing today's issues."[8] Changes in world politics, they say, contribute to a condition of "complex diplomacy," about which theory has little or nothing to say.[9]

Changes in diplomatic conduct compound the difficulty. "Of all branches of human endeavour," Harold Nicolson wrote eighty years ago, "diplomacy is the most protean."[10] Nicolson had in mind the difficulty of capturing analytically the multifaceted character of that experience. He explained that whatever one's perspective—historical, legal, interpretive, or experiential—"always there is some element . . . which escapes reality, always there is some aspect which refuses to be recorded or defined."[11] Models of diplomacy, prerequisites to drawing out generalizations, require stable and researchable parameters. If the model's attributes are changeable, vary in significance, or are uncertain, the ability to generalize is weakened or at worst becomes impossible. Nicolson recognized the problem in the protean diplomatic experience. "Above all," he concluded, when weighing the difference between diplomatic appearances and reality, "there is the danger of mistaking actual values, of attributing to circumstances which seem significant an importance which they did not in fact possess, of underrating other circumstances, apparently trivial, which at the time acted as determinant factors."[12]

A second gap between IR and diplomacy analysts comes from a mutual disrespect for each other's theoretical needs. IR texts do not address what John Mearsheimer has termed "vagaries of diplomacy,"[13] partly because students of diplomacy themselves have lacked interest in discovering regularities and partly because, having identified structural regularities in the international system, IR theorists have not understood diplomats as agents whose choices are consequential.[14]

For their part, diplomacy texts examine diplomatic conduct in insular terms, often failing to link diplomatic phenomena with more enduring characteristics of world politics that are basic for international theory. One of these is the condition of international anarchy. As Martin Wight has argued, "international theory is the theory of survival. What for political theory is the extreme case (as revolution, or civil war) is for international theory the regular case."[15] Arguing for the significance of diplomacy in world politics, diplomacy texts do not make the case for a diplomatic "master-institution."

These differences between students of diplomacy and IR analysts are not irreconcilable, however. The former do not dismiss the possibility of reaching empirically grounded generalizations of diplomatic practice, and most of the latter are not wedded to one theoretical outlook but can and do refine their outlooks on the basis of interchange between those employing different theoretical perspectives. Both groups incorporate continuities as well as changes into their analyses; there is no a priori reason that diplomatic statecraft should be more resistant to theory than are other phenomena in international relations. Nicolson's observation about changes in diplomatic conduct does not distinguish that phenomenon from any other researchable topic, and certainly does not mean that generalizing about diplomacy is impossible. These ideas suggest that the two groups should be able to cooperate to gain better insights into diplomatic behavior and its consequences. At best, theory-building on a case comparison basis should help ensure that cooperation.

I. NATURE OF THIS STUDY

This book aims to bring diplomacy into the theoretical mainstream. I accept Nicolson's characterization of diplomacy as "protean" as a challenge in this regard. Assuming that diplomatic statecraft exhibits regularities backed by appropriate empirical data and methodology, I defend the search for those regularities. This text outlines a focused comparison method to identify regularities and shows how using that method is fruitful.

Such a method is especially attractive when theory is weak or missing.[16] It does not require a working model of diplomatic conduct. This is fortunate because the present study does not affirm any particular theoretical paradigm. It examines diplomatic behavior from many angles, with a primary interest in how states employ communication and negotiation to enhance national gains and mitigate national losses.[17] It argues that introducing a large and varied array of cases for detailed comparison supports optimism about theory-building that is lacking in Nicolson's writing. The study does not aim at new information about diplomatic behavior or at redefining the boundaries of diplomacy as a subject.

The study does, however, aim to enhance interchange between, and to reconcile, world politics and diplomacy agendas—to allow issues of diplomatic communication and negotiation to penetrate mainstream IR theoretical thinking and to permit IR theory to assist in identifying regularities in diplomatic statecraft. The two sides need to work together to enhance theory.

When they do not work together, as at present, theory can stand for the obvious, as when Kerr and Wiseman note that "by tracing . . . continuities and changes in [diplomatic] practices across time and space, we can begin to *theorize* that diplomacy concerns more than sovereign states."[18] And failure to theorize leaves research priorities unclear. Discussing diplomatic practices, another diplomacy text argues that even less important diplomatic dialogue matters. "Diplomatic talk is anything but inconsequential," they write. "Cheap talk and rhetorical strategies, for example, have major consequences for the outcomes of negotiations."[19] But if "cheap" and "valuable" talk are equally important, neither can have theoretical significance.

The next section of this chapter discusses two definitions of diplomacy, locates the definition employed in this study, and then describes how IR and diplomacy texts use these definitions differently. The chapter then considers important changes in diplomatic practice that make it more difficult to propound generalizations about diplomatic behavior. One is the movement away from cabinet diplomacy and toward diplomatic conduct as an aid for private needs. A second is the shift in national objectives away from the primacy of war-making and toward peaceful dispute management. And a third deals with the difference between deductive theorizing, the norm thus far in developing diplomatic and international theory, and the inductive approach employed here. The chapter concludes with an overview of the book's structure.

II. DEFINING DIPLOMACY AS A FIELD OF STUDY

Fifty years ago, Richard N. Rosecrance distinguished between two definitions of diplomacy, both still in use.[20] The narrower of the two, defining diplomacy as "the process by which governments, acting through official agents, communicate with one another," deals with the diplomatic aspect of foreign policy. Understood in this way, diplomatic regularities may be probed in recruitment patterns, trends in diplomatic practice, types of communication channels, modes of communication, and the balance between negotiating and nonnegotiating responsibilities of diplomats. This definition also attends to the impact of globalization and the rise of international and transnational actors in world politics upon diplomatic contacts.

Alternatively, diplomacy has been defined as "modes or techniques of foreign policy affecting the international system." In this conception, diplomatic analysis extends beyond the behavior of diplomats to the translation of policy interests to policy outcomes, bargaining and negotiation strategies, efforts to influence foreign publics, nondiplomatic contacts between governments, and the use of diplomatic leverage to affect other countries. This approach would also explore how diplomacy affects, and is affected by, linkages between nations and the character of the international system.[21]

Following the second of these definitions, the present study views diplomacy as an intangible asset and influence technique that assists in managing bilateral and international problems. Diplomacy, on this understanding, is a technique and strategy that, pursuant to national objectives, facilitates the interaction of states to deal with their common problems. It is distinct from force use strategy but shares with it an applied, calculated orientation intent on accomplishing an objective in the most efficient way. This strategic outlook, which contributes much variety to diplomatic behavior, is a key to negotiating and managing conflict.[22]

IR and diplomacy analysts acknowledge the significance of both conceptions. However, IR texts characteristically give more weight to the broader definition of diplomacy, while diplomacy texts are more wedded to the narrower definition. This difference has consequences for receptivity to theory. The narrow definition logically highlights nuances of detail and the difficulty, or even impossibility, of abstracting from those nuances. By contrast, the broad definition highlights both the need for abstraction and an optimism about its feasibility. A brief survey of IR and diplomacy texts will suffice to clarify this contrast.[23]

A. International Relations Textbooks

IR textbooks explore diplomatic communication and strategy as policy instruments of states. John T. Rourke and Mark A. Boyer view diplomacy as "applied power" and as "a far-ranging communications process, including many channels in addition to ambassadors and other such diplomats. . . . Although . . . presented here as an individual instrument of foreign policy . . . diplomacy is conducted along the scale of methods ranging from the overt use of economic and military muscle through the argumentation of skilled diplomats."[24] Karen A. Mingst and Ivan M. Arreguín-Toft likewise discuss diplomacy as translating the potential power of states into effective power. "Traditional diplomacy," they write, "entails states trying to influence the behavior of other actors by negotiating, by taking a specific action or refraining from such an action, or by conducting public diplomacy."[25]

The IR texts also associate diplomatic behavior with peaceful pursuits. Of the four texts I consulted that dwell on this theme, three discuss diplomacy and military force as alternative instruments in chapters addressed to the "State" or "Foreign Policy." In these texts, diplomacy is applied to objectives similar to those for which military force is applied, but with the aim of convincing a target country without force use.[26] One text discusses diplomacy along with other nonviolent instruments in a chapter entitled "Power, Statecraft, and the National State: The Traditional Structure" and allocates military force to a separate chapter. An American foreign policy text that narrowly defines diplomacy "in its classic sense of 'the formalized system of procedures and process by which sovereign states . . . conduct their official relations'" immediately afterward discusses diplomacy as the key element of "foreign policy strategy" enhancing the core value of peace.[27] "International Institutionalism is diplomacy's most closely associated IR '-ism,'" it writes. "International Institutionalism views world politics as 'a cultivable "garden,"'" in contrast to the Realist view of a global 'jungle.'"[28]

In this view, diplomacy as institution encourages cooperation because states and other actors communicate; when they continually interact, cooperation is their self-interest.[29] As a result, the international system becomes more ordered. "Diplomacy," Adam Watson writes, "is an organized pattern of communication and negotiation, nowadays continuous, which enables each independent government to learn what other governments want and what they object to. In a developed international society it becomes more than an instrument of communication and bargaining. It also affects its practitioners."[30]

The value of diplomatic interaction need not depend on building an international society; as we will see, "the Realist view of a global 'jungle'" attaches great importance to building world order diplomatically. Diplomacy directed to manage conflicts can reduce the chances of war and build on common interests. As such, diplomacy has *independent potential* to enhance state objectives as well as the international system, an idea that is a common theme in IR texts.

One IR text, by Walter C. Clemens Jr., goes further to build diplomatic choices into a theoretical framework focused on an environment in which the "fitness" of states or the international system is determined by the ability to manage complex challenges. The current challenge—complex interdependence—occurs in an international system more peaceful than in the past yet with a larger number of issues crowding the diplomatic agenda. It is characterized by the absence of a hierarchy of issues, many channels of communication, and an unwillingness of states to employ force against other states. In this framework, diplomatic choices will determine whether the international system is closer to a "garden" or to a "jungle." States may seek the largest relative benefits for themselves, solve a mutual problem through cooperation, or create a framework for mutual gain. They may also reject diplomacy or defect from cooperation.[31]

B. Diplomacy Texts

Most diplomacy texts acknowledge the importance of diplomatic negotiation but are mainly concerned about communication and representation. One study defines diplomacy as "the institutionalized communication among internationally recognized representatives of internationally recognized entities through which these representatives produce, manage and distribute public goods."[32] Another's focus is "the transformation of diplomatic method," which, it asserts, "involves far fewer variables than the study of the entire structure of international politics or the making of foreign policy."[33] Adjustments of diplomatists to global developments "represent attempts by international actors to meet changing needs."[34] A third text emphasizes how understanding the outlooks of diplomatists is complicated by "a gap between those who theorize diplomacy (scholars) and those who practice it (professional diplomats). Scholars tend to see the big picture without understanding the pressures of daily diplomatic life [while] diplomatic practitioners [are] often unaware of the larger picture." The gap is one reason why, in their view, students should "reflect more deeply on the uses and *limits* of theory."[35] According to Paul Sharp, the main traditions of international theory poorly understand "the operations of diplomacy and diplomats," properly the main focus of diplomatic study.[36]

Diplomatic studies do not link diplomacy with peace strategy or process. Instead, they view peace as a standard diplomatic element that emerges when separate, distinct groups wishing to have relations with each other do not wish to fight. "There can be no diplomacy when people are completely separate and, hence, unaware of one another. It is when they know each other exists that relations become possible. It is when people want those relations with one another, but also want to keep apart, that the conditions of separateness are created. . . . [T]here is very little in the way of peaceful relations of separateness without diplomacy."[37]

In practice, whether diplomacy is peaceful is determined by the policies it supports, and therefore students of diplomacy insist that "the study of diplomacy has to pay attention to policy formation."[38] "Diplomacy certainly has the general tendency—and lots of potential—for peaceful solutions of conflicts," Corneliu Bjola and Markus Kornprobst write. "But diplomacy is not always innocent. The declaration of war, for instance, is as much a diplomatic act—very much an institutionalized communicative act—as mediation and negotiation of peaceful resolution of conflicts."[39] They also direct attention to winners and losers in diplomatic outcomes that are fundamentally about *"producing, managing and distributing public goods* . . . that are important for the well-being of a community."[40]

The fundamental idea here is that ensuring peace is not primarily a diplomatic responsibility. Harold H. Saunders argues that "citizens outside as well as within governments are both instigators and resolvers of conflict," and therefore political change is likely to require public involvement. He writes that "negotiation" may mislead by suggesting that the problem is finding a way to start negotiation. Instead, "the real problem is how to start a political process that can change relationships and lead to the end of violence, to peace, and to reconciliation. The methods used in that process may or may not include negotiation."[41] For example, the Israeli-Arab peace process pushed in the 1970s by Secretary of State Henry Kissinger was designed to help governments "reshape the political environment." Formal negotiations between Israel and the Palestine Liberation Organization were made possible by dialogues that had taken place outside of official channels for decades.[42] In the Israeli-Arab peace process, governments were given the capability of leading change in popular attitudes, but publics can also pressure governments to intensify peace efforts.

The preoccupation with diplomats and their ideas, on the one hand, conflicts with the dispersion of responsibility *away* from diplomats, on the other. Students of diplomacy handle this conflict by emphasizing change in diplomatic practice, in terms of new actors, practices, and changes in traditional diplomacy, and as a consequence of broader international developments such as globalization. "We see little evidence for the claim that globalization spells the death of diplomacy," write Kerr and Weisman. "Indeed, we see evidence that diplomacy, redefined, is everywhere: public diplomacy, citizens diplomacy, sports diplomacy, city diplomacy."[43] However, the emphasis on change suggests that students of diplomacy understand their focus to be examining the impact of nondiplomatic developments on diplomacy rather than the impact of diplomacy on those developments.

III. OLD AND NEW DIPLOMACY, AND THE PURSUIT OF THEORY

Studying diplomacy using a state-centered definition of diplomatic practice appears at first glance a throwback to a much-earlier time. It fits an "old" diplomacy model, based on cabinet government, in which independent public attitudes and influences on governments did not exist and in which diplomats worked as they had traditionally, "with a broad consensus within a narrow circle," as Stephen D. Kertesz explains.[44] It was the heyday of diplomacy as "master-institution."

The old model was undermined by the end of the First World War, when the authority of diplomats was questioned and formerly elite diplomatic channels were transformed, Kertesz notes, into a "theater of diplomacy . . . part of a world context which embraces new social forces, institutions, and values, including ideology."[45] In this new environment, "the entire diplomatic profession was blamed for being unable to halt the drift towards war and strong calls to action were heard for a fundamental revision of diplomatic practices and institutions." The distinctive feature of international relations, its lack of a central authority, was ignored, as "essentials of liberal democracy" that had been applied to domestic affairs were now being applied to foreign policy.[46]

Students of international relations joined in the critique, "exclud[ing] diplomacy or [taking] for granted what it continued to accomplish, while highlighting its shortcomings. Diplomatic theory, in particular, acquired an air of obsolescence."[47] The intellectual and policy consequences of the critique diminished the incentive to engage in diplomatic theory-building, either to enhance awareness of linkages between different types of diplomatic behavior and policy outcomes or to push for changes in policy on the basis of projected diplomatic effectiveness. Neither liberal nor realist was motivated to examine diplomacy in new ways or to ask new questions about it. Diplomacy could hardly serve as a "master-institution" under these circumstances.

The "new" diplomacy blurred the division between domestic and foreign policy politics. Publics, through their influence on elected officials, used diplomatic relationships to enhance their own nongovernmental interests. Governments shared in the gains associated with diplomatic conduct with publics, and they were held responsible for losses in dispute management to nongovernmental political interests as well as to governmental entities. In addition, governments were often subject to conflicting domestic and international imperatives. Electoral and party politics significantly affected diplomatic priorities, broadening issues for diplomatic communication and negotiation.

An example of this new diplomacy is the 2016 trip taken by President Barack Obama to Vietnam. While the United States and Vietnam share security interests in relation to Chinese maritime claims in the South China Sea, private interests affect the diplomatic agenda. "Twenty years ago," according to an account by the secretary of state and two coauthors, "there were fewer than 60,000 American visitors annually to Vietnam. Today, there are nearly half a million. Twenty years ago, our bilateral trade in goods with Vietnam was only $450 million. Today, it is 100 times that. Twenty years ago, there were fewer than 1,000 Vietnamese students in the United States. Today, there are nearly 19,000."[48] Publics in this instance expect their diplomats to increase interdependence between the two countries, and that expectation affects diplomatic practitioners, who represent nongovernmental as well as governmental interests.

Does the reality of the new diplomacy overshadow or undermine theoretical study predicated on a state-centered definition? Does the gap between old and new diplomacy vitiate the pursuit of theory? Three arguments can be used to answer these questions in the negative. The first, given by Harold Nicolson a century ago, is that the difference between the old and new models of diplomacy is less significant than it appears. "The more I have considered the subject," Nicolson wrote at the end of the First World War, "the less have I come to believe in any real opposition between [the old and new diplomacy]. Diplomacy essentially is the organized system of negotiation between sovereign states. The most important factor in such organization is the element of representation—the essential necessity in any negotiator that he should be fully representative of his own sovereign at home."[49]

A second answer is driven by theoretical interests. We have noted that both of the definitions of diplomacy we have provided can be the basis for pursuing theory. But *enlarging* the scope of diplomacy as a subject must be distinguished from *narrowing* the analytical focus to study causal impacts. Some diplomacy texts equate the idea of theory with an unattainable *comprehensive* theory. As we will see, theories searching for generalizations at a more particular, limited level—such as the one being developed in this book—are more feasible. In any event, attending to causal linkages allows analysts to highlight both the newer and older dimensions of diplomatic statecraft. Theoretical analysis can test the view of diplomats as "master-institution of international relations," conforming to the traditional diplomatic role, or as depending on outside domestic or international influences, as favored by analysts sympathetic to newer "people-factor" diplomatic conduct.

The third answer highlights Hans J. Morgenthau's contribution to reviving interest in diplomacy as an instrument of peace after World War II. Morgenthau, who inaugurated political realism as an IR paradigm, took issue with the earlier devaluing of diplomacy by governments and publics and provided a framework for thinking about how states could, and indeed needed, to strengthen peace. Emphasizing the intrinsic potential of diplomatic statecraft, he argued in a backward-looking diplomatic portrait that diplomacy was as important for contemporary international peace as it was when it demonstrated—as a "master-institution"—its ability to keep peace in the century prior to the First World War. He also asserted that diplomacy was allowed to become "obsolete" and overwhelmed by "the crusading spirit of the new [popular] moral force of nationalistic universalism."[50]

Morgenthau did not advance a theory of peace, leaving it to others to detail and generalize about peace strategies. His prolific commentary about postwar American diplomatic behavior was incomplete and at times superficial because, not being privy to confidential diplomatic records, he based his assessments entirely on publicly available information. His conceptualization about diplomacy was not precise, he overrated the constraints on diplomacy, and he underrated its independence. However, the claim of one stand-alone diplomacy text that "diplomacy and diplomats stump realists" is incorrect.[51] Diplomacy and diplomats were the foundation of Morgenthau's thinking about international politics, and he provided a focus for theorizing about diplomatic statecraft.

IV. LINKING DIPLOMATIC STRATEGY WITH POLICY OBJECTIVES

The foregoing makes clear that contemporary realist and liberal international relations analysts link diplomacy with peace objectives. Morgenthau and the realists view diplomatic statecraft as necessary to prevent war in an anarchical international system characterized by weak international institutions and international law. By contrast, liberal internationalists envision the current international system as one in which "a group of states, conscious of certain common interests and common values, form a society" in which states understand they are bound by common rules and engaged in common institutions.[52] Adam Watson, who understands diplomacy in light of a "developed international society," argues that it is "an activity which even if often abused has a bias towards the resolution of conflicts. It is a function of the diplomatic dialogue to mitigate and civilize the differences between states, and if possible to reconcile them, without suppressing or ignoring them."[53]

The huge priority given by contemporary diplomats to peace-building and peace preservation can be understood through either of these paradigms. "Mediators, peacekeepers, diplomats, NGO staffs and volunteers, citizen diplomats, businesspeople, peace activists—all have put a tremendous effort into ending the world's wars," Joshua Goldstein writes. "And, more often than is generally recognized, they have succeeded."[54] Yet the goal of diplomacy to restrain violence should not be taken to mean that the diplomatic process is necessarily itself restrained. Goldstein cites a veteran peacemaker acting on behalf of the UN secretary-general as saying that "90 percent of diplomacy is a question of who blinks first."[55] Thomas C. Schelling, stressing the confrontational element in diplomacy, portrays states "continually engaged in demonstrations of resolve, tests of nerve, and explorations for understandings and misunderstandings . . . through a diplomatic process of commitment that is itself unpredictable. . . . The resulting international relations often have the character of a competition in risk-taking, characterized not so much by tests of force as by tests of nerve."[56]

Diplomatic nerve is needed to counter resistance to making accommodations that yield agreement. As Goldstein notes, "Conflicts . . . going on for a decade or more . . . are harder for diplomacy to resolve" because the antagonists are accustomed to stalemate and to block peace efforts.[57] Successful peace diplomacy, however, owes much to newer modes of diplomatic agreement. As Walter Clemens describes, these include the "Win-Win Cooperator," which aims at absolute benefits and sees agreement as a common objective, and the "Conditional Cooperator," in which the parties protect themselves against deception while taking actions to enlarge the potential for joint benefits.[58] More generally, attention to contemporary cases must focus on how diplomats have approached wars in ways leading to successful peacemaking and how their strategies have failed.

But, as diplomacy texts imply, a theoretical focus on diplomatic technique and strategy should not be wedded to the primacy of one diplomatic objective. While including the study of interstate peacemaking, it must also address how, pursuing national objectives, technique and strategy support warmaking. In fact, both realists and liberals very tentatively move beyond the primacy of peace.

Hedley Bull, acknowledging that an international system that is not an international society can exist, asks about diplomatic practice when "a sense of common [state] interests is tentative and inchoate; where the common rules perceived are vague and ill-formed, and there is doubt as to whether they are worthy of the name of rules; or where common institutions—relating to diplomatic machinery or to limitations in war—are implicit or embryonic."[59] Morgenthau goes further: he identifies a premodern period of international history in which war was a higher priority for states than peace, and therefore international society was certainly missing. "When war was the normal activity of kings," he observed, "the task of diplomacy was not to prevent it, but to bring it about at the most propitious moment. On the other hand, when nations have used diplomacy for the purpose of preventing war, they have often succeeded."[60]

Two questions are raised by these contrasting objectives: First, was diplomatic strategy different when war, rather than peace, was the key state objective? And second, does the difference between the priorities of war and peace vitiate comparative case analysis, or are there commonalities in each era that transcend those differences and suggest generalizations? Some tentative answers encourage, rather than discourage, efforts to generalize about diplomatic technique and strategy despite the shift in priorities.

In the absence of international society, diplomacy would not have been invested in building on prior cooperation.[61] Diplomatic conduct would have been more direct, less complex, more unpleasant, more governed by suspicion, and more subject to deadlock. We may assume that most diplomacy was of the "Win-Lose Hard-liner" type aimed at relative advantage.[62] Territorial objectives, with one side winning as the other loses, contributed heavily to war but were not likely to be part of the diplomatic agenda. Status questions, often a prelude to war, were discussed diplomatically at length. Garrett Mattingly writes about the diplomacy of the seventeenth century: "Whenever they came together, French and Spanish ambassadors disputed precedence, sometimes with bitter words and dangerous diplomatic gestures, sometimes with the undignified jostling of coaches, sometimes with drawn swords. Naturally the smaller powers followed suit, and the whole story of diplomacy . . . is filled with this pointless squabbling."[63]

Alliance-building was also a prelude to hostilities in this early period, but alliances were usually short-lived and undependable. Defection was common, as allies would often be offered, and would accept, greater advantages to associate with former enemies than to remain in the alliance. The potential for defection would enlarge suspicion between states and lessen the value of diplomatic communication.[64]

Yet diplomatic behavior in the premodern and modern eras is still comparable. Preventing war became more important because of the cost of close combat and immobile tactics. "When all the technical factors pushed warfare in the direction of close combat," Frank Hinsley has written of the eighteenth century, "the limited administrative and economic techniques of even the leading states—not to speak of their bankruptcy—made them prefer to avoid the pitched battles and heavy casualties which decisive action in close combat conditions necessarily entailed."[65] And as preventing war became more important, governments were likely to depend on diplomacy to achieve that objective.

Beyond this, negotiation is said to have been the "chief function" of the diplomatic representative in this early period:

> [The diplomat] was the man counted on to influence the policies, or perhaps simply the attitudes, of the government to which he was sent in a sense favorable to his own; to minimize frictions, to win concessions, to achieve co-operation (or, what was sometimes just as valuable, the appearance of co-operation), and if worst came to worst, to sound the first warning that the situation was getting out of hand, and that other pressures were required. In this game . . . all [was] subordinated to the patient stalking of objectives of high policy in a series of moves planned far ahead, yet kept flexible enough to meet any possible check or opportunity."[66]

This cursory survey suggests that negotiation between states—and the diplomatic practice entrusted to implement it—transcends the priority of achieving peace or making war. The practice of negotiating, both in premodern and in modern systems, often prevented a rupture in relations that could rule out achieving specific national objectives. Ruptures in the contemporary system would likely be perceived as costlier than they were earlier because of rising collaborative interests in the context of complex interdependence among states. Some analysts argue that contemporary international society supports newer networks of knowledge-based experts, so-called epistemological communities, assisting states in identifying interests, promoting debate about issues, and facilitating negotiation of mutual problems when common state interests are highly developed.[67] But the negotiating process remains uncertain even in international society and requires analysis on its own terms.

V. DEDUCTIVE AND INDUCTIVE INTERNATIONAL THEORY

Two types of international theory can isolate and explain diplomatic tendencies. One, derived deductively, is based on paradigms that guide the formulation of detailed generalizations that are tested against specific features of diplomatic practice. Theory is always at hand in paradigms, but challenging theory requires challenging preconceptions and beliefs that are consistent with it. Historically, this approach has predominated. A second theory-building approach is inductive, uninformed by paradigm and not guided by preexisting assumptions of state behavior. Considering cases of a specific type, the analyst using this approach constructs theory based on commonalities and differences between the cases. Much less dramatic and appreciated than the first, this is the approach employed in the present study.

A. Deductive Theory-Building

Paradigmatic deductive theory has been used to understand the "diplomatic community" as the manifestation of the international state system.[68] Its earliest manifestation was international law, but Martin Wight has argued that international theory as international law could not explain growing international cooperation. "International law," he wrote, "seems to follow an inverse movement to that of international politics. When diplomacy is violent and unscrupulous, international law soars into the regions of natural law; when diplomacy acquires a certain habit of co-operation, international law crawls in the mud of legal positivism."[69] Historically, theorists were gradually weaned away from natural law and toward positivism. Early in the seventeenth century, lawyers such as Hugo Grotius had formulated rules between nations that equated international and natural law as a set of ethical rules Christian men should support through the force of reason.[70] Lawyers later came to agree that state compliance with international law depended entirely on sovereign independence.

States ignored natural law norms,[71] and therefore divisive and belligerent diplomatic practice had a larger impact in the premodern period than unifying natural law theory did. Frank Hinsley has argued that the legal theorists lagged behind state practice when they persisted in emphasizing the collective European political system; only later did they recognize that state autonomy had come to overshadow the collective.[72] According to Hinsley, it was only in the mid-eighteenth century "that international lawyers made the transition from emphasizing Christendom, with its law between laws [that is, between territorially based municipal laws], to insisting that international law was the law between Europe's component states."[73]

Positivism, consistent with state autonomy, highlighted the uniqueness of international politics as a "state of nature"—a political system without a government. But positivism was inconsistent with the growth of state cooperation. Wight explains:

> It is curious that a theory which starts from the axiom of legal self-sufficiency . . . which sees the will of sovereign states as the exclusive source of international law, and defines international law as nothing but such rules as states have consented to—should have flourished in an age when the conception of Europe as a cultural and moral community acquired a new vigour, and the diplomatic system of the Concert maintained standards of good faith, mutual consideration and restraint higher probably than at any other time in international history.[74]

Critiquing his own paradigm by applying it to increasingly cooperative diplomatic conditions, Wight demonstrated the limits of paradigmatic thinking.

B. Inductive Theory

Avoiding paradigms, inductive theory explains diplomatic practice in much more limited fashion than does its deductive counterpart. Focused comparison, one example of inductive theory-building, seeks diversity within a sample of cases, either in case outcomes or, where outcomes are similar, in pathways by which actors manage common policy problems. Each case in the small sample is studied as unique within a framework of common questions—selected according to the interest of the analyst—to clarify variances. "It is the task of theory," Alexander George writes, outlining this focused comparison method, "to identify the many conditions and variables that affect historical outcomes and to sort out the causal patterns associated with different historical outcomes. By doing so, theory accounts for the variance in historical outcomes; it clarifies the apparent inconsistencies and contradictions among the 'lessons' of different cases by identifying the critical conditions and variables that differed from one case to the other."[75]

The focused comparison's heavy descriptive approach permits only a relatively small number of cases to be studied. The analyst can compensate somewhat for her limited case sample by being alert to the broader importance of particular cases and by highlighting cases containing policy conflicts or tensions.[76] However, since more than one type of influence is involved in these cases and their relative strengths are unclear, focused comparison analysis is not likely to support strong causal inferences.[77] The following shows how case comparisons can assist the search for generalizations about diplomatic statecraft.

Assume an analyst wishes to study diplomatic norms as an independent offset to war-making. She would choose cases in which leaders had strong incentives to make war but did not necessarily do so. The period following the French Revolution would be appropriate for studying growing tension between diplomatic and military trends—that is, conflict between pursuing diplomatic norms of collaboration with a major foreign power, on the one hand, and curtailing cooperation in favor of belligerence, on the other. During this time, states experienced growing international cooperation and reliance on diplomacy, which divided the era from the premodern period, yet also a lingering high incidence of war. Focused case comparisons would pose common questions about this issue to a sample of cases occurring in this period, with the aim of comparing the relative strength of diplomatic and military values.

The political theorist Edmund Burke, who critiqued at length British diplomatic statecraft toward the revolutionary French regime following the start of the War of the First Coalition against France in 1792, provides a window into how this conflict affected one major state.[78] Though the British government joined the alliance of Austria and Prussia against France early in 1793 and then besieged the French port of Toulon, it did not break diplomatically with the French regime, which had not made war against it. Burke, discussing diplomacy's place in world politics,[79] acknowledged diplomatic norms, referring to "the similitude through-out Europe of religion, laws, and manners,"[80] and the "body of old conventions . . . the *corps diplomatique* . . . form[ing] the digest and jurisprudence of the Christian world [i]n [which] are to be found the *usual* relations of peace and amity in Civilized Europe."[81] These norms discouraged making a diplomatic break with France.

However, Burke argued for a diplomatic break. "This pretended [French] republic is founded in crimes," he wrote, "and exists by wrong and robbery [which] far from a title to any thing, is war with mankind. To be at peace with robbery is to be an accomplice with it."[82] He also contended that diplomatic intercourse was futile because the "exterior aggrandizement of France [was the regime's] ultimate end."[83]

This example suggests that the explanatory power afforded by focused comparison is much narrower and less dramatic than deductive theory-building. It cannot be decisive, given that considerable variation would be expected in cases taking place in a revolutionary period. And it would need to be followed up with additional probes of the incentives for peace and for war. Yet the argument for such patient, undramatic work remains strong. Explanation is weaker or nonexistent without case comparisons. As Gary King and his associates note, "Good description is better than bad explanation."[84] And focused comparison avoids the difficulties encountered when using deductive international theory to explain diplomatic practice.

VI. PLAN OF THIS STUDY

The chapters of this book collectively introduce a theoretical approach to diplomatic statecraft. Chapter 2 addresses gaining a "point of view" as a preliminary step to theorizing about diplomacy. It defines a diplomatic viewpoint contrasting with theoretical paradigms set forward by Johan Galtung and the security community school of thought. Chapter 3 initiates use of the focused comparison method by testing the importance of diplomatic communication, widely assumed to be central to diplomatic conduct and technique. It does so by examining cases in which countries fail to communicate in order to see whether and how those countries' relationships are affected. Chapter 4 focuses on diplomatic technique. It attempts to see whether, as expected, allied states are likely to choose a strategy of accommodation rather than a tougher, one-sided bargaining strategy. The fifth chapter, a gateway to the balance of the study, distinguishes between diplomacy as cause and effect, a major source of theoretical linkage. The chapter distinguishes two types of cause-and-effect theorizing—reflective and manipulative—and provides examples of each. With respect to diplomacy as effect, the chapter probes the potential for adapting to rising constraints on diplomatic action.

Chapters 6 and 7 illustrate diplomacy as a causal factor in world politics. Chapter 6, "Diplomatic Mediation as an Independent Variable," examines a series of successful mediations to compare the processes and problems encountered in mediation efforts. Chapter 7, "To Arms Control or Not: Lessons of Focused Case Comparisons," examines two long-lasting armaments competitions, one with extensive arms negotiations and another without any negotiations, to explain why diplomacy figured so prominently in the former but not in the latter.

Chapter 8, dealing with diplomacy as effect, examines a series of cases in which diplomatic statecraft preferences were at odds with belligerent domestic public opinion. It probes how diplomatic officials reacted and adapted to such conflict. Finally, chapter 9, an "interim report," underscores the preliminary character of the research reported upon here and the feasibility of follow-up work. Elaborating on the way the text has sought to develop diplomatic theory, the chapter defends the study's openness to a wide variety of deductive viewpoints, examines the impact of inductive analysis on its diplomatic inquiry, and argues for the focused comparison method as a contributor to diplomatic theory-building.

NOTES

1. Paul Sharp, *Diplomatic Theory of International Relations* (Cambridge: Cambridge University Press, 2009), 11.

2. Paul Sharp, "Diplomacy in International Relations Theory and Other Disciplinary Perspectives," in *Diplomacy in a Globalizing World*, ed. Pauline Kerr and Geoffrey Wiseman (New York: Oxford University Press, 2013), 65.

3. Hans J. Morgenthau, *Politics among Nations*, 4th ed. (New York: Knopf, 1967), 519.

4. Martin Wight, *Power Politics*, ed. Hedley Bull and Carsten Holbraad (New York: Holmes & Meier, 1978), 113.

5. Karen A. Mingst and Ivan M. Arreguín-Toft, *Essentials of International Relations*, 5th ed. (New York: Norton, 2011), 68–69; emphasis in original.

6. Steven L. Lamy, John Baylis, Steve Smith, and Patricia Owens, *Introduction to Global Politics* (New York: Oxford University Press, 2011), 11, 64.

7. Jean-Robert Leguey-Feilleux, *The Dynamics of Diplomacy* (Boulder, CO: Lynne Rienner, 2009), 11.

8. Pauline Kerr and Geoffrey Wiseman, "Introduction," in Kerr and Wiseman, *Diplomacy*, 1–2; emphasis in original.

9. Geoffrey Wiseman and Pauline Kerr, "Conclusion," in Kerr and Wiseman, *Diplomacy*, 343. Wiseman and Kerr claim that their "complex diplomacy" concept "emerges inductively from the combined efforts of the books' [*sic*] authors" (ibid.).

Paul Sharp, who writes at length about theory (see Sharp, *Diplomatic Theory*), is ambivalent about its use to explain diplomatic phenomena. On one hand, he argues that the need for "good diplomacy" increases "where people live in groups that feel separate from one another and want to be so," and "good diplomatic theory of all types will be at a premium" ("Diplomacy in International Relations Theory," 51–52). On the other hand, he writes that "a sense is growing that attempts to establish the right sort of international or global order with the right sort of membership create as many problems as they solve. If this is so, then the attempts of theorists to make sense of what diplomacy and diplomats do in accordance with their respective theoretical positions on how the world is constituted and works may become less important than they are at present" (ibid., 66).

10. Harold Nicolson, *Peacemaking: 1919* (New York: Grosset & Dunlap, 1965 [1933]), 3.

11. Ibid.

12. Ibid., 4.

13. John Mearsheimer, "Disorder Restored," in *Rethinking America's Security*, ed. Graham Allison and Gregory F. Treverton (New York: Norton, 1992), 226.

14. Brian C. Rathbun complains that IR theorists have not given adequate attention to choices faced by diplomats as agents: "Reducing important outcomes to structural features beyond agents' control, such as the ability to send costly signals, prominent traditions in international relations theory have long treated diplomacy implicitly or explicitly as automatic, unproblematic, and ultimately unimportant." *Diplomacy's Value* (Ithaca, NY: Cornell University Press, 2014), 1.

15. Martin Wight, "Why Is There No International Theory?," in *Diplomatic Investigations*, ed. Herbert Butterfield and Martin Wight (London: George Allen & Unwin, 1969), 33.

16. For an earlier effort to employ the focused comparison method to study an interstate problem in which theory was lacking altogether, see Barry H. Steiner, *Collective Preventive Diplomacy* (Albany: State University of New York Press, 2004).

17. A most valuable source for diplomacy case studies is the Case Study Program of the Institute for the Study of Diplomacy, Georgetown University, accessed online at isd.georgetown.edu.

18. Introduction to essays in part 1 of Kerr and Wiseman, *Diplomacy*, 13; emphasis added.

19. Corneliu Bjola and Markus Kornprobst, *Understanding International Diplomacy* (London: Routledge, 2013), 204.

20. *International Encyclopedia of the Social Sciences*, vol. 4, edited by David L. Sills, 187–91 (New York: Macmillan and Free Press, 1968), s.v. "Diplomacy."

21. Philip M. Burgess, "Commentary," in *Instruction in Diplomacy: The Liberal Arts Approach*, ed. Smith Simpson (Philadelphia: American Academy of Political and Social Science, 1972), 158. Harold Nicolson employed the *Oxford English Dictionary* definition of diplomacy as "the management of international relations by negotiation; the methods by which these relations are adjusted and managed by ambassadors and envoys; the business or art of the diplomatist." *Diplomacy* (London, 1939), cited by Geoffrey A. Pigman in "Debates about Contemporary and Future Diplomacy," in Kerr and Wiseman, *Diplomacy*, 1, 70. Nicolson's linking of diplomacy with negotiation is also cited in Mingst and Arreguín-Toft, *Essentials*, 130; and in Bruce W. Jentleson, *American Foreign Policy*, 4th ed. (New York: Norton, 2010), 294. A compendium of studies about diplomatic practice that also discusses the evolution of diplomatic theory is *The SAGE Handbook of Diplomacy*, ed. Costas M. Constantinou, Pauline Kerr, and Paul Sharp (Los Angeles: Sage, 2010).

22. Bernard Brodie, the pioneer nuclear strategist, wrote, "Strategy is a 'how to do it' study, a guide to accomplishing something and doing it efficiently." *War and Politics* (New York: Macmillan, 1973), 452.

23. The diplomacy texts used in this survey include Kerr and Wiseman, *Diplomacy*; Leguey-Feilleux, *Dynamics of Diplomacy*; and Bjola and Kornprobst, *Understanding International Diplomacy*. The IR texts consulted include Mingst and Arreguín-Toft, *Essentials*; Lamy et al., *Introduction to Global Politics*; John T. Rourke and Mark A. Boyer, *International Politics on the World Stage*, *Brief*, 8th ed. (Boston: McGraw Hill, 2010); and Walter C. Clemens Jr., *Dynamics of International Relations*, 2nd ed. (Lanham, MD: Rowman & Littlefield, 2004). Also consulted was Jentleson, *American Foreign Policy*.

24. Rourke and Boyer, *International Politics*, 147.

25. Mingst and Arreguín-Toft, *Essentials*, 129.

26. Raymond Aron, cited in Lamy et al., *Introduction to Global Politics*, 132.

27. Jentleson, *American Foreign Policy*, 13, citing Alan K. Henrikson, "Diplomatic Method," in *Encyclopedia of U.S. Foreign Relations*, ed. Bruce W. Jentleson and Thomas G. Paterson (New York: Oxford University Press, 1997), 2:23.

28. Jentleson, *American Foreign Policy*, 13.

29. Mingst and Arreguín-Toft, *Essentials*, 79.

30. Adam Watson, *Diplomacy* (Philadelphia PA: ISHI Publications, 1986), 20.

31. Clemens, *Dynamics*, xxiii, 30ff.

32. Bjola and Kornprobst, *Understanding International Diplomacy*, 4.

33. Leguey-Feilleux, *Dynamics*, 12.

34. Ibid., 13.

35. Introduction to part 2 essays in Kerr and Wiseman, *Diplomacy*, 49; emphasis added. Contributing to the gap between scholars and diplomat practitioners, it appears, is the latter's dislike of being generalized about. As Sharp notes, "Diplomats tend not to like 'theory'—in the sense of formulating general, and often abstract, propositions, which help people explain and understand how they relate to one another and how they might do so." Sharp, "Diplomacy in International Relations Theory," 52.

36. Sharp, *Diplomatic Theory*, 9.

37. Ibid., 84, 93.

38. Bjola and Kornprobst, *Understanding International Diplomacy*, 6.

39. Ibid., 4.

40. Ibid., 5; emphasis in original.

41. Harold H. Saunders, "Prenegotiation and Circum-negotiation: Arenas of the Peace Process," in *Managing Global Chaos*, ed. Chester A. Crocker, Fen Osler Hampson, with Pamela Aall (Washington: United States Institute of Peace Press, 1996), 421.

42. Ibid., 423.

43. Wiseman and Kerr, "Conclusion," 338.

44. Stephen D. Kertesz, "Commentary," in Simpson, *Instruction in Diplomacy*, 29.

45. Ibid.

46. Bjola and Kornprobst, *Understanding International Diplomacy*, 29, citing Harold Nicolson, *The Evolution of Diplomatic Method* (London: 1988 [1954]). The distinction between old and new diplomacy is made in Wiseman and Kerr, "Conclusion," 341–42.

47. Sharp, "Diplomacy in International Relations Theory," 65–66. An appraisal of the "new diplomacy" is provided in E. L. Woodward, "The Old and New Diplomacy," *Yale Review* 36 (Spring 1947): 405–22.

48. John Kerry, John McCain, and Bob Kerrey, "Lessons and Hopes in Vietnam," *New York Times*, 24 May 2016.

49. Nicolson, *Peacemaking: 1919*, 4.

50. Morgenthau, *Politics among Nations*, 531.

51. Sharp, "Diplomacy in International Theory," 55. The Kerr and Wiseman volume speaks with two voices on realism. Summarizing one theoretical outlook on diplomacy at the end of their study ("Conclusion," 341), they write, "In the influential structural realist view of international relations, diplomacy and diplomats are generally overlooked." But the essay by Paul Sharp in this volume asserts that structural realists are concerned with diplomatic communication ("Diplomacy in International Relations Theory," 55).

52. Hedley Bull, *The Anarchical Society* (New York: Columbia University Press, 1977), 13.

53. Watson, *Diplomacy*, 20.

54. Joshua A. Goldstein, *Winning the War on War* (New York: Dutton, 2011), 178.

55. Ibid., 182.

56. Thomas C. Schelling, *Arms and Influence* (New Haven, CT: Yale University Press, 1966), 93–94; this suggests that Schelling does *not* include diplomacy among "conventions [and] traditions that restrain participation in games of nerve" (120). For the contrary view that diplomacy is an institution, see Leguey-Feilleux, *Dynamics*, 1.

57. Goldstein, *Winning the War*, 185.

58. Clemens, *Dynamics*, 35. These are presumably what Bjola and Kornprobst have in mind when noting that diplomacy is about "producing, managing and distributing public goods" (*Understanding International Diplomacy*, 5).

59. Bull, *Anarchical Society*, 15. The tentative character of common interests may have been compensated for in the premodern European system by the fact that, at that time, Europe, in the form of Latin Christendom, "still thought of itself as one society," as Garrett Mattingly points out. *Renaissance Diplomacy* (Baltimore, MD: Penguin, 1964), 16. See also below, section 5.

60. Morgenthau, *Politics among Nations*, 549. Significantly, Morgenthau made this observation only on the second to last page of his book.

61. This is in contrast to the contemporary period. As Watson has noted, "There is

today more diplomacy, and it is more complex, than ever before." Watson, *Diplomacy*, 34.

62. Clemens, *Dynamics*, 34–35.

63. Mattingly, *Renaissance Diplomacy*, 218.

64. The present writer has argued with reference to the contemporary period, by contrast, that the decision of states to defect from commitments to others "logically *requires* taking account of existing diplomatic channels." Barry H. Steiner, "Diplomacy and International Theory," *Review of International Studies* 30 (2004): 501; emphasis in original.

65. Frank H. Hinsley, *Power and the Pursuit of Peace* (Cambridge: Cambridge University Press, 1963), 179.

66. Mattingly, *Renaissance Diplomacy*, 219.

67. For example, Peter M. Haas, ed., *Knowledge, Power, and International Policy Coordination* (Columbia: University of South Carolina Press, 1997). This theme is developed in chapter 2 of this book.

68. Wight, "Why Is There No International Theory?," 22.

69. Ibid., 29.

70. Ibid., 30; Hinsley, *Power and the Pursuit of Peace*, 165.

71. Wight, "Why Is There No International Theory?," 30.

72. Hinsley, *Power and the Pursuit of Peace*, 167ff.

73. Ibid., 164.

74. Wight, "Why Is There No International Theory?," 30.

75. Alexander L. George, "Case Studies and Theory Development: The Method of Structured, Focused Comparison," in *Diplomacy: New Approaches in History, Theory, and Policy*, ed. Paul Gordon Lauren (New York: Free Press, 1979), 44. See also Gary King, Robert O. Keohane, and Sidney Verba, *Designing Social Inquiry* (Princeton: Princeton University Press, 1994), 44–45, 226–28. On Kerr and Wiseman's use of inductive reasoning, see endnote 9.

76. On heuristic case study, see George, "Case Studies and Theory Development," 52; and Alexander L. George and Andrew Bennett, *Case Studies and Theory Development in the Social Sciences* (Cambridge, MA: MIT Press, 2005), 75.

77. King, Keohane, and Verba, *Designing Social Inquiry*, 228.

78. "Three Letters . . . on the Proposals for Peace with the Regicide Directory of France," 1796, included in *The Works of the Right Honourable Edmund Burke*, vol. 4 (London: Henry G. Bohn, 1845), 331–554.

79. According to Alexander Ostrower, Burke used "diplomacy" as a collective noun, referring to a diplomatic corps. *Language, Law, and Diplomacy: A Study of Linguistic Diversity in Official International Relations and International Law*, vol. 1 (Philadelphia PA: University of Pennsylvania Press, 1965), 107.

80. Burke, "Letter I: On the Overtures of Peace," in *The Works of the Right Honourable Edmund Burke*, 399.

81. Burke, "Letter II: On the Genius and Character of the French Revolution as It regards Other Nations," in *The Works of the Right Honourable Edmund Burke*, 433; emphasis in original.

82. Burke, "Letter I," 404.

83. Burke, "Letter II," 436.

84. King, Keohane, and Verba, *Designing Social Inquiry*, 45.

2

Toward a Diplomatic Viewpoint

The historian John Lewis Gaddis recalls how one of his articles was turned down by a major IR journal on the grounds that he indulged in "paradigm pluralism." "Not allowed," the reviewer's report said. "You can only have one paradigm at a time."[1] Gaddis responded that a plurality of paradigms might converge to bring a closer fit between representation and reality, even a common point of truth. But plural approaches may be justified even if convergence does not result. Stephen M. Walt asserts that "members of the security studies profession should actively strive to retain the intellectual and methodological diversity of our field."[2]

This chapter adds to diversity in two ways. First, it introduces a conceptual framework that supports the work of subjecting diplomatic behavior to theoretical inquiry. The framework facilitates raising questions that stimulate case-based analysis. It identifies a distinctive perspective about diplomatic statecraft, yet is open to its protean character. The justification for this exercise is that a point of view must guide efforts at generalization. Other perspectives yield valuable insights about diplomatic issues and behaviors, as we will see, but the framework introduced here provides a unified focus, identifies diplomatic issues missed by other viewpoints, and builds where appropriate on those other viewpoints.[3]

The framework, applied to diplomatic conflict management and resolution, highlights two distinctions: between diplomatic statecraft as an independent variable and as a dependent variable, and between contestation and negotiation as diplomatic strategies. Diplomacy is independent when it has causal importance, a development affirmed by comparing its impact with contrary forces in such environments as crisis management and third-party mediation.

Diplomacy is dependent when it responds or adjusts to other causal influences, such as domestic political pressures or initiatives from the international environment.[4] Diplomatic contestation seeks relative advantages, while negotiation identifies bases for mutual accommodation.[5]

The chapter also contributes to diversity by providing a preliminary test of the logic and focus of its framework against two established approaches: peace studies literature, represented in the writing of Johan Galtung, and security community literature, pioneered by Karl Deutsch and strongly revived in the last fifteen years by Emanuel Adler and others. Both of these approaches emphasize that (1) peace is not enforceable but emanates from the social solidarity and common needs of peoples; and (2) regional networks and associations are indispensable in resolving conflicts and preventing war. The Galtung school of thought focuses on managing continuing and often intractable conflict between and within states, while the security community school addresses transnational and interstate interactions that produce new solidarities and durable governance structures. This "paradigm encounter" validates the diplomatic framework, but, by making explicit the divergences and commonalities with the other approaches, it also displays the framework's strengths and weaknesses.

The chapter begins by elaborating the diplomatic viewpoint. Then, after a brief summary of the Galtung and security community approaches, those approaches are subjected to the diplomatic viewpoint, highlighting aspects of those approaches that fit diplomatic viewpoint concepts and critiquing those approaches from that same vantage point. A concluding section summarizes what has been learned.

I. THE DIPLOMATIC POINT OF VIEW

The diplomatic point of view addresses diplomacy as independent variable, as dependent variable, and as strategy. Underlying these three dimensions is the definition of diplomacy as the pursuit of state interests by official agents through communication and the exchange of information between states.[6] Diplomacy is distinct from particular state objectives, from foreign policy more generally, from strategic conception, and from the outcome or impact of diplomatic initiatives.[7]

Independent diplomacy is rooted in the autonomous pursuit of statecraft by political executives seeking a basis of accommodation with other states. It presumes concentrated power and authority by executive leaders, whose impact, in the form of "diplomatic potential" or "diplomacy as capability," can be measured. It must be understood in light of contrary tendencies that interfere or challenge diplomatic pursuits. Thus, Martin Wight understands as the task of diplomacy "to circumvent the occasions of war, and to extend the series of circumvented occasions; to drive the automobile of state along a one-way track, against head-on traffic, past infinitely recurring precipices."[8] The diplomatic search for accommodation may be greatly handicapped or even overwhelmed by contrary tendencies (such as war preparations or mistrust), but it is also capable of anticipating and sidestepping those tendencies to enhance the chances of diplomatic success.

Government-to-government diplomatic undertakings can be pressured or impeded by nondiplomatic developments, such as public opinion, ideology, or weapons innovation. These other developments constrain or limit what is diplomatically feasible. For example, realists nostalgic for autonomous state actors in the classical diplomatic period have lamented the loss of diplomatic flexibility in democratic political systems.[9] Ideological conflict polarizes states and interferes with the search for diplomatic accommodation. Arms racing, which makes attaining military security more difficult, shapes and interferes with diplomatic efforts at arms limitation. Executive officials and diplomats may adapt to constraints, shifting diplomatic activity in strategy or tactics to protect and preserve diplomatic functions or requirements. Harold Nicolson, characterizing diplomacy as the most "protean" of human endeavors, appears to have had diplomatic adaptation in mind.[10]

Diplomatic strategy is employed to seek national objectives. A strategy of contestation entails a tough bargaining position that seeks a result superior to that gained by other states. A second strategy, negotiation, approaches diplomacy as a mutual problem-solving exercise entailing considerable cooperation between states. A diplomatic point of view defines contexts in which one or the other strategy is more expected and then studies cases of a particular type to inquire whether the expectation is warranted. For example, diplomacy between allies would be expected to highlight negotiation rather than contestation; diplomacy between adversaries would tend to emphasize contestation. To focus on the choice of strategy, cases of a common type—such as alliances and polarized antagonisms—are selected.

Table 2.1 summarizes the threefold framework described here. We now apply this framework to the Galtung and security communities literature.

II. THE GALTUNG PEACE APPROACH[11]

The Galtung approach is based on a categorically strong commitment to peace between countries in conflict. Peoples and countries must aspire to "positive" or "transformational" peace that transcends and heals conflict, and

Table 2.1.   The Diplomatic Viewpoint

1. Independent Diplomacy
   A. Autonomous behavior
   B. Uphill effort
   C. Conflicting effects affect achievements

2. Dependent Diplomacy
   A. Constraints or limits from a variety of sources on executive statecraft
   B. Adaptation to constraints

3. Diplomatic Strategy
   A. Contestation—the search for diplomatic advantage
   B. Negotiation—the search for diplomatic accommodation

not merely "negative" peace, the absence of violence. When parties fail to cope with conflict in a manner that transforms the parties, their relationships erode. "Conflict is a synonym for violence," Galtung has written. "Conflict arises when there are incompatible goals, 'issues,' contradictions; as human as life itself. If the conflict is sufficiently deep and not resolved or transformed, then it may enter a violent phase. *Conflicts cannot be prevented; but violence can be prevented.* Conflict energy can be channeled in positive, nonviolent, constructive, transforming directions. That is our task."[12]

Galtung would not exclude any intervention aimed at defusing conflict. The least desirable—though sometimes necessary—peace efforts create situations of "negative peace"—as two of his associates termed them, "war-provoking 'peaces' "—in which disputes conducive to war are not settled and can fester.[13] Peace treaties managed by the imposition of superior power (as in the treaties concluding the First World War) are examples of "negative peace." To have lasting importance, peace efforts should aim at settling disputes conducive to war. Peace transcending conflict—"positive peace"—is aimed at people rather than at states and elites. It requires "broad social involvement in building peace" using divergent viewpoints and maximizing inclusiveness.[14]

"Only when dialogue, as the foundation upon which peace is to be built, is brought together with *peace theory* and *peace action* . . . does an authentic peace process develop," Galtung's collaborators write. "Dialogue (between parties, between parties and an outside mediator, conflict worker, peace worker . . . and between actors and parties at all levels . . .) + theory (creativity, capacity to come up with 'solutions'/alternatives/ideas for transforming the conflict . . .) + action (listening, empowerment of peace actors . . .) = *peace praxis*. What is crucial is *process*: how, where, when, why, and who/

what. What is needed: *to start!*"[15] Such a peace process rejects superior force or coercion as an instrument and aims at peace by peaceful means. "*Conflict and peace*, in theory and practice," Galtung writes in emphasizing the importance of process, "are about improving the quality of the relation [between conflicting entities], by such means as peaceful conflict transformation, conciliation, cooperation for mutual and equal benefit, and harmony. All of them [are] relations."[16]

A. Diplomacy as Independent Value

Galtung is ambivalent about statecraft. Because the effects of force are horrendous, he supports autonomous government-to-government diplomacy when stopping violence is urgent. "Where [governmental] mediation (when successful) is useful," his collaborators write, "is in bringing an end to fighting, a clarification of the positions and interests of both sides and the necessity to go beyond conflict as a destructive and damaging relationship."[17] As Galtung himself put it in 2012, "*Peace, at least negative, is the normal human condition.*"[18] On the other hand, the Galtung approach criticizes such diplomacy for not addressing structures and cultures that cause conflict and war. For example, the Oslo Accords between Israel and the Palestinian National Authority "did not deal with any of the questions most relevant to [their] conflict, or the underlying structures and mindsets behind it."[19] It contributed to "*meta-conflict*, about winning, only one outcome, one party prevails," as when the Oslo agreement "transformed [the 'peace process'] into a cover for continued expansion and expropriation of land and denial of even the most basic human rights to the Palestinian people."[20]

A diplomatic viewpoint takes note of other costs in imposing peace. First, diplomatic urgency does not invariably make for rapid or successful diplomatic action in civil strife, where intrastate violence is very intense. Small powers will have much to say about the impact of great power diplomacy. In ethnic conflict, according to I. William Zartman, "governments are loath to regard external intervention of any kind as friendly—all the more so because mediatory intervention necessarily implies some compromise on part of the government (as well as the dissidents) and some criticism of government practices."[21] In what is being characterized at present as "a painstakingly assembled peace process" developed by a number of states "with deep stakes" in the five-year-old Syrian civil war, the opening of cease-fire discussions has been delayed by how the Syrian opposition is to be represented, and the United Nations mediator thought confidence-building measures should precede a cease-fire.[22] In a prolonged, slow-moving prenegotiation phase, conflicts between state intervenors can overshadow issues of how to end the fighting.

Second, the strongest states generally prefer to promote international order by seeking, on their own as well as with lesser powers, to generate a durable peace process for divided small states.[23] However, the cooperation of great powers indispensable to imposing peace may have to be obtained slowly and painstakingly. When deadlock prevents the major states from acting collectively (as in the current Syrian civil war and in the Bosnian civil war of the 1990s), they will often act unilaterally to demonstrate their stake in a conflict as a precursor to acting collectively.

The diplomatic viewpoint studies how the great power relationship evolves from deadlock to cooperation, and from cooperation to responsible action. The major states are not likely to retreat from international responsibility after having acted in concert, such as when arranging cease-fires between small-power antagonists. The so-called Minsk accords following Russian-assisted rebellion in Eastern Ukraine are regarded as a success in curbing fighting between Ukrainian separatists and proregime militias, but now the interveners—initially European leaders but later also the United States—are attending to humanitarian, economic, and political arrangements for the disputed Eastern Ukraine area to ensure that the cease-fire endures.[24]

B. Dependent Diplomacy

Galtung incorporates dependent diplomacy when he envisions a far more dangerous international system than now exists, one in which, because of international pressures, governments cannot protect their inhabitants against violence. In such a case there would be tension between the *reality* of negative peace and *aspirations* for positive peace. Diplomatic statecraft would reflect international pressures on national governments calling forth strong defense postures, while, at the same time, publics demand positive peace.

A positive peace process is independent of state involvement and government-to-government diplomacy, but it presupposes protection against violence that the state ordinarily provides. By reducing popular insecurity, the state *allows* creative peace dialogue to emerge and proceed.[25] However, Galtung also treats negative peace as a variable: "The less unreconciled trauma and unresolved conflict, the more solid the negative peace."[26]

But making negative peace presents governments with a dilemma: to resolve conflict they are likely to aim at moderates more sympathetic to peace than at extremists, yet by doing so they ignore hard-line spoilers who are most willing and able to undermine peace agreements. This was a problem, for example, in the aftermath of the Oslo Accords between Israel and the

Palestinian Authority, when hard-liners assassinated the Israeli prime minister and led to an upsurge in terrorism. This, in turn, led to a right-wing Israeli government that "threatened to destroy the entire [peace] process."[27] Negative peace was weakened, and positive peace could not be obtained.

A greater weakness in negative peace is that all governments form part of what Galtung characterized as the "war system . . . based on a faultline between governments and people, with death as a likely outcome; with other governments or one's own as perpetrator."[28] The "war system faultline" undermines negative peace by encouraging very competitive diplomacy, based on each state's need for extreme vigilance about the intentions and capabilities of other states. The diplomacy is linked to preventive war and war preparations as instruments to gain maximum advantage over other states.[29] There is historical precedent for the international system affecting statecraft in this way; prior to the Napoleonic Wars, statecraft was employed primarily as a war tool rather than as an instrument to prevent war, as it is currently used.[30] But states whose diplomacy was historically shaped by the war system contained politically insignificant publics. In Galtung's conception, contemporary state leaders are pulled in opposite directions over the priority they should give to war and war preparation.

The result is a double statecraft dependency in which international and domestic pressures on diplomacy are themselves in conflict, creating a second dilemma. If statecraft defends peace interests, it becomes vulnerable to foreign state behavior; if it defends war values, it will be attacked at home. Tragically, in each instance negative peace is weakened and positive peace becomes more remote.

C. Diplomatic Strategy

Galtung defined negotiation in 2012 as "struggle by violent verbal means . . . continuation of war by verbal means."[31] That is, though intended to promote agreement, diplomacy intensifies the conflict between states and poses a desire to prevail more than to accommodate. It cannot move beyond negative peace. Galtung describes the setting of diplomatic negotiation: "Two parties, diplomats dressed alike, opposed across tables, paid to promote national interests—not the same as peace—trained in verbal skills to negotiate ratifiable treaties, with rules defining beginning and end of the process."[32]

A diplomatic viewpoint finds Galtung's understanding of diplomacy as antagonistic too narrow. Even when state relations are hostile, antagonists would not be likely to practice only a strategy of diplomatic contestation, especially if they are looking to prevent hostilities. Where the danger of war is high and antagonists wish to reduce war risks, they may settle, as in the

Cuban missile crisis, for a "least effort" agreement that could be reached quickly.[33] Galtung himself is optimistic about coping with conflict and accentuates the prevalence of peace: "Consider a world with 10 states, 45 dyads and a year with war in two dyads, one state in both. A 'belligerent year'? It was 43/45 = 96% peaceful, and we may learn more from the 43 peaces about what kept them at peace, even if only negative than from the 2 wars."[34] Some peace dyads are likely to be explained by the ability of even hostile states to practice accommodation, and if antagonistic states can practice accommodation, allies should rely on it even more.[35]

Galtung may have characterized diplomacy as "violent verbal means" not because he understood diplomacy as mostly antagonistic, but because of his desire to accentuate the weaknesses of negative peace, and particularly of an imposed negative peace. For example, the coercive diplomatic strategy used by the major powers to end the 1990s civil war in Bosnia-Herzegovina, entailing "imposition of 'great power' *diktat*," brought on by NATO air strikes against Serbian positions (1995), ignored other policy prescription alternatives and instead laid the foundations for a " 'Cold War' peace which ended fighting by placing a layer of concrete, in the form of NATO troops, upon otherwise unresolved conflicts and traumas."[36] It is well-known, furthermore, that diplomatic statecraft supports objectives that weaken peace. "Rhetoric and appeals aside," an associate of Galtung has written, "the very powers which most often claim to stand for peace and justice in the world are often those in violation of them."[37]

In response, the diplomatic viewpoint would separate the choice of diplomatic *strategy* from the foreign policy *objectives* that diplomacy is intended to support. To be sure, more ambitious objectives are likely to lead to larger interstate disputes and to greater contestation. However, the choice of strategy should not be appraised by whether objectives are peaceable; diplomatic analysis must instead compare the incentives to choose alternative diplomatic strategies and the feasibility of using those strategies to attain given national objectives.

At one time, Galtung studied diplomatic statecraft in detail. Addressing at one point the means-serving aspect of diplomatic statecraft, he wrote that bilateral, nonantagonistic diplomatic practice was in decline and that newer sources of information and of interstate conduct would undercut the diplomatic generalist. "Bilateral, government-to-government diplomacy will be considerably reduced, and mainly be used between antagonists," he wrote in 1965, suggesting it would be replaced by multilateral diplomacy, consular services, and "internationalization of news communication."[38]

Yet accommodative strategies have at least an equal claim to state priority as strategies of contestation, and if peoples can accommodate in positive peace, so also can states accommodate in negative peace. Instead, Galtung may have emphasized diplomatic antagonism because he felt diplomacy was most *consequential* for antagonistic state relationships. Alternatively, his idea that diplomacy between antagonists has residual importance is linked to the difficulties and necessity of maintaining negative peace. According to this interpretation, Galtung critiqued negative peace in relation to positive peace but touted it in relation to diplomacy. Authoritative and secure communication channels would especially be needed to manage interstate crises. But a diplomatic viewpoint would argue that proliferating alternative forms of communication *increase* the utility of diplomatic channels even in noncrisis environments, as governments find it harder to obtain from the plethora of information available to them reliable indicators of the intentions of other states as well as methods of signaling their intentions to them.

Table 2.2 summarizes the views of the Galtung school and the diplomatic viewpoint on the threefold diplomatic framework outlined earlier.

III. SECURITY COMMUNITIES[39]

Security communities have three characteristics: (1) shared identities and values; (2) many-sided direct relations, including face-to-face encounters; and

Table 2.2.   The Galtung-Diplomatic Viewpoint Encounter

	Galtung	*Diplomatic view response*
1. Independent Diplomacy	A. Diplomacy is related to negative peace	A. Impediments to gaining negative peace
	B. Diplomacy is unrelated to positive peace	B. The responsibility of great power statecraft is to gain negative peace
	C. Positive peace requires cessation of the use of force (negative peace)	
2. Dependent Diplomacy	A. The war system	A. The realities of negative peace clash with aspirations for positive peace
		B. Diplomatic statecraft is doubly constrained.
3. Diplomatic Strategy	A. "Violent verbal means" suggests contestation.	A. Accommodation (negotiation) should not be neglected.
	B. Antagonism as residual diplomacy	B. Distinguish interests from diplomatic strategies.

(3) long-term reciprocity responses and altruism between community members.[40] They arise when governments cope with the conflict-causing effects of increasing transactions.[41] While relatively rare,[42] a security community was regarded by Deutsch and others as a highly significant integrator of states and peoples that was often overlooked by studies of interstate conflict.

Karl Deutsch and his associates initially employed the North Atlantic alliance area as a prototype security community. "For the first time in history," Deutsch wrote in 1968, "war within Western Europe is being looked upon by its governments and peoples as illegitimate and improbable, and as not worth preparing for in any major way. In this sense, Western Europe has become a security community."[43] Political leadership has an important role in creating a security community. "For Deutsch," Amitav Acharya explains, "a security community is the end product, or terminal condition, of a process of integration which is driven by the need to cope with the conflict-causing effects of increased transactions. The growing volume and range of transactions—political, cultural, or economic—increase the opportunities for possible violent conflict among actors."[44] Transactions also create the potential for common kinship and experiences that unify formerly disparate peoples into national groupings. "From 1913 to about 1957," according to Deutsch, illustrating this point, "there had been a trend toward the structural integration of the economic and social fabric of Western Europe, as shown by the growing proportions of cross-boundary trade, mail correspondence, travel and university attendance within the area." However, he found that this objective trend was halted after 1957, raising doubts about the future of European regional identity and integration.[45]

In the last twenty years there have been two important changes in the security community research agenda. One is the identification of security-building in other areas. The relationship between the United States and Israel has been conceptualized as a noncontiguous security community.[46] And regions that are not security communities have been identified as building security community. For example, the continent-wide Organization for Security and Cooperation in Europe (OSCE), not yet a security community, is said to form a new model of "comprehensive," "indivisible," and "cooperative" security that is linked to peaceful change, including the peaceful end of cold war.[47]

A second change is methodological. Deutsch deemphasized the role of elites in community-building, stressing instead broader shifts in attitudes, the development of common definitions of needs and outlooks, and the overcoming of racial and ethnic differences as the primary basis for community.[48] Contemporary analysts are much more concerned with elites as agents of

political change. "While communication between peoples, learning processes, and the thickening of the social environment plays a crucial role in the
evolution of political communities," Emanuel Adler and Michael Barnett
write, "these are but propensities until agents transform them into political
reality through institutional and political power."[49]

A related change is an emphasis on the state and its security interests.
Deutsch and his followers downplayed security issues, believing that large
security burdens weakened security communities.[50] For their part, Adler and
Barnett write, "To make the connection between growing transnational networks and transformations in security practices requires taking state power
seriously. . . . The issue at hand . . . is to focus on state power without
overshadowing the presence of transnational forces that might encourage
states to adopt a different security architecture."[51] Acharya points out, for
example, that the Association of Southeast Asian Nations (ASEAN) member-
country elites earlier used nationalism against colonial rulers to consolidate
their rule, and they later directed security perceptions inward, giving higher
priority to preventing intrastate war than to forestalling external threats.
"Communities can be constructed," he concludes, "even in the absence of
cultural similarities or economic transactions between groups through the
creation and manipulation of norms, institutions, symbols, and practices that
significantly reduce the likelihood of conflictual behavior."[52] Since norms of
peace can be significant even in the absence of social and economic integration, the security community focus should be on those norms and not on how
they originated.[53]

A. Independent Diplomacy

Independent diplomatic statecraft can be significant—although modest and
undramatic—early in the process of building security communities. According to Adler and Barnett, diplomacy appears to be most independent as an
initiative that emerges early in the political association across political
boundaries, before security community is even an objective. At that stage,
"governments . . . begin to consider how they might coordinate their relations
in order to: increase their mutual security; lower the transaction costs associated with their exchanges; and/or encourage further exchanges and interactions. Accordingly, we expect to see various diplomatic, bilateral, multilateral
exchanges, something akin to 'search' missions, that are designed to determine the level and extent of cooperation that might be achieved."[54]

As associations mature, diplomacy tends to be less independent, as more
channels of communication and more constraints on diplomacy develop.
Diplomacy is envisioned by security community analysts as reinforcing, not

interrupting, normative changes in interstate association. Acharya, for example, notes that multilateralism in ASEAN, a practice originating for the members with the negotiation of ASEAN itself, "serves as a social and psychological barrier to extreme behavior," although members customarily use bilateral channels to deal with their disputes. Norms of behavior include "strict non-interference" in members' internal affairs and commitment to the pacific settlement of disputes. Consensus and regional autonomy also comprise part of ASEAN's "collective identity."[55]

A diplomatic point of view allows not only for diplomatic reinforcement of regional norms but also for diplomatic *challenges* to them. In the security community framework, a military alliance such as NATO can help develop a security community. "A core state or coalition of states is a likely facilitator and stabilizer" of the initial phase of coordinating relations to increase mutual security, write Adler and Barnett, and "development of a security community is not antagonistic to the language of power; indeed, it is dependent on it."[56] Military allies "recognize or discover that they have joint interests that require collective action, and can mutually benefit from some modest coordination of security policies."[57]

Yet differences between the United States and its NATO allies have worked against regional norms, straining solidarity effected by social mobilization and assimilation as well as governmental decisions. During superpower cold war, the European allies questioned the basic norm of mutual protection from the alliance, and specifically the American pledge to assist European allies in the event of attack by the Soviet Union. The allies questioned whether American government resolve to defend the allies would be strong enough to permit the use of nuclear weapons if that step endangered American cities by promoting Soviet retaliation against them. They also questioned whether American nuclear weapons used against an invading Soviet army might be too destructive, in which case they preferred nuclear nonuse.

A second alliance issue, the sharing of weapons technology, was also acrimonious. One observer in 1963 found it "surprising to what extent the relations between the main allies, the United States, Britain, and France have in fact come to depend upon such military questions as the sharing of nuclear weapons."[58] He went on to note that even advanced NATO military integration was a source of problems "because changes in institutional arrangements have lagged behind developments in weapons systems and alterations in the distribution of power in the alliance."[59] Cultural and economic compatibility have been less important than policy interests in coping with the intricacies and difficulties of NATO contingency planning.

To gauge the larger importance of these intra-alliance issues, the diplomatic viewpoint would inquire about the source of security association

norms—specifically, whether they emanate primarily from social and transactional solidarities or from governmental elites. If nonelite sources are the
key, tensions between interstate elites, and the evolution of elite ideas, will
be of relatively minor importance; governments would anticipate interstate
disputes, create mechanisms to overcome them, and accommodate differences. Adler and Barnett, however, highlight "the critical role of social learning . . . on the basis of new causal and normative knowledge" provided by
policy elites.[60] "While social learning can occur at the mass level," they write,
"and such changes are critical when discussing collective identities, our bias
is to look to policymakers and other political, economic, and intellectual
elites that are most critical for the development of new forms of social and
political organization that are tied to the development of a security community."[61] This suggests greater changeability in norms. Deutsch and his team
also seemed to accept this view. Finding no evidence in scientific journals of
increased internationalism in the sixty-year period up to 1954, they attributed
its absence to political and administrative obstacles to the movement across
national boundaries, concluding in 1957 that "men will have to work toward
the building of larger security-communities without the benefit of any clear-
cut automatic trend toward internationalism to help them."[62]

A diplomatic point of view, affirming that norms are mostly established at
the governmental level, directs attention to how these norms adjust to policy
shifts and interstate deadlock. For example, the poor chemistry between
Israeli prime minister Benjamin Netanyahu and U.S. president Barack Obama
suggests they would be unable to accommodate their differences. Would
U.S.-Israel security community be sustainable under this condition? Perhaps
tensions at high policy levels would have only minor effect on mass solidarities, as the responsiveness of American and Israeli populations to each other
and their social solidarity remain strong. Considerable interaction between
lower-level American and Israeli officials also compensates for tension at the
highest policy levels.[63]

But if norms of American-Israeli community are shaped primarily at the
policy level, diplomatic tensions could stimulate doubts about common outlooks and expectations. Israeli elites, for example, have become more sensitive to American criticism of Israeli policy toward the Palestinians, an issue
that is likely to be more rancorous in the future. Rising insularity on the part
of both American and Israeli populations—the desire to be left alone and not
to be responsible for the welfare of foreign states—forms a potential challenge to the American-Israel security community; it will become still more
significant if leaders appeal to their respective populations as a substitute for
diplomatic cooperation.

B. Dependent Diplomacy

As has been suggested, multiple agents of change—and interdependence rather than independence—characterize the members' relations in a mature interstate association. Increasing congruence between political institutions and the social and economic forces they serve, both in the domestic arena and internationally, characterize this interdependence, shaping community norms, shared viewpoints, and mutual responsiveness. "Multiple channels that existed [earlier] are extended and intensified," Adler and Barnett write, "and states and their societies are increasingly embedded in a dense network of relations collectively portrayed as 'friendly.' " Trust is deepened even before a common identity is created.[64] The primary norm is avoiding war. Acharya writes that "a security community usually implies a fundamental, unambiguous and long-term *convergence* of interests among the actors in the avoidance of war."[65] The identification of interests often goes far beyond this, however. Emanuel Adler outlines an "inside-out" model of international security in which security is defined as comprehensive (including a broad range of factors such as culture and human rights), indivisible, and cooperative (including the peaceful resolution of disputes and institutional initiative).

At the peak of the association, when a common identity develops between association members, multilateral and consensus decision-making predominates.[66] External and domestic values converge as a security community develops in an extensive social environment that contributes to new understandings of security itself. The OSCE, for example, is said to have brought about "a transformation of the cognitive, institutional, and material context within which post–Cold War domestic and international politics takes place."[67]

The diplomatic viewpoint would not equate national self-interest with convergent interests, but instead would anticipate that foreign and domestic pressures on government could be at odds with the diplomatic statecraft that executive officials wish to exercise on their own. Diplomatic statecraft would then be limited by these pressures yet could be adapted to them. The convergent interests of community members, and domestic pressures, limit diplomatic statecraft if they conflict with diplomatic priorities. How will these tensions be resolved? Political integration in a pluralistic community—peace among the participating units—could help resolve these tensions.[68] Alternatively, the absence of such integration could increase them—for example, subjecting executive officials to tensions between domestic pressures to prevent or end warfare, on the one hand, and more classic, vigilant, and expedient behavior directed to security threats from abroad, on the other. Nonintegrated communities with large social and economic disparities would likely be more turbulent than their integrated counterparts, and a greater challenge for leaders, because they are more conducive to popular dissatisfaction.[69]

The "two-level games" literature, which details how leaders tackle disparate foreign and domestic responsibilities, does not address security integration between states.[70] Its model takes the process of ratifying interstate agreements as the "crucial theoretical link" between domestic and international politics, defining leaders' ability to gain domestic ratification of interstate agreement (their "win-set") by how many "potential agreements . . . would be ratified by domestic constituencies in a straight up-or-down vote against the status quo of 'no agreement.' "[71] In this model, a leader's influence in domestic politics is enhanced "by exploiting his or her freedom to act autonomously within the domestic win-set."[72]

The diplomatic view counsels distinguishing sharply between dependent (non-autonomous) and independent (autonomous) diplomatic statecraft. For example, if the domestic win-set is a constraint on statecraft, then capitalizing on it would be adapting to the constraint. Analysis of diplomacy as dependent variable also requires going beyond the ratification process to include all external and domestic pressures pushing a statecraft agenda that is at odds with governmental preferences.

Third, insisting that constraints on statecraft are not Gulliver-like limitations on diplomatic behavior, the diplomatic viewpoint can build on the security community approach. Adler and Barnett note that "social learning . . . is more than 'adaptation' or 'simple learning,' that is, when political actors choose more effective means of achieving ends as a response to changes in the international environment." They say it refers to the "capacity and motivation of social actors to manage and even transform reality by changing their beliefs."[73] The diplomatic view, focusing on the political leader and not the social actor, would understand adaptation in utilitarian fashion, as improved diplomatic effectiveness toward a given objective or objectives.

C. Diplomatic Strategy

Processes of security community highlight and require interstate cooperation. "The idea of cooperation in a security community is deeply embedded in a collective identity," Acharya notes, "which is more than just the sum total of the shared interests of the individual actors."[74] Interstate cooperation and convergence of interests presume an accommodative diplomatic strategy. Referring to OSCE, for example, Adler notes that the institutional rubric is very significant in "stimulating cooperative behavior through a plethora of face-to-face interactions on a large variety . . . of subjects."[75]

He elaborates on "seminar diplomacy," by which he means "all types of multilateral diplomacy (meetings of diplomats, practitioners, civil servants, and academic experts, the use of experts in diplomatic missions) aimed at promoting political dialogue and international cooperation (political, social, economic) and preventing or managing conflict by means of consensual technical or normative knowledge."[76] Such repeated face-to-face interactions undoubtedly increase interstate trust, as does the "pedagogical" approach of such seminars, emphasizing community-building and unifying persons with varying competences to enhance collective understanding of norms of interstate relations and of democratic polities.[77] The broad OSCE agenda fosters statecraft that entails "preference for practitioners and experts over traditional diplomats as [seminar] delegates" and that is linked to political change in Europe.[78] According to one highly informed source, "all the major developments associated with the end of the Cold War . . . *began* with dialogue."[79]

On the other hand, if the seminar diplomacy dialogue is most useful as an *early* legitimizer of political change, implementing such change is bound to be slow and problematic. Traditional diplomatic behavior is likely to impede shifts in norms and invite hard bargaining to bring about such changes. For its part, the diplomatic point of view highlights how states employ less compromising diplomatic methods even as agreed-upon behavioral norms exist. States appear paradoxically more willing to take risks when their relationship is subject to rules of conduct, for then leaders perceive risk-taking to be less likely to lead to a breakdown in relations.[80] If so, the convergence of interests and the buildup of norms in integrated communities should also contribute to the willingness to accept risk to enhance relative gains between states.

Two notable recent examples of diplomatic contestation being applied in an environment of convergent interests may be cited. The first is former Italian prime minister Matteo Renzi, whose tough stance in relation to the European Union (for example, on the refugee problem) protected him at home against political change and may have been designed to provide Italy with greater leverage over its national budget.[81] The second is the former Greek minister of finance, Yanis Varoufakis, who confronted the European Union regarding his country's debt repayments by refusing to accept demands from the Eurogroup, the committee comprising finance ministers of countries using the euro, for greater Greek economic austerity.[82]

Table 2.3 summarizes the contrasting security community and diplomatic outlooks.

Table 2.3.   Security Community and Diplomatic Viewpoint Encounter

	Security community	Diplomatic view response
1. Independent diplomacy	A. Early diplomacy as "search mission" B. Leaders mostly guide development of security community	A. Concern with diplomatic challenges and not just reinforcements B. Elite clashes can hamper norms and community
2. Dependent diplomacy	A. Convergence of objectives	A. National self-interest distinct from convergent interests B. Implementation of peaceful change is difficult C. Diplomatic adaptation to the constraint of convergent interests
3. Diplomatic strategy	A. Accommodation as strategy of choice B. "Seminar diplomacy" as a technique of peaceful change	A. Contestation is used opportunistically when common norms are well developed

IV. CONCLUSIONS

A diplomatic viewpoint is necessary to guide theorizing about diplomatic statecraft. This chapter has used paradigm "dialogue" primarily to deepen that viewpoint because a diplomatic point of view can only be developed by demonstrating how it is different from other perspectives. The dialogue has proceeded on two levels. First, I have built on the Galtung and security community approaches by seeking elements in those approaches corresponding to the threefold conceptual framework of the diplomatic viewpoint: independent diplomacy, dependent diplomacy, and diplomatic strategy.

Independent Diplomacy. The Galtung and security community approaches highlight independent diplomacy by allowing for new diplomatic directions. Although he critiques diplomatic statecraft that supports negative peace, Galtung supports it on the grounds that cessation of fighting is essential for human needs. Perhaps the greatest weakness in Galtung's approach from a diplomatic point of view is its ambivalence about diplomacy. The security community school allows for "diplomatic search missions" to identify potential arenas for political integration. Both approaches acknowledge that diplomacy can impede interstate peace.

Dependent Diplomacy. The Galtung and security community approaches highlight constraints on diplomatic statecraft. Galtung discusses a "war system" in which negative peace is difficult to obtain; this introduces a double constraint on diplomacy in which international values weakening peace are in tension with domestic values seeking peace. Diplomatic adaptation to such contrasting pressures would likely be very difficult. The security community school raises the question of how diplomacy adapts to the convergent interests of state and nonstate actors in a regional grouping. From the diplomatic vantage point, the security community literature seems to rely too heavily on elite cooperation as a political integrator.

Diplomatic strategy. The Galtung approach emphasizes diplomatic contestation, while the security community orientation generates diplomatic negotiation. Neither appears to reject diplomatic experience, but each extracts from diplomatic experience what best validates its primary concerns.

Second, I have critiqued the Galtung and security community approaches, using them to define a diplomatic viewpoint. Because the Galtung and security community literatures—one focusing on the difficulties of resolving disputes and the other on the benefits of integrative norms of behavior—are themselves quite different from each other, they pose a double challenge to the diplomatic viewpoint. The challenge is useful for identifying features of the diplomatic viewpoint that, because they have been useful in both paradigm encounters, have enduring importance and deserve emphasis in future study.

The diplomatic viewpoint separates from the Galtung and security community approaches, first, because the diplomatic function is centered on the state rather than on nonstate actors, newer interstate elite collaboration, and citizens of states. It also differs from them because it dwells on the changeability of state behavior and strategy rather than emphasizing the steadier norms of negative and positive peace, the primary concerns of the Galtung and security community orientations. The diplomatic viewpoint also affirms, however, the long-standing importance of the state and of state strategy and tactics—and it attempts to generalize about them—in relation to the growing prominence of nonstate activity and norms of cooperation. Its most serious inadequacy revealed here appears to be its difficulty in understanding the adjustment of statecraft to international and domestic constraints.

NOTES

1. John Lewis Gaddis, *The Landscape of History* (New York: Oxford University Press, 2002), 108.

2. Stephen M. Walt, "Rigor or Rigor Mortis? Rational Choice and Security Studies," *International Security* 23 (Spring 1999): 48, cited in Ethan B. Kapstein, "Two Dismal Sciences Are Better than One—Economics and the Study of National Security," *International Security* 27 (Winter 2002–2003): 159.

3. For an earlier effort to search for a point of view for diplomatic statecraft, see Barry H. Steiner, "Diplomacy and International Theory," *Review of International Studies* 30 (2004): 493–509.

4. An extended discussion of the independent/dependent variable distinction is found in chapter 5 of this book. An early effort to make this distinction is Barry H. Steiner, "Diplomacy as Independent and Dependent Variable," *International Negotiation* 6 (2001): 79–104.

5. For analysis of contestation and negotiation as competing diplomatic strategies, see chapter 4.

6. For definitions of diplomacy, see Hedley Bull, *The Anarchical Society* (New York: Columbia University Press, 1977), 162–164; Hans J. Morgenthau, *Politics among Nations*, 4th ed. (New York: Knopf, 1967), 135–39; Brian C. Rathbun, *Diplomacy's Value* (Ithaca, NY: Cornell University Press, 2014), ix, 1–4; and Paul Gordon Lauren, Gordon A. Craig, and Alexander L. George, *Force and Statecraft*, 4th ed. (New York: Oxford University Press, 2007), 153–54. See also chapter 1 of this book.

7. Rathbun, *Diplomacy's Value*, ix.

8. Martin Wight, *Power Politics*, ed. Hedley Bull and Carsten Holbraad (New York: Holmes & Meier, 1978), 137.

9. Lauren, Craig, and George, *Force and Statecraft*; Morgenthau, *Politics among Nations*, 519ff.

10. Harold Nicolson, *Peacemaking 1919* (New York: Universal Library, 1965), 3.

11. Sources consulted on this approach include Johan Galtung and Carl G. Jacobsen, eds., *Searching for Peace* (London: Pluto, 2000); Galtung, *A Theory of Peace: Building Direct Structural Cultural Peace* (Bergen, Norway: Kolofon, 2013); and Galtung, *Solving Conflicts* (Honolulu: University of Hawaii Institute for Peace, 1989).

12. Johan Galtung, "Transcend: 40 Years, 40 Conflicts," in Galtung and Jacobsen, *Searching for Peace*, 107; emphasis in original.

13. Kai Frithjof Brand-Jacobsen, with Carl G. Jacobsen, "Beyond Mediation: Towards More Holistic Approaches to Peacebuilding and Peace Actor Empowerment," in Galtung and Jacobsen, *Searching for Peace*, 254.

14. Ibid., 253, 256–57.

15. Ibid., 256–57; emphasis in original.

16. Galtung, *Theory of Peace*, 8; emphasis in original.

17. Brand-Jacobsen, "Beyond Mediation," 237.

18. Galtung, *Theory of Peace*, 47; emphasis in original.

19. Brand-Jacobsen, "Beyond Mediation," 240.

20. Ibid., 257; emphasis in original.

21. William Zartman, "Negotiations and Prenegotiations in Ethnic Conflict: The Beginning, The Middle, and the Ends," in *Conflict and Peacemaking in Multiethnic Societies*, edited by Joseph V. Montville (New York: Lexington, 1991), 512.

22. Somini Sengupta, "Dispute over Opposition's Seat at Table Threatens to Push Back Syria Peace Talks," *New York Times*, 19 January 2016.

23. For the distinctive role of great powers in the international system, see Bull, *Anarchical Society*, 206–7.

24. Neil MacFarquhar, "American Envoy to Hold Talks with Russians on Peace Deal for Ukraine," *New York Times*, 18 May 2015.

25. We have already noticed Galtung's view that peace, even negative peace, is the "normal human condition."

26. Galtung, *Theory of Peace*, 242.

27. Brand-Jacobsen, "Beyond Mediation," 236.

28. Galtung, *Theory of Peace*, 212.

29. For analysis of the assumption that states seek maximal advantage in their relationships with other states, see Arnold Wolfers, "The Actors in International Politics," in *Discord and Collaboration*, by Arnold Wolfers (Baltimore, MD: Johns Hopkins University Press, 1962), 14ff.

30. Morgenthau, *Politics among Nations*, 549.

31. Galtung, *Theory of Peace*, 48–49.

32. Ibid., 48.

33. This idea is discussed in Steiner, "Diplomacy and International Theory," 502.

34. Ibid., 47.

35. For a test of the prevalence of diplomatic accommodation between allied states, see chapter 3.

36. Brand-Jacobson, "Beyond Mediation," 242; emphasis in original.

37. Ibid., 232.

38. Johan Galtung and Mari Holmboe Ruge, "Patterns of Diplomacy," *Journal of Peace Research* 2 (1965): 126–27. See also Bull, *Anarchical Society*, 174. Morgenthau maintained that newer and more regularized forms of communication between states contributed to a decline in the ability of diplomats "to make important contributions to the foreign policies of their countries." (*Politics among Nations*, 525–26).

39. Emanuel Adler and Michael Barnett, eds., *Security Communities* (Cambridge: Cambridge University Press, 1998); Karl W. Deutsch, Sidney A. Burrell, Robert A. Kann, Maurice Lee, Jr., Martin Lichterman, Raymond E. Lindgren, Francis L. Loewenheim, and Richard W. Van Wagenen, "Political Community and the North Atlantic Area," in *International Political Communities: An Anthology* (Garden City, NY: Anchor Books, 1966); Karl W. Deutsch, *Nationalism and Its Alternatives* (New York: Knopf, 1969); and Deutsch, *The Analysis of International Relations* (Englewood Cliffs, NJ: Prentice-Hall, 1968).

40. Emanuel Adler and Michael Barnett, "A Framework for the Study of Security Communities," in Adler and Barnett, *Security Communities*, 31.

41. Amitav Acharya, "Collective Identity and Conflict Management in Southeast Asia," in Adler and Barnett, *Security Communities*, 204. For an earlier argument that rising interactions between states increase the likelihood of friction and war, see Quincy Wright, *A Study of War* (Chicago: University of Chicago Press, 1965 [1942]), 1284–87.

42. Adler and Barnett, "Framework," 37.

43. Deutsch, *Analysis of International Relations*, 188.

44. Acharya, "Collective Identity and Conflict Management," 204.

45. Deutsch, *Analysis of International Relations*, 188. A searching study of the status of European integration in the early 1960s moving beyond transactional indicators is

Ernst B. Haas, "International Integration: The European and the Universal Process," *International Organization* 15 (Autumn 1961), reprinted in *International Political Communities*, 93–129.

46. Adler and Barnett, "Framework," 33.

47. Emanuel Adler, "Seeds of Peaceful Change: The OSCE's Security Community-Building Model," in Adler and Barnett, *Security Communities*, 119.

48. In *Nationalism and Its Alternatives*, chapter 1, Deutsch discussed elites only very briefly (on 11–12), while giving much more attention to kinship and peoplehood.

49. Adler and Barnett, "Framework," 43.

50. Deutsch, "Political Community," 39.

51. Adler and Barnett, "Framework," 14.

52. Acharya, "Collective Identity and Conflict Management," 205–6.

53. Ole Waever, "Insecurity, Security, and Asecurity in the West European Non-War Community," in Adler and Barnett, *Security Communities*, 75.

54. Adler and Barnett, "Framework," 50.

55. Acharya, "Collective Identity and Conflict Management," 208–12.

56. Adler and Barnett, "Framework," 53.

57. Ibid., 50.

58. Modelski, "A Study of Alliances: A Review," in *Alliance in International Politics*, ed. Julian R. Friedman, Christopher Bladen, and Steven Rosen (Boston: Allyn and Bacon, 1970), 66.

59. Ibid.

60. Adler and Barnett, "Framework," 43.

61. Ibid., 44.

62. Deutsch, "Political Community," 6.

63. A recent development understandable in terms of Israeli-American security community was the 2016 compromise over egalitarian prayer at the Western Wall in Jerusalem. One prominent participant was quoted as saying, "This would not have happened had it not been for strong growing pressure from American Jewry. . . . [T]his . . . was a response to very concrete pressure conveyed to Israel through diplomatic representatives, Jewish federations and key donors." Isabel Kershner, "A Compromise at the Western Wall, but a Wider Divide among Jews," *New York Times*, 3 February 2016. (The compromise was rejected the following year by the Israeli government.)

64. Adler and Barnett, "Framework," 53.

65. Acharya, "Collective Identity and Conflict Management," 201; emphasis in original.

66. Adler and Barnett, "Framework," 55.

67. Adler, "Seeds of Political Change," 150. See also Adler, "The Emergence of Cooperation: National Epistemic Communities and the International Evolution of the Idea of Nuclear Arms Control," in *Knowledge, Power, and International Policy Coordination*, ed. Peter M. Haas (Columbia: University of South Carolina Press, 1992), 101–46.

68. Deutsch, "Political Community," 12.

69. For the idea of a "weak state," which fits these characteristics, see Patrick J. McGowan, "Coups and Conflict in West Africa," *Armed Forces and Society* 32 (October 2005): 5–23.

70. Peter B. Evans, Harold Karan Jacobson, and Robert D. Putnam, eds., *Double-Edged Diplomacy* (Berkeley: University of California Press, 1993).

71. Andrew Moravcsik, "Introduction: Integrating International and Domestic Theories of International Bargaining," in Evans, Jacobson, and Putnam, *Double-Edged Diplomacy*, 23.

72. Ibid., 24.

73. Adler and Barnett, "Framework," 43–44.

74. Acharya, "Collective Identity and Conflict Management," 200–201.

75. Adler, "Seeds of Political Change," 121.

76. Ibid., 138.

77. Ibid., 139.

78. Ibid., 141.

79. Ibid., 142; emphasis added.

80. Steiner, "Diplomacy and International Theory," 506.

81. Jim Yardley, "Pushing for a Place at Europe's Power Table," *New York Times*, 29 January 2016.

82. Yanis Varoufakis, *Adults in the Room: My Battle with the European and American Deep Establishment* (New York: Farrar, Straus and Giroux, 2017); and Ian Parker, "The Greek Warrior," *New Yorker*, 3 August 2015, 44–57.

3

When Diplomatic Communication Is Missing

Communication is an essential part of diplomacy and interstate relationships. "Diplomacy facilitates communication between political leaders of states and other entities in world politics," Hedley Bull has written. "Without communication there could be no international society, nor any international system at all. Thus the most elementary function of diplomatists is to be messengers."[1] Others have argued that communication has diplomatic primacy. As George F. Kennan wrote,

> Essentially what the diplomat does is only to maintain communication with other governments about the behavior of the respective countries in ways that have reciprocal impacts and are of interest to the governments. . . . He is only the clerk and the recorder—a secretary of sorts—not an independent agent. For every real promise or commitment he expresses to a foreign government regarding the behavior of the U.S. on the international scene, he must have the sanction of some domestic authority. . . . Strictly speaking, there are no diplomatic means, divorced from the real elements of national power and influence, which are all—in the U.S.—remote from diplomatic control.[2]

Messaging has historically linked groups or states that were inherently separated. "At the heart of the diplomatic tradition," writes Paul Sharp, "lies the assumption that people live not as such, but as peoples in various sorts of groups. . . . The diplomatic tradition thus presents peoples as living in *conditions of separateness* from one another, and even where they are not physically separated, a sense of separateness remains a dimension of their relationships."[3] Making communication possible between separated entities, the diplomat has been the custodian of the link between those entities, a role that extended beyond merely conveying messages. The diplomatic channel would also convey the moods, contexts, and intentions of those sending messages, ensure confidentiality, and offer the opportunity to try out new, untested ideas.[4] And it entailed security protection—which Kennan characterized as a "cushion of safety that normally existed in the ability of governments to talk with one another over the diplomatic channel."[5]

Kennan seems to have had in mind that diplomatic communication was desirable whatever the goals of states or the character of their relations. In principle, it would assist in avoiding crisis, clarifying intentions, and retarding defection from cooperation. But what if communication is not available to or used by separated, adversarial state entities? If diplomatic communication is significant, significant consequences should follow from its absence. For example, the absence of diplomatic communication should add to the attractiveness of force use between adversaries deadlocked over vital interests. On the other hand, the absence of communication is not necessarily conducive to war, because disputes and interests will vary.

The "prisoners' dilemma" (PD) game, the basis for much commentary, is used to describe and understand the problematic consequences resulting from the inability of states to communicate. PD is taken as a metaphor to demonstrate how, because of international anarchy, an inability to communicate undermines states' ability to cooperate and contributes to a worsening of their relationship as each is forced to assume the other is hostile. In the game metaphor, states are analogized to bank robbers under suspicion by law enforcement who are prevented from communicating with each other. Whatever their need to cooperate, each has a strong incentive in the absence of communication to incriminate the other in the belief that the other would do likewise. As a result, both parties are worse off.[6] The problem with the PD metaphor is that it does not reveal whether the result would have been different if the parties had been permitted to communicate; to make the case in this context for the metaphor's significance, a positive must be inferred from a negative. On the other hand, it is unwarranted to assume from the metaphor that communication is invariably insignificant; countries may prefer to communicate even when unable to do so.[7]

Yet diplomatic communication seems less important when adversaries coexist despite being unable to communicate. For example, at the onset of diplomatic crisis, when channels of communication would seem to be most useful, the credibility of those channels may be questioned for permitting the crisis to arise.[8] And, for adversaries, communications may be less consequential than shared interests, such as their mutual fear of using force. States that do not communicate diplomatically may avoid being drawn into a mutually defeating PD interaction. Conforming to commonly accepted expectations and norms may itself serve as a message. Again, absence of diplomatic communication does not imply that diplomatic communication is unimportant or inconsequential.

As these observations suggest, this chapter does not challenge the central function of communications in international relations. Instead, by contrasting disputes conducive to war with those that are not, the chapter limits the discussion to exceptional instances of missing diplomatic communications. Probing how states and factions interact in the absence of communications, the analysis focuses on alternative techniques for pursuing conflicting interests and how those techniques might hypothetically appear to the adversaries if communication were available to them.[9]

I. OBJECTIVES

This chapter tests the supposed importance of formal diplomatic communication against a series of cases of conflict lacking such communication. An appreciation of diplomatic communication is deepened by probing the consequences of its absence, and outlier cases refine an understanding of the general importance such communication plays in world politics.

Our outlier cases can be located on a spectrum of diplomatic communication. At one extreme, no formal diplomatic channels exist, and states are unable to communicate. Moving toward the center of the spectrum, channels exist but are unused for one or more reasons. Farther to the right is the diplomatic norm, in which channels are formally employed for a "cushion of safety" on the significant issues of concern to states, but the diplomats do not have a personal chemistry to draw them together. Finally, at the opposite extreme, personal chemistry prevails, and diplomats not only have the "cushion of safety" but empathize with each other despite their differences.[10] Our concern in this chapter is limited to the first two of these positions.

We ask whether diplomatic communication would have made a difference in helping state and nonstate entities avoid crisis, clarify opponents' intentions, and retard defection from cooperation. The chapter uses the hypothetical impact of communication in these cases as a standard by which to understand the value of diplomatic communication. Communication may be missing for a variety of reasons, including missing diplomats, the absence of a message, complacence, inflexible commitment, or mistrust. When the diplomatic channel is missing, countries may communicate tacitly by conforming to accepted norms of behavior. When the channel is available, other influences may override its potential.

Three perspectives—political realism, liberal internationalism, and applied diplomacy—are introduced here to generate diverse linkages between diplomatic communication, international norms, and state interests. They also generate explanations for, and consequences of, the *absence* of communication in particular conditions. Political realism and liberal internationalism are mainstays in the international relations literature, and the two approaches debate the strength of international norms in the absence of world government. Realists and liberal internationalists agree that diplomatic channels are not significant primarily in themselves but reflect the use to which they are put and the broader features of the international environment. The third perspective, applied diplomacy, shows how diplomatic channels, which assist in managing conflict between states, can paradoxically intensify interstate rivalry and competitiveness.

II. PERSPECTIVES ON DIPLOMATIC COMMUNICATIONS

The following summarizes insights of our perspectives on the significance of diplomatic communication and on the consequences of its absence. Links drawn between the two are will be especially helpful in comparing the cases.

A. Political Realism

For the realist, diplomatic communication has the double purpose of supporting the search for national advantage and of restraining that search through mutual cooperation. Realist understanding of diplomatic channels is shaped by the understanding that international institutions and norms are weak, and that this weakness encourages competition between states for national advantage. Diplomatic communication is especially needed, according to the realist, because weak international institutions make it difficult for states to cooperate, because states are highly competitive and combative, and because governments must cope with dangerous consequences of self-interested but defensive behavior.

As this suggests, the larger the scope for interstate competition, the greater the need for and usefulness of diplomatic communication. According to Hans J. Morgenthau, communication was most useful historically when governments needed to stay in frequent contact, even though their messages were sparse.[11] The role of the permanent diplomatic representative declined, Morgenthau maintains, as the volume of communications exploded through the telephone, satellite, and telegraph, and through special representatives, scholars, the mass media, and transnational forces.[12] However, the value of the diplomatic safety net in the new communications environment presumably lay increasingly in the *authoritative* character of interstate communications.

Realists also acknowledge the adaptability of diplomacy to the needs of states. Initially, diplomacy was primarily an instrument of competition. "When war was the normal activity of kings," Morgenthau writes, "the task of diplomacy was not to prevent it, but to bring it about at the most propitious moment."[13] When adapted for war, diplomacy valued information for deception and for identifying the war-related strengths and weaknesses of the adversary.[14] When diplomacy later became primarily used to prevent war, it was reoriented to gain cooperation between adversaries.[15] Realists would then understand the inability to communicate diplomatically as having made the effort to cooperate more difficult.

B. Liberal Internationalism

The liberal internationalist highlights an international society of states sustained by "a pattern of activity that sustains the elementary or primary goals of the society of states, or international society."[16] Historically, norms of order have been sustained and strengthened through a series of ordering institutions, including diplomatic statecraft, international law, and the balance of power.[17] Convergent interests of states, which sustain cooperation, are an additional benefit of the broad foundation of international order. Convergent state interests strengthen incentives to cooperate, as, for example, in international regimes, when states seek to "establish stable mutual expectations about others' patterns of behavior and . . . develop working relationships that will allow the parties to adapt their practices to new situations."[18]

Resident embassies, facilitating diplomatic communication, followed the emergence of powerful and independent states, free from external danger and secure from the establishment of universal monarchy.[19] Diplomacy "fulfils the function of symbolizing the existence of a society of states," especially given the declining role of a common diplomatic culture.[20] "The diplomatic corps," writes Paul Sharp, making the same point, "is one of the very few tangible expressions of the international society or community to which everyone routinely makes reference."[21]

But diplomatic channels are not *uniquely* important for international order. Hedley Bull notes that "the diplomatic institutions of today presuppose an international society, [but] international society does not presuppose them in the same way."[22] Because diplomatic channels share the ordering role with international law and the balance of power as norm-strengthening institutions, he argues, all the functions of diplomacy "could in principle be fulfilled in other ways than by a mechanism of professional diplomacy of the sort we have now."[23] If diplomatic communication is not available, its loss is therefore less consequential for state needs than the realist maintains, because other mechanisms provide substitutes to maintain international norms. The adaptive character of international norms and institutions would then presumably help channel and manage interstate conflict when diplomatic channels were unavailable.

C. Applied Diplomacy

The diplomatic perspective seeks "a process of interaction for the greater good through nonviolent methods," and it undertakes to assist states in employing those methods.[24] It gives special attention to state incentives to cooperate and to the productive use of those incentives. It also addresses impediments to state cooperation and seeks to improve negotiating results by overcoming them diplomatically.[25]

Although this perspective regards interstate communication as indispensable for interstate cooperation, it also draws attention to problems experienced when states cannot communicate. They may lack an authoritative channel for communicating because of the intensity of their competitiveness or because multiple channels of communication provide opportunities to communicate new objectives, making outcomes indeterminate.[26] These scenarios seem to rule out a diplomatic safety net between states.

The opposite problem is partly a consequence of a diplomatic safety net. With well-developed diplomatic rules and procedures, and ample opportunity for communication, states may become too wedded to one-sided understandings of each other. They can become overly confident about their norms and procedures, rely on overly selective assumptions about their opponents' intentions, take more liberties in relation to each other, and fail to anticipate behavior incompatible with their optimistic assumptions.

The diplomatic perspective understands these scenarios differently than the realist and the liberal internationalist. The realist and the liberal internationalist would be pessimistic about the potential for cooperation when interstate competition is intense or when, in Thomas Schelling's words, states have a "common inability to keep their eyes off certain outcomes," but the advocate for diplomatic process would suggest that deadlock and fewer commonalities would make states more cautious.[27] When communication is poor, states would understand that they have less room for flexibility. Each would have an incentive to practice self-restraint and would avoid assuming the worst about its antagonist.[28]

Realists and liberal internationalists would agree that a safety net is strengthened with the growth of common rules and procedures, reassuring states that they can control the risks of their behavior. A paradox highlighted by the diplomatic point of view, however, is that the state relationship giving the liberals highest confidence about cooperation and stability can, if states overvalue it, be conducive to the competitive behavior cited by the realists. A safety net can lead to too much trust in an adversary's intentions—to overconfidence that an interstate relationship can withstand more venturesome behavior. Eventually, the relationship is endangered as the adversary objects to the behavior.

For example, the tendency of superpowers to take risks in the Mideast during the cold war has been linked to the perceived depth of the diplomatic safety net between the United States and the Soviet Union. According to Harold H. Saunders,

> With the safety net of . . . a diplomatic framework to fall back on, [the United States and Soviet Union had] been willing to use the Arab-Israeli conflict as a vehicle in their competition, but each side has recognized some limits of tolerance in the other's willingness to accept setbacks. . . . Interestingly, they were most cautious in 1967 and 1983 when their bilateral relationship was least well developed. They were most daring in terms of their own competitive military involvement in 1970, when they had begun to develop enough of a relationship to be more confident of their ability to avoid confrontation but were still testing each other in the process of building that relationship.[29]

In Saunders's analysis, the growth of the safety net led the superpowers to become less cautious in their actions toward the other.

In sum, our three perspectives generate contrasting expectations about the consequences of severing diplomatic communication. The realist, for whom diplomatic contact provides the main resource for accommodation between states, forecasts dire consequences from the absence of communication. No satisfactory alternative exists to enable states to gauge each other's intentions and restrain competitive behavior. The liberal internationalist is less concerned about the absence of diplomatic communication and relies on other international institutions and on the convergent interests of states to underpin international cooperation. The negotiation specialist is confronted by paradox: well-developed state relationships contribute to bolder behavior that intensifies conflict, while less developed norms may contribute to uncertainty and to cautious behavior. These conclusions reverse the realist and liberal internationalist logics. The realist worries most about the absence of communication, but the negotiation specialist argues that the absence of communication may be more conducive to caution. The liberal internationalist highlights order based on norms of cooperation, but the negotiation student suggests that such norms may be linked to disorder.

Table 3.1 illustrates the contrasts between our three perspectives.

Table 3.1.   The Three Perspectives

	General characteristics	Purpose of diplomatic communications	Consequences of no diplomatic communications
Political Realism	1. Competitive state behavior 2. Weak international institutions	Unique need for authoritative contact	Dire results
Liberal Internationalist	1. International unity 2. Many ordering institutions	Diplomacy does not provide unique needs	Convergent interests and norms sustain cooperation
Applied Diplomacy	1. Seek greater good for states 2. Overcome impediments to cooperation	Well-developed relations can be problematic	Cautionary behavior lessens danger

III. PROBING DIPLOMATIC COMMUNICATION

We display differences between the three perspectives by asking three questions about diplomatic communication.

(1) Are adversarial states lacking diplomatic communication at greater risk of confronting each other than states that communicate diplomatically?

The realist argues that diplomatic communication is needed to restrain competition between states and reach mutual accommodation. Inability to communicate makes interstate confrontation more likely. The liberal internationalist, informed by a stronger foundation of rules and ordering institutions between states, questions this outlook and argues that in an international society, broader characteristics of the international system will ordinarily ensure that adversarial conflicts would not worsen in the absence of diplomatic communication. Nondiplomatic institutions would prevent conflicts from intensifying merely because of neglect and drift. The diplomatist points out that diplomatic communication does not in itself rule out confrontation, as competition between states is intensified in a process intended to yield accommodation. For example, a step-by-step approach to maximize the effort at agreement between adversaries would ideally begin *prior* to negotiation, to identify obstacles and issues to be overcome and to build confidence. Yet even with the best preparation, negotiations often lead to confrontation over details that would be largely ignored in the absence of negotiations. Nongovernmental interests that may oppose governmental negotiators contribute to such confrontation.[30]

2. Are states more flexible in their perceptions of each other when they communicate diplomatically than when they do not?

The realist argues that the safety net of diplomatic communications can facilitate shifts in gauging opposing state intentions. Absence of communications makes shifts in interpreting adversary intent more difficult, adding to uncertainty and insecurity. The liberal internationalist, informed by shared state membership in an international society, questions why the inability to communicate diplomatically should lead to uncertainty and insecurity. In an international society, a diplomatic safety net is not a prerequisite to gauge foreign state intentions or to provide reassurance about the will and ability to cooperate. The difficulty in interpreting foreign state intentions is not due primarily to the lack of communication channels but instead to the incentive to free ride for self-interested purposes on cooperative international norms. The diplomatic process perspective observes that a well-developed state relationship, with authoritative diplomatic channels, may be associated with inflexible assumptions leading to overconfidence about the intent of an adversary, particularly in its potential to cooperate. But if diplomatic communication may harden perceptions of an opponent, the failure to communicate, while diminishing confidence about adversary intent, may have a smaller effect on state security than the realist maintains, contributing to caution and restraint rather than insecurity.

3. How important are diplomatic communications for discouraging defection from commitments and norms? Are states more likely to defect when they lack diplomatic channels to communicate their views?

Diplomatic communication can discourage or retard defection from an interstate relationship because it represents value to that relationship that a defector would hesitate to forfeit. The potential for cooperation in such a relationship is increased by available diplomatic channels, and the attractiveness of defection is reduced. Conversely, absence of diplomatic communication, removing the hesitation factor, makes defection more attractive to satisfy unilateral state objectives because the diplomatic potential for cooperation is smaller. With communications lacking, the cooperation potential is smaller and defection becomes more attractive.

The PD metaphor also explains why the absence of diplomatic communication makes defection attractive: even allied actors feel their security is threatened in the absence of communication by the incentive of their partner to defect, and that danger increases their own incentive to defect from their partner. This view presumes that defection is inevitable because the absence of communication means there is no diplomatic relationship to protect. An opposing idea is that countries are very confident of their positions and that the absence of diplomatic channels emboldens them to defect by challenging each other. Lack of communication brings defection because the horizon of cooperation is constricted.

The realist, touting the value of diplomatic statecraft, links defection with state interests and opportunity, asking not only what goals defection is designed to realize but what value the diplomatic relationship compromised by the defection behavior holds. According to the realist, diplomatic communication discourages defection from commitments and norms because states will logically take account of predefection relationships before defecting and ask, "Defection from what?"

Liberal internationalists and diplomatists do not consider defection from commitments and norms a central problem, and therefore they are not preoccupied with the link between diplomatic communication and defection. The liberal internationalist portrait of an international society suggests that strong international rules and procedures discourage defection. States that defect then "free ride" on norms, pursuing a narrow self-interest on the assumption that other states will not. The liberal, presuming that norms of order will endure, believes the international system can absorb such self-interested behavior.[31] For the diplomatist, defection is unlikely whatever the status of diplomatic communication. When authoritative channels exist, there is no incentive for defection because a diplomatic process can enable adversaries to achieve mutual gains. If channels do not exist, they can be created for this purpose.

IV. CASES IN WHICH DIPLOMATIC COMMUNICATION IS MISSING

We now present five cases in which adversaries lack diplomatic communication. The cases are not intended to be fully representative of the missing communication universe but rather to introduce variety to the manner in which conflict is managed in the absence of communication. Subsequent analysis will seek commonalities between the cases, abstracting from their differences.

1. Libya (2011–2014)[32]

Following the end of superpower cold war, great power efforts to prevent and mitigate civil violence were undermined by the absence of protection for major-state diplomats in unstable developing countries lacking central government. In many such countries, warring factions could not assure those diplomats the personal security they required, and, when the major states lacked vital interests in such countries—for example, not being committed to fight a particular antagonist—the inability to protect diplomats led to diplomatic withdrawal. For example, following the ouster of the Libyan leader Muammar Qaddafy, the United Nations and major Western powers withdrew their diplomats and closed their missions in Libya. "We cannot care more than you do," the British ambassador wrote in an online message to a Libyan pleading for international assistance.[33] Polarization between factions and the absence of central government in civil strife such as Libya is particularly volatile with factions unified by antagonism toward their domestic opponent.

2. Soviet-American Relations (1952)[34]

Official Soviet-American communication was minimal during the several months in 1952 during which George Kennan served as American ambassador to Moscow. "I did not ask for an appointment with Stalin," Kennan later reflected. "The main reason was simply that, being effectively without instructions, I had nothing to say to him. Why, I thought, take up the time of a busy man for no good purpose at all and only invite embarrassment in case he opened up any serious question?"[35]

Kennan was concerned at this time about sustaining superpower peace despite the failure to communicate diplomatically. Specifically, he worried about whether the Pentagon "had the bit in its teeth" in pursuing its objectives. "How was I to account for, or to explain," he reflected later, "the overriding priority that Washington appeared to give to the gathering of military intelligence over whatever other usefulness, and particularly whatever usefulness in the task of *preventing* a war, the embassy might have had?"[36] Kennan recounted hearing about a plan to strengthen American military capabilities near the Soviet frontier and wondered, in light of public American assertions about the requirement to build up military strength toward a "peak of danger" that was supposed to arrive in 1952, whether Soviet leaders' suspicions about American intentions would be heightened by learning about such a plan.[37]

3. German-Polish Relations (1939)[38]

Immediately preceding the outbreak of the Second World War, Poland rejected communication with Germany to forestall negotiations on Germany's demands on the Polish city of Danzig. Germany had demanded concessions in Danzig, where there was a large German population, but in a war of nerves between the two countries the Polish government, fearing that negotiations with Germany were likely to lead to a settlement favorable to Germany, rejected such negotiations for more than five months prior to the outbreak of war in September 1939. The Poles dismissed Hitler's war threat as a bluff, but they also believed that their allies, Britain, France, and Italy, would pressure Poland to make concessions over Danzig once the issue was open for discussion. "Poland's Western allies were . . . an additional reason for her diplomatic immobility," writes A. J. P. Taylor. "It was obvious that Great Britain and France would give way over Danzig, if the Poles once opened the door to negotiation. Therefore they kept it closed."[39]

4. Anglo-French Relations (1750s)[40]

Prior to the Seven Years' War, which began in 1756, British and French leaders rejected discussions of their conflicting territorial ambitions in North America. Reports of fighting in Maine and the Ohio Valley, reaching London and Paris in 1754, were perceived by the British and French governments as their opponent's testing and probing of intentions rather than desiring general war. According to Patrice Higonnet, Anglo-French diplomacy at that time was limited "to create the element of surprise and justification for the limited counterblows which the two countries in turn decided to strike." Negotiations to end the fighting were also suppressed by the anticipated need for later discussions, following limited force use designed to impress the opponent. "Since the idea was to impress rather than to destroy the opponent, cordiality had to be maintained at all cost." The result, notes Higonnet, was a discrepancy between each belligerent's desire for peace and the unwillingness of either side to attempt diplomatically to prevent war.[41]

5. Anglo-French Arms Competition (1840–1866)[42]

Samuel Huntington distinguishes two modes of balancing power: an "external" method of diplomatic realignment and an "internal" method cultivating "the inherent power of the [state] units."[43] The first and older of these required a so-called balancer that could shift its weight toward the side that seemed weaker; in cases where no balancer existed or where bilateral antagonisms were not amenable to a balancer, the second method became more prominent. In the nineteenth century, according to Huntington, increasing state reliance on internal strength resulted in arms competitions between major powers of comparable military strength in which diplomacy played little or no role. Competitors in armaments, motivated by the need for more favorable force goals relative to their opponent, have no inherent need for diplomacy yielding mutual arms restraint. The long-term Anglo-French naval competition waged in the absence of diplomacy between 1840 and 1866 is a classic example of such a rivalry.

V. CASE ANALYSIS

We now attempt to answer our prior questions using our case material, seeking commonalities amid the variety of cases. Our main preoccupation is whether communication would have made a difference, had it been available.

1. Do our five cases suggest that a greater danger of confrontation prevails when adversaries lack the ability to communicate than when they do communicate?

Three of our examples, the Libyan civil war, the German-Polish standoff, and the eighteenth-century Anglo-French episode, illustrated the onset of crisis and the absence of crisis management to control it. Drift in relations and confrontation in these instances led to violence. Heightened war risks made crisis management and mutual self-restraint vital to dampen conflicts.[44] The absence of diplomatic communication ruled out crisis management in these instances. By contrast, the Soviet-American episode and the nineteenth-century Anglo-French naval race did not illustrate heightened war risk. Free from crisis, they did not necessitate crisis management or the communication that made crisis management possible.

It is doubtful whether communication would have stemmed the drift to hostilities in the first group. Adversaries did not desire communication or crisis management in those cases, suggesting that the risks of interstate confrontation emanated not from the inability to communicate but from state interests and assertiveness. German demands on Poland precipitated a crisis that could not be managed because the Poles suppressed communications with Britain and France. Britain and France rejected communications to deal with their New World problems. Post-Qaddafy factions in Libya rejected communications with each other.

Crisis management was suppressed in these instances for a variety of reasons. The Poles suppressed communications with Germany to escape German demands for Danzig that were anticipated to come through Britain and France. British and French leaders believed their relationship was stable, though it was highly competitive. Anglo-French rivalry in the New World took the form of probing and testing rather than direct demands. The absence of crisis management in that instance was not related to conflict but instead reflected the contentious character of the international environment and the weakness of international norms in that era. Libyan violence appears linked to the settling of old ethnic scores and the absence of domestic institutions for coping with disputes.

Cases in the second group require an explanation of their stability despite the absence of communications. Stable Anglo-French and superpower relationships suggested that norms of behavior, bringing international order to bear on states, were a significant alternative to communication in those instances. Anglo-French relations could be collaborative despite naval competition, as when England and France allied in 1853 to protect the Ottoman Empire against Russian expansion, and they also negotiated a trade agreement in 1859. In the superpower case, beyond the mutual fear of nuclear war, shared norms developed about outstanding issues that did not require communication or negotiation.[45] The major powers in these instances wished to avoid hostilities, and their cautious behavior enabled them to avoid unintended effects. " 'Conservative' behavior of the existing great powers," Herman Kahn has written of the superpower cold war period, "reflect[ing] the facts of power and risks of escalation," came about from this caution.[46] We conclude from these observations that, as in the first group, diplomatic communications would not have made a difference in the result.

2. Would communication have changed threat perceptions that adversaries held of each other?

The tentative conclusion is that threat perceptions would not have changed because they were stable. Libyan and Polish perceptions were shaped by insecurity—toward opposing domestic factions in the Libyan case and toward Germany in the Polish example. In the superpower case, the American understanding of the Soviet Union was necessarily limited by the closed character of Soviet decision-making. Uncertainty from lack of information about Soviet intentions led the Americans to shape their threat perceptions of the Soviet Union on logical foundations.[47] Ambassador Kennan and American intelligence estimates used logic to support their conclusion that the Soviet Union did not desire war with the United States.

Finally, in the Anglo-French cases, stable threat perceptions selectively accorded with national objectives. As long as those objectives did not change, diplomatic discussions would not have been likely to make a significant difference in the adversaries' orientation toward each other. In the mid-eighteenth century, British and French perceptions were stable though their relationship was unstable. They viewed each other as determined to preserve peace, when in reality both were striving opportunistically and militarily for territorial expansion. Their selective perceptions were conditioned by their competition for New World territory. A century later, stability in Anglo-French orientations were linked to rivalry for favored naval position, with the French introducing ironclad warships in an effort to displace the British as the leading naval power. They then each overrated the hostility of the other to accord with their determination to gain naval preeminence. On the British side, three so-called panics about French attack against England from across the English Channel gave public expression to English fears—encouraged by the British government—about French hostility.[48] This hostility was compartmentalized, however; as indicated, during the competition Britain and France negotiated a treaty to reduce tariffs between themselves.

3. Could diplomatic communication have affected the likelihood of defection?

Our cases illustrate three ways in which missing communication can affect the chances of defection: (a) Missing communication can reflect a low value for diplomacy more generally and undermine cooperation. (b) Diplomacy can be valued despite missing communication, with defection conditioned on diplomatic demands that fail because communication is absent. (c) Despite the absence of communication, cooperation can be encouraged and defection discouraged by self-restraint or tacit respect for rules.

The first of these, illustrated by the Libyan example, reflects the longest insecurity shadow from the absence of communication, and the greatest risks of defection. In this pattern, states and factions lack diplomatic inhibitors to war-making because there is little or nothing diplomatic to protect. In the Libyan civil war, the PD effect was intensified. Ethnic, religious, cultural, and linguistic groups viewed their security needs in opposition to the needs of others; in the resulting security dilemma, the efforts by one group to strengthen itself defensively were necessarily viewed as threatening by other contenders.[49] Because of the high risk of defection, the potential utility of communication is high. Barry Posen concludes, for example, that "groups

drifting into conflict should be encouraged to discuss their individual histor-
ies of mutual relations."[50] However, we conclude that diplomatic communication in the Libyan case would have done little to stop defection from mutual
suspicion.

Defection is also very likely in our second pattern, but because of
offensive-mindedness rather than the security dilemma. The interwar Polish-
German and eighteenth-century Anglo-French cases resemble Schelling's
understanding of a "diplomatic process of commitment" and "competition in
risk-taking."[51] In the Polish-German case, the diplomatic process was one-
sided. In this pattern, diplomacy serves the interests of a state making
demands on its opponent, but the adversary, rejecting the demands, attaches
no importance to diplomacy. The state, perceiving the demands as vital, conditions its defection to their fate, while the adversary, indifferent to the defection as well as the demands, ensures the failure of the demander's initiative.
Because each side was strongly committed and undeterred by the prospect of
defection, diplomatic communication—that is to say, two-sided diplomatic
engagement—was unlikely to make a difference.

The Anglo-French case entailed two-sided diplomatic commitment.
England and France competed for New World territory prior to the Seven
Years' War, and their diplomacy was put to the use of territorial competitiveness. Their defection was limited rather than total, confined to areas of their
territorial ambitions. Diplomatic communication was unlikely to blunt their
offensive-minded national objectives.

Finally, the superpower example and both Anglo-French examples illustrate how mutual interest in preventing defection constrains adversaries even
in the absence of diplomatic communication. In these cases, a diplomatic
relationship is preferred to defection even when it is far from ideal. Offensive
and defensive military dispositions were affected by less-than-ideal diplomatic relationships. We recall Kennan's concern in the superpower case about
the danger that American behavior toward the Soviet Union could be controlled by defensive-minded American military interests, which might appear
provocative and offensive-minded to Soviet leaders. British panics about
French invasion in the later Anglo-French case mobilized domestic militia
forces but did not lead, so far as is known, to redistributing the British fleet
toward the French coast.[52]

Beyond this, diplomatic communication might have *worsened* the Anglo-
French and superpower relationships. In the actual cases they were able to
avoid discussing the basis for conflict and competition in a manner that might
have inflamed tensions. Nineteenth-century Anglo-French naval rivalry arguably endured for a long period because the contenders decided that they
should not communicate about their naval objectives or the means to satisfy

them.[53] Failure to communicate also suggests mutual interest in preserving flexibility in pursuing rivalry.[54]

VI. REVIEWING THE PERSPECTIVES

Each of our perspectives—political realism, liberal internationalism, and applied diplomacy—is vindicated to a degree in the case analysis.

A. Political Realism

Two conclusions from our cases are consistent with realism. First, *state interests opposed communication and crisis management*. In this respect, pursuit of national advantage trumped the potential of diplomacy—both emphasized by the realist—to manage conflict. This conclusion is of particular interest in relation to those examples—the Libyan and Polish-German cases—in which conflict was conducive to war and factions risked war contrary to international norms. In those instances, states and factions, rejecting communication, also ruled out the crisis management technique that their conflict condition objectively required. In the cases of the superpowers and nineteenth-century Anglo-French rivalry, in which war danger was not high and crisis management was not needed, a stable relationship did not require diplomatic communication. Threat perceptions in those cases were also shaped by interests, and continuity in threat perception enhanced stability.

However, when adversary relations were stable and there was no war danger, *a cost of the absence of diplomatic communication was a worsened security dilemma*. To be sure, the absence of communication did not *create* the rivals' security dilemma, and the security problem likely would have been present had communication occurred. Failure to communicate did, however, add to the burdens and difficulties of the adversaries in relation to each other: it took away a means by which they could come to appreciate how their own defensive military precautions were read as offensive-minded by their opponent. This conclusion affirms the security importance realists attribute to diplomatic communication.

B. Liberal Internationalism

The liberal internationalist perspective is vindicated by the conclusion that *diplomatic communication is not a prerequisite for stable state relationships*. Through a convergence of state interests, norms provide a framework that transcends diplomatic communication as states pursue their interests cooperatively. In the superpower and nineteenth-century Anglo-French conflicts, norms of behavior appear to have substituted for communication in underpinning stable relations. As has been noted, security could be diminished for each rival, even with stable relations between the adversaries.

Second, *international norms can substitute for diplomatic communication in discouraging defection from cooperation, even if actual cooperation is minimal.* Defection depends on a belief that a particular relationship is unsustainable, especially for urgent and high-stakes conflict. On the other hand, norms of an international society work to deter defection. The stronger the norms, presumably the more they will deter defection. We cannot conclude, however, that our cases provide strong affirmation of the power of international norms: superpower norms in 1952 and nineteenth-century Anglo-French norms were not very well developed. Crisis management in the Soviet-American rivalry became normative only in the 1962 Cuban missile crisis, and norms of Anglo-French naval rivalry were much weaker than the Concert norm of blunting war-making by Russia against the Ottoman Empire in the 1850s.[55] In each case, however, the adversaries appeared to wish to avoid war with each other. This may be contrasted with the neglect or absence of norms in our cases that were conducive to war, whether because of internal divisions (Libya) or because of overriding state interests (eighteenth-century Anglo-French rivalry and Polish defensiveness against German demands).

C. Applied Diplomacy

The applied diplomacy perspective cautions, first, that *the absence of diplomatic communication is often not decisive for state relations.* In our more problematic cases (the Libyan, eighteenth-century Anglo-French, and Polish-German conflicts), overconfident adversaries, seeking state advantage, were overly opportunistic and competitive, and, viewing their opponents selectively, miscalculated their opponents' resistance.

Second, *states also compensate for the absence of diplomatic communication by acting cautiously.* In the less dangerous cases (the superpower and nineteenth-century Anglo-French conflicts), states practiced self-restraint when diplomatic communication was not available. States acted prudently to avoid competition in national resolve when they lacked information about the objectives and resistance potential of their adversaries.

VII. CONCLUSIONS

This chapter has focused on examples in which adversary governments and factions rejected diplomatic communication. We have highlighted differences between our examples, such as between instances in which relations deteriorated in the absence of communications and those in which stable relations were maintained in spite of that absence. Through counterfactual analysis, we analyzed whether the missing communication was significant. Despite focusing on an atypical set of examples, our presumption has been that if, as widely conceded, diplomatic communication is highly important for states and factions of states, the absence of such communication should also be important.

Of the three perspectives employed in this chapter, the political realist outlook is closest to the conventional wisdom about the importance of diplomatic communication. Realists maintain that adversaries who lack diplomatic communication have more difficulty cooperating and are more likely to wage war against each other. We have introduced counterfactual analysis to see whether communication would have made a significant difference. Using such analysis, our cases do not support the realist idea that communication would have made a significant difference for state and factional relationships. The variability in our cases does not affect this conclusion. Our volatile cases, characterized by an increasing danger of war, do not suggest that states and factions would have made use of diplomatic communication to address and manage their differences. And our stable cases show that adversary states at times had no need to address those differences, as insecurity can at times be controlled despite the absence of diplomatic communication.

This finding suggests a disconnect between the *prevailing* importance of diplomatic communication in *most* state relationships and the limited importance of such communication in the exceptional cases discussed here. For all its productive uses, diplomatic communication has its limits. States and factions may attach higher priority to their objectives than to using existing or new communication channels to discuss them. And the perceived importance of those objectives is reflected in the fact that attaining them may often be more difficult in the absence of communication channels than when such channels are employed.

Communication is not only of limited value objectively; it may also be discounted by states that had already decided on hostilities, were frustrated by continuing deadlock, or chose to depend on alternatives to diplomatic communication, including norms of international law and the balance of power. The more important those norms are, the less consequential the diplomatic channel for avoiding war.

In addition, adversaries adapt to their relationships. Political realists, we have noted, highlight state preoccupation with one-sided advantage. Such an advantage may be attainable through diplomatic communication, as the study of crisis management presumes. Alternatively, it may not be attainable diplomatically: adversaries may conclude that *avoiding* communication is preferable to capitalizing on a diplomatic safety net.

NOTES

1. Hedley Bull, *The Anarchical Society* (New York: Columbia University Press, 1977), 170.

2. Cited by W. W. Rostow, *The Division of Europe after World War II: 1946* (Austin: University of Texas Press, 1981), 67.

3. Paul Sharp, *Diplomatic Theory of International Relations* (Cambridge: Cambridge University Press, 2009), 10; emphasis in original.

4. Bull, *Anarchical Society*, 179. Dean Rusk writes that "governments must be able to try out ideas on each other and quietly explore the various elements of an agreement before those elements become public." *As I Saw It*, ed. Daniel S. Papp (New York: Penguin, 1990), 562.

5. George F. Kennan, *Memoirs: 1950–1963*, vol. 2 (Boston: Little, Brown, 1972), 139.

6. Robert Jervis, "Cooperation under the Security Dilemma," *World Politics* 30 (January 1978): 167–214.

7. Barry H. Steiner, "Diplomacy and International Theory," *Review of International Studies* 30 (2004): 501.

8. Robert Jervis, *The Logic of Images in International Relations* (Princeton: Princeton University Press, 1970), 95.

9. For a discussion of the use of hypotheticals, see Philip Tetlock and Aaron Belkin, *Counterfactual Thought Experiments in World Politics* (Princeton: Princeton University Press, 1996); and I. William Zartman, *Cowardly Lions* (Boulder, CO: Lynne Rienner, 2005), 9–14.

10. An excellent example of the latter, about which nothing further will be said here, was the relationship between American Secretary of State Dean Acheson and British Ambassador Oliver Franks. See Henry Brandon, *Special Relationships* (New York: Atheneum, 1988), 75ff.

11. Hans J. Morgenthau, *Politics among Nations*, 4th ed. (New York: Knopf, 1967), 525.

12. Ibid.

13. Ibid., 549.

14. Ibid., 524.

15. Ibid., 549.

16. Bull, *Anarchical Society*, 8.

17. Ibid., passim.

18. Robert O. Keohane, *After Hegemony* (Princeton: Princeton University Press, 1984), 89.

19. Geoffrey Butler and Simon Maccoby, *The Development of International Law* (London: Longmans, Green, 1928), 74, cited in Bull, *Anarchical Society*, 167–68.

20. Bull, *Anarchical Society*, 172, 183.

21. Paul Sharp, "Practitioners, Scholars and the Study of Diplomacy," *Foreign Service Journal*, January/February 2015, 41.

22. Bull, *Anarchical Society*, 167.

23. Ibid., 179.

24. Victor A. Kremenyuk, "Preface," in *International Negotiation: Analysis, Approaches, Issues*, ed. Kremenyuk (San Francisco: Jossey-Bass, 1991), xiii.

25. Ibid., xiv. See also I. William Zartman and Maureen R. Berman, *The Practical Negotiator* (New Haven: Yale University Press, 1982); and Roger Fisher et al., *Coping with International Conflict* (Upper Saddle River, NJ: Prentice-Hall, 1997). On preparatory meetings between the negotiating parties to build a cooperative orientation, and to counter frustrations that develop over a negotiating process, see Daniel Druckman and Robert Mahoney, "Processes and Consequences of International Negotiations," *Journal of Social Issues* 33 (1977): 60–87, esp. 68 and 70.

26. Thomas C. Schelling has characterized states as "continually engaged in demonstrations of resolve, tests of nerve, and explorations for understandings and misunderstandings . . . through a diplomatic process of commitment that is itself unpredictable." Schelling, *Arms and Influence* (New Haven, Yale University Press, 1966), 93–94. Hedley Bull notes that one reason for the absence of diplomatic relations historically has been that "relations are so hostile as to make the exchange of ambassadors impossible." Bull, *Anarchical Society*, 173.

Schelling has pioneered the concept of tacit interstate bargaining when diplomatic channels are not available for hostile states to communicate. "When *some* agreement is needed," Thomas Schelling has written, "and when formal diplomacy has been virtually severed, when neither side trusts the other nor expects agreements to be enforceable . . . any agreement that is available may have a take-it-or-leave-it quality." Schelling, *Arms and Influence*, 139, emphasis in original. Such a situation, in which war is averted only when states desperately signal to each other, is beyond the scope of this chapter, which focuses primarily on barriers to traditional means of communication rather than on the ability of states to compensate for the absence of such means. On the role of multiple channels of communication, see ibid., 140–41.

27. Thomas C. Schelling, *The Strategy of Conflict* (Cambridge, MA: Harvard University Press, 1960), 73.

28. Steiner, "Diplomacy and International Theory," 501.

29. Harold H. Saunders, "Regulating Soviet-U.S. Competition and Cooperation in the Arab-Israeli Arena, 1967–86," in *U.S.-Soviet Security Cooperation*, ed. Alexander L. George, Philip J. Farley, and Alexander Dallin (New York: Oxford University Press, 1988), 575, 578–79. Excessive trust in the intentions of an adversary has also been linked to faulty national intelligence estimation. For example, the United States and the Soviet Union each failed to correctly anticipate their opponent's behavior with respect to the emplacement of offensive Soviet missiles in Cuba in 1962. See Sherman Kent, "A Crucial Estimate Relived," in *Sherman Kent and the Board of National Estimates: Collected Essays*, ed. Donald P. Steury (Washington: Center for the Study of Intelligence, Central Intelligence Agency, 1994), 173–88; and Albert Wohlstetter and Roberta Wohlstetter, "Controlling the Risks in Cuba," *Adelphi Paper*, no. 17 (London: Institute of Strategic Studies, 1965).

30. See, for example, Robert D. Putnam, "Diplomacy and Domestic Politics: The Logic of Two-Level Games," *International Organization* 42 (Summer 1988): 427–60.

31. Robert Jervis, who studied the nineteenth-century Concert of Europe, argued that the Concert "may have contained the seeds of its own destruction. Since world politics did not seem so dangerous, pushing harder seemed sensible to individual states. . . . But seeking individualistic gains raised doubts in others' minds as whether moderation and reciprocation would last." Jervis, "Security Regimes," in *International Regimes*, ed. Stephen D. Krasner (Ithaca, NY: Cornell University Press, 1983), 184.

32. This case has been examined from my file of articles from the *New York Times*.

33. David D. Kirkpatrick, "Strife in Libya Could Presage a Long Civil War," *New York Times*, 25 August 2014.

34. This case is based upon Kennan, *Memoirs*.

35. Kennan, *Memoirs*, 121–22.

36. Ibid., 136–37, emphasis in original.

37. Ibid.

38. A. J. P. Taylor, *The Origins of the Second World War* (New York: Atheneum, 1985), 215ff.

39. Ibid., 251.

40. Patrice Louis-Rene Higonnet, "The Origins of the Seven Years' War," *Journal of Modern History* 40 (March 1968): 57–90.

41. Ibid., 71, 78.

42. An extended discussion of this case may be found in chapter 7. See also Samuel P. Huntington, "Arms Races: Prerequisites and Results," in *Public Policy*, ed. Carl J. Friedrich and Seymour E. Harris (Cambridge, MA: Harvard University Graduate School of Public Administration, 1958), 41–58, included in *The Use of Force*, ed. Robert J. Art and Kenneth N. Waltz, (Boston: Little, Brown, 1971), 365–401.

43. Ibid., 367.

44. On crisis management, see Paul Gordon Lauren, Gordon A. Craig, and Alexander L. George, *Force and Statecraft*, 4th ed. (New York: Oxford University Press, 2007), 220ff.

45. For the development and significance of superpower norms of behavior in the cold war, see Alexander L. George, Philip J. Farley, and Alexander Dallin, eds., *U.S.-Soviet Security Cooperation* (New York: Oxford University Press, 1988).

46. Herman Kahn, *On Escalation* (New York: Praeger, 1965), 262–63.

47. Barry H. Steiner, "When Images and Alarm Collide: The Significance of Information Disparity," *International Journal of Intelligence and CounterIntelligence* 28 (2015): 319–46.

48. Richard Cobden, "The Three Panics," in *Political Writings*, vol. 2 (London: Ridgway, 1867), 214–435.

49. "Because so much conflict has been identified with 'group' identity throughout history, those who emerge as the leaders of any group and who confront the task of self-defense for the first time will be skeptical that the strong group identity of others is benign." Barry R. Posen, "The Security Dilemma and Ethnic Conflict," in *Ethnic Conflict and International Security*, ed. Michael E. Brown (Princeton: Princeton University Press, 1993), 106.

50. Ibid., 120.

51. See endnote 26.

52. This was unlike the shift in British naval dispositions that occurred during the

much better-known Anglo-German naval race (1898–1914). On this competition, see E. L. Woodward, *Great Britain and the German Navy* (Oxford: Clarendon, 1935).

53. Whether the British and French failure to communicate on armaments was linked to their mutual determination to pursue long-term naval competition—and, if there was such linkage, how their diplomatic reticence depended on this urge to compete—requires more study.

54. David Schoenbaum notes that Allied reticence on the German question during and after the Second World War "confirms a certain sense of urgency—but for summit diplomacy and open options, not agreement per se." Schoenbaum, "The World War II Allied Agreement on Occupation and Administration of Postwar Germany," in George, Farley, and Dallin, *U.S.-Soviet Security Cooperation*, 39.

55. On norms of crisis management during the superpower cold war period, see Coral Bell, *Conventions of Crisis: A Study in Diplomatic Management* (London: Oxford University Press, 1971). For norms in the nineteenth-century Concert period, see F. H. Hinsley, *Power and the Pursuit of Peace* (Cambridge: Cambridge University Press, 1963), 213ff.

4

Bargaining, Negotiation, and Convergent Interests

One of the most important functions of diplomacy is reconciling state differences to produce agreement. As Adam Watson observes, "Diplomacy . . . has a bias towards the resolution of conflict."[1] Frederic Pearson and J. Martin Rochester note that "the essence of diplomacy remains bargaining [which] can be thought of as a means of settling differences over priorities between contestants through an exchange of proposals for mutually acceptable solutions. There must be conflict over priorities in order for bargaining to take place."[2]

But bargaining is also understood as a diplomatic strategy aiming at national advantage, in contrast to enhancing mutual benefits for disputing states: "*Bargaining* in statecraft is normally regarded as a *contest* in which each side attempts to maximize its own gains at the expense of the other. . . . *Negotiation* . . . is the term usually employed in statecraft to describe *more formal discussions and structured procedures for collaborative problem solving.*"[3] This is the central distinction adopted in this chapter.[4]

Contestation and negotiation are usually integrated as pathways to accommodation, as when an initial standfast position is followed by a more compromising fallback approach. But bargaining and negotiation also compete as strategies for bringing about accommodation.[5] I. William Zartman describes the "Negotiator's or Toughness Dilemma": "The tougher the negotiator, the greater her chance of getting an agreement close to her position but the less her chance of getting an agreement at all, whereas the weaker a negotiator, the greater his chance of getting an agreement but the less his chance of getting that agreement close to his position."[6]

Understanding how diplomats deal with this dilemma is one of the most important researchable issues in diplomatic engagement. "It is only by look-ing into negotiators' behavior," Zartman writes, "that negotiated outcomes can be explained."[7] But the analyst seeking to understand diplomatic strategy must acknowledge the enormous scope of behavior appropriate for study. According to one careful overview, diplomatic interplay "includes all actions or communications, by any party to the negotiation, either made within the negotiating situation or intended to influence its outcome," such as prelimi-nary negotiations, the formulation of alternatives and resistance points, efforts to persuade, and threats and promises.[8] A theorist must narrow her attention within this large range of possibilities.

As a first step, two approaches may be distinguished. One is to examine contestation and negotiation as conflicting pathways to accommodation. They can be viewed as instrumental, and their impact can be tracked. A second approach focuses on why these strategies were adopted, irrespective of their results. Such an approach would compare actual choices between toughness and weakness in specified instances with logical expectations about the result. It would permit closer study of the variability of each case within its case type. Theory can be pursued inductively within that case type by asking similar questions of each of the cases.[9]

This chapter takes the latter approach, using alliance relationships, and specifically instances in which allies cooperate against a common enemy, as its context, thus providing an empirical basis for theorizing.[10] Allies attempt to maximize their gains relative to each other while also engaging in collabo-rative problem-solving designed to provide mutual benefits. But their opposi-tion to a mutual enemy should be highly consequential for their choice of dominant strategy. They would be expected to be more committed to com-mon action and collaboration, and less to contestation, because their security objectives will then be more salient and more highly valued than their con-flicting goals. Alignment without a mutual third state threat lacks such salience and affords more opportunity for contestation strategy.[11]

This chapter hypothesizes that when allies have a common enemy, they will be able to successfully counter contestation strategies with collaboration. Confirmation of the hypothesis would reflect alliance strength and enlarged scope for the "realm of the possible" in alliance relations.[12] It would show that alignments not only are disciplined by their countries' objectives but also adapt *to* them by a strategy of collaboration rather than contestation. It would indicate that, at least in a special class of cases, state objectives are a *pre-dictor* of their diplomacy. This chapter tests this hypothesis empirically.

If, on the other hand, contestation is shown to be more important than collaboration in our cases, alliances would be demonstrated to be relatively weak, as diplomacy impedes cooperation. Self-interested strategies are said to yield more diplomatic rewards than collaboration yields. Zartman writes that "the bargainer who opens negotiations with a high request, has a small rate of concession, has a high minimum level of expectation, and is very perceptive and quite unyielding, will fare better."[13] If this is so, the propensity to obtain advantage should apply also to alliance partners.[14] Furthermore, a collaborative-minded diplomatic orientation appropriate to alliance will not assist agreement if it is applied to a firm ally. "Concession-making," according to one study of the negotiating process, "may not be interpreted as a cooperative gesture but rather as evidence of the opponent's weakness."[15]

Even allies against a common enemy may doubt each other. Rising suspicions or shifts in allied interests contribute to contestation by making joint action and planning more difficult. Close alignment linkages may also make allies more adventuresome, as when one ally uses alignment as leverage to demand and gain one-sided benefits from the other. Strong alignment ties may make the allies more self-satisfied and complacent, neglecting the needs of their partner; alternatively, alliances can stimulate the search for unilateral advantage in negotiation because allies may have a background of deep suspicions or be unable to find diplomatic forms to express their solidarity.

The next section makes more precise the context chosen for analysis in this chapter. Using two prototype examples, it distinguishes between alliance as a special outcome of *regular* diplomatic interplay between allies, unaffected by third parties, and as an outcome of *special* circumstances, in which solidarity between allies emerges from geopolitics and the influence of third parties. We test our hypothesis by analyzing alliances directed to a third state. The chapter then builds on this distinction in terms of three diverse theoretical perspectives, highlighting how they regard our central question of bargaining versus negotiation in alliances whose members share security interests.

The chapter tests contestation as a competitor to negotiation in six contemporary cases. Four questions are asked of each of six profiled case studies, and then detailed comparisons and contrasts answer those questions. A recapitulation of our contrasting viewpoints and a summary of the analytic findings conclude the chapter.

Case analysis finds considerable contestation and one-sided gain in those alliances, but collaboration is required to manage them. Contestation never undermined alliance in the cases, but it occasionally weakened alliance efficiency and brought about a questioning of the allies' common interests. The alliances were protected against contestation in two major ways. When allies' common interests were strong—especially when the common enemy was engaged in war, but at times when it was not a military threat—the allies depended less on diplomatic crisis management to cope with contestation.

When common interests were weaker, crisis management became more important.

The force of these conclusions is limited by the relatively narrow base of the cases selected for analysis. First, comparing alignments having complementary interests with those containing common interests would provide a more demanding and instructive test of the impact of contestation on alliances. The former demands less cooperation than the latter, but the effect of contestation on them is uncertain. Alliances with complementary interests may absorb contestation more easily if there is less at stake, or they may be more easily upset than alliances based on convergent interests. The latter type of alignment, with higher stakes than the former, may require more effort to cope with contestation. Alternatively, contestation may be accepted as the price of sustaining vital common interests.

Second, the contemporary case sample probed here leaves out the tendency in earlier periods for alliances to be more unstable and prone to shift than those in the present era.[16] Since the 1940s, alliances have generally been long-lasting. Because allies in earlier periods were more accustomed to shifts, a study that more ambitiously included cases from earlier periods might, by linking contestation to the greater propensity for alliance shifts, produce conclusions different from those produced here.

I. TWO TYPES OF ALLIANCE-BUILDING

This section argues that alliance-building stimulated by third-party action is more likely to spur collaborative diplomacy than is alliance in the absence of a mutually threatening third party. Convergence of interest stimulates cooperation. Even if their relations had been hostile, the allies' perception of a new common enemy shifts their policies toward cooperating against that threat. In the absence of third-party threats, the interests of the allies are likely to be less harmonious and less receptive to reciprocal alliance initiatives. Progress toward alliance will then be halting and inconsistent, as bargaining and contestation push aside proposals for common action.[17]

We discuss two dimensions of alliance-building—images and diplomatic process—to clarify this distinction. Positive images have been linked to negotiating success. Jack Sawyer and Harold Guetzkow maintain that those images "influence substantially both (a) the actions one party takes toward the other, and (b) the interpretations he places upon the acts of the other."[18] For example, positive images increase the likelihood of collaborative initiatives and alliance-building. Alignment, for its part, logically encourages positive images, as the stakes for cooperation increase. Allies have strong reason to work for agreement—to demonstrate, in Zartman's words, "a genuine interest in trying to help the other side reach its objective while retaining his own objective and making the two appear compatible."[19] And by enhancing favorable interpretations of an ally's behavior, positive images enlarge receptivity to bargaining initiatives and increase their impact, facilitating mutually desired diplomatic interaction. They enlarge, that is, "the means of persuasion to bring about . . . movement [of offers, acceptances, minimum negotiating points], against any defense or countermove."[20] Negative images, by contrast, foster hostility and deadlock, making it difficult or impossible for one negotiating party to take constructive initiatives or to persuade others; during Soviet-American cold war, for example, contestation by one side invited a response in kind.[21]

The argument is, first, that allies with convergent, identical interests will have more enduring positive images of each other than will allies with complementary interests. Convergent interests provide a stronger foundation for collaboration than do complementary ones. The requirement of containing, or balancing against, their opponent is likely to shape what Sawyer and Guetzkow term "superordinate" interests, which are unattainable by each ally acting separately and require cooperation between the two.[22] Positive images, and negotiation and agreement, are also encouraged by close association between convergent allies' policymakers and diplomats.

Second, convergent interests will facilitate and simplify the diplomatic process more effectively than complementary interests. Ordinarily, states are subject to a two-step diplomatic process: they must agree on a diplomatic agenda—that is, determine which issues they will address diplomatically— before they can attempt substantive negotiations.[23] Complementary interests do not escape such a process: allies are free to employ contestation and hard bargaining at each step, and their divergence may cause deadlock at either step. But convergent interests underpin a common agenda, enabling allies to address common and divergent concerns directly without having to identify common interests beforehand.

In short, alignment with convergent interests makes self-evident *what* the parties should address, and their *need* to do so, enhancing the negotiation process and enabling allies to proceed immediately to accommodate and operationalize joint benefits consistent with those interests, rather than haggling over their diplomatic agenda. Clarifying the diplomatic agenda through bedrock common interests, such alignment positions the allies to focus on implementation and to avoid endless talk and deadlock.

A. Alignment with Regular Interplay

Diplomatic interplay between states may reveal compatible security objectives in the absence of a mutually threatening third state. Interests of the cooperating states are then likely to be complementary rather than convergent, as in the secret Franco-Russian alliance of January 1894, characterized by A. J. P. Taylor as "a turning-point in the history of Europe." The pact's "serious intention, so far as it had one," according to Taylor, "was to keep Germany neutral while the two partners pursued their several objects elsewhere."[24]

1. Images

Positive French images of Russia and positive Russian images of France were present in the 1890s but were hardly categorical; the French, for example, used loans to Russia "to sweeten her for an alliance," but Russia was still known as the oppressor of the Poles and France as the champion of antiauthoritarianism.[25] The impact of positive images was diluted by general insecurity and diplomatic caution, and by the shifting diplomatic agenda. "Both France and Russia had feared that they would be isolated in the face of a hostile coalition," reports Taylor, "and this fear drove them together. But each Power was still looking over its shoulder."[26] Positive images provided little protection against contestation and resistance to cooperation. In the autumn of 1892 Franco-Russian relations cooled when the French president charged that the Russian ambassador to France had been involved in a Panama Canal scandal; just a year before agreement on the Franco-Russian alliance, the Russian monarch Alexander III caused the French president to apologize for making the charge.[27]

2. Diplomatic Process

Contestation in Franco-Russian relations was predictable at the diplomatic agenda stage because of the difference in Russian and French objectives. Russia worked against British naval supremacy in the Mediterranean while demanding that the French not make war against Germany to recover Alsace and Lorraine. French insistence that a Russian army provide a balance against Germany became the foundation for the Franco-Russian military convention of August 1892, while an earlier Franco-Russian military entente of August 1891, aimed by Russia against England, committed France to diplomatic action against England at Constantinople. Each side advocated its own version of the military convention and disregarded the other.[28]

B. Alliances Produced by Third-Party Threat

Hostile images allies hold toward a third state are a powerful motive for building alliances. The larger their negative image of the third state, the more the allies can sustain problems in their own relationship. A classic example is the rapprochement in the 1970s between China and the United States generated to deal with the threat both perceived from the Soviet Union.

1. Images

For decades after 1949, when the Communists were victorious in the Chinese civil war, American images of the Communist Chinese mainland regime and Chinese attitudes toward the United States had been overwhelmingly negative. "By March 1969," according to Henry Kissinger, "Chinese-American relations seemed essentially frozen in the same hostility of mutual incomprehension and distrust that had characterized them for twenty years."[29] The need for a new approach was made evident to both countries following Chinese-Soviet clashes in Northeast Asia along the Ussuri River in March 1969, followed by additional incidents in April, May, and August 1969. Kissinger writes that, "ironically, it was heavy-handed Soviet diplomacy that made us think about our opportunities" after the Soviet ambassador to the United States delivered a long briefing about Chinese atrocities in the first of the clashes.

Kissinger insisted that American planners take account of the Chinese role in the "power equation," noting that "it was usually more advantageous to align oneself with the weaker of two antagonistic partners, because this acted as a restraint on the stronger."[30] He also sought improved communications with China and argued that an American rapprochement with China would contribute to Soviet conciliation of the United States. By August, President Nixon informed his cabinet of his view that the Soviet Union was more aggressive than China and that the United States should commit to prevent the Soviets from defeating China militarily.[31] An authoritative Chinese official on April 1 publicly listed the Soviets and the United States as equal threats to China, "fulfilling," according to Kissinger, "one of the preconditions of triangular diplomacy, that the United States should not be the principal enemy."[32]

2. Diplomatic Process

Prior to 1969, the primary Chinese-American diplomatic problem was not contestation but the lack of diplomatic contact. Once the strategy of triangular diplomacy was set and new contacts were made, Chinese-American relations became mostly collaborative. Both sides sought a framework for normalizing Chinese-American relations, and although differences remained over the terms of normalization, particularly on the status of Taiwan, they were of much smaller moment than the strategic calculations the two countries shared.[33] Convergence of Chinese-American interests toward the Soviet Union was clear, and the understanding that China and the United States could work together to strengthen the convergence neutralized prior mistrust and prevented contestation from impeding improved relations.

Table 4.1 summarizes the two types of alliance-building.

II. THREE PERSPECTIVES ABOUT BARGAINING

The perspectives introduced in the last chapter—political realism, liberal internationalism, and applied diplomacy—understand contestation and negotiation in diverse ways. We now review those perspectives in this context.

A. Political Realism

Contestation is consistent with the realist emphasis on "the struggle for power among sovereign nations," which necessitated "bringing the different elements of national power to bear with maximum effects" on specific areas of the international arena to serve the national interest.[34] It is also the primary diplomatic strategy for increasing the influence of a country beyond what its power makeup would lead an observer to expect.[35] Limitations to the exercise of power, something the realist is also sensitive to, increase the importance of collaborative diplomacy.[36] Diplomatic advantages sought in negotiation are often denied; Joseph E. Nye and Robert Keohane write that "political bargaining is the usual means of translating potential into effects, and a lot is often lost in the translation."[37] And too much haggling for advantage can be counterproductive if it isolates states and impedes their ability to work with others.[38]

The realist encourages the study of tension between collaboration and contestation in an alliance. "Glancing through the treaties of alliance of the

Table 4.1.   Two Types of Alliance-Building

Alliance type	Strategy	Chief barrier to alliance	Outcome
1. No common external threat	Contestation and collaboration	Diplomatic complexity	Complementary interests
2. Common external threat	Contestation followed by collaboration	Prior hostility	Convergent interests

seventeenth and eighteenth centuries," Hans J. Morgenthau writes, "one is struck by the meticulous precision with which obligations to furnish troops, equipment, logistic support, food, money, and the like, were defined."[39] Such far-reaching collaboration, apparently aimed at lessening mistrust between states, deemphasizes diplomatic contestation logically dictated by the struggle for power and mistrust between states. On the other hand, mistrust between allies may lead them to bargain for advantage: they may find it difficult to collaborate, may not be reassured about their respective ability to implement shared goals, or may be unwilling to share information.

B. Liberal Internationalism

The liberal internationalist posits that an international society provides order by sustaining the most important goals of states. An international society, writes Watson, "provides diplomacy with its full possibilities and sets its limitations."[40] It enables an "intensifying search by independent states for areas of consent in which they can act together . . . to solve common problems," but it also legitimizes independent state action.[41] Indeed, Watson defines diplomacy as *"negotiation between political entities which acknowledge each other's independence."*[42] Hedley Bull, on the other hand, portrays international society as not requiring diplomatic cooperation, and when he elaborates on the diplomatic component of international society, he stresses bargaining produced by conflicting state interests.

Bull critiqued the post-WWI diplomatic emphasis on what he termed "international technical management . . . in which the central concern is not conciliation of the different interests of states but collaboration to maximize a common interest."[43] He believed that diplomacy's most important function, "the attempt, through the 'application of intelligence and tact,' to identify the interests of states and bring about conciliation between them where possible," declined for this reason. "Diplomacy," he writes, "is undermined . . . by situations in which states regard their interests as being identical. In these situations . . . [t]heir common problem is not the political or diplomatic one of reconciling different interests or demands but the technical one of finding the most efficient means of achieving a given end."[44] In this process, bargaining would evidently slow down a more open and shared diplomatic process, giving collaborative efforts a subordinate role. Alliances, for their part, cannot improve on the stability of an international society posited by the liberal internationalist. When aimed against a third state or coalition, alliances may even weaken international stability if, striving for what Watson describes as "a sufficient degree of coherence between the inevitably somewhat divergent interests of its members," the allies neglect interalliance negotiation and dialogue.[45]

C. Applied Diplomacy

The applied diplomatic approach rejects that diplomatic engagement is a zero-sum pursuit, plays down mistrust as a negotiating problem, and does not rely on the cooperative framework of an international society. It aims at integrative, positive-sum negotiating outcomes rather than relative negotiating benefits. It does this by using the negotiating process to build confidence between the parties, to question negotiating assumptions, to make diplomatic interaction more open and transparent, and to employ a joint problem-solving approach. Prenegotiations ensure that a negotiator "is likely to enter negotiations with a more cooperative orientation than one who has engaged in extensive strategy planning on a unilateral (own-team) basis."[46] The idea that the positive sum of the goods and values of agreement may not be enough to cover the parties' requirements justifies strengthening and enhancing mutual interests in the negotiating process.[47]

The applied diplomatic approach also desires to transform the parties' subjective attitudes toward their conflict. "Zero-sum perceptions," write Zartman and Berman, "are characteristic of a conflict before it becomes the subject of negotiations; the secret of negotiation is to change that perception and in the process to change the stakes into items that can be used to benefit both parties."[48] According to Sawyer and Guetzkow, "Even . . . genuine conflict of interests may be heightened or mitigated by psychological factors, and . . . these may influence its eventual outcome."[49] This approach is alert to how differences in the way negotiating parties see a set of issues could contribute to a peaceful settlement.[50] Alternatively, states may overplay commonalities and collaborative potential, becoming complacent and taking for granted that alliance objectives will be fulfilled while giving less attention to their implementation.

In short, the political realist, viewing world politics primarily as a battle between states for national advantage, must explain alliance cooperation as a special case. Alliances highlight self-restraint and reassurance about cooperative intentions, but can be impaired by excessive search for national advantage. The liberal internationalist emphasizes norms of international society and concerns with international order, but also state contestation for national advantage. Competition for advantage by states seems to necessitate interstate collaboration distinct from common concerns for international order. The applied diplomacy perspective, aiming at integrative, mutually beneficial positive-sum negotiating outcomes, downplays bargaining and contestation that do not lead to positive-sum outcomes. It also highlights that gaining diplomatic agreement can be difficult, even when allies share interests. Common interests may contribute to overconfidence about bringing about mutual benefits and to complacence in operationalizing them.

The differences between our three perspectives are described in table 4.2.

III. QUESTIONS FOR THE CASES

Four common questions, enumerated below, were asked of our cases.

1. What motivated the allies' convergence of interests, and how urgent was that motivation? Did the allies reflect the same urgency about their common interests?

How much do the allies' common interests, and their willingness to jointly implement them, depend on the threat they perceive from their common enemy? Alliance solidarity is likely to be high when they believe that threat is significant. In the initial alignment period, for example, solidarity is likely to be considerable, as alignment responds to and, to some degree, repairs the allies' prior insecurities. The allies may also have different levels of urgency in acting on their common interests: one ally may be in more immediate jeopardy from the common enemy than the other, and the latter may find it difficult to satisfy its ally's need for troops and weapons while still protecting itself against the same enemy.

Table 4.2.   Perspectives on Diplomatic Bargaining

Perspective	Guiding bargaining	Character of negotiating process	Implications for allies with common interests
Political Realism	National interest and national advantage	Competitive	Cooperation as a special case; precision of commitment
Liberal Internationalism	State independence	Shared responsibility and competition	Bargaining likely despite common interests
Applied Diplomacy	Promoting positive outcomes and changed attitudes	Shared responsibility	Allies have unique negotiating problems

2. How efficient was the allies' collaboration? Was that efficiency diminished by contestation and self-interest?

Convergent interests mean little unless they are translated into concrete joint programs of cooperation. But efficiency of cooperation often falls short of the ideal. The allies may have been deeply suspicious of each other, their solidarity may have diminished, or, despite their alignment, they may remain committed to unilateral advantage. These are conducive to contestation strategies, which conflict with the spirit of convergence and may further damage alliance solidarity and cooperation. The interest here is the extent to which contestation affected negotiation and implementation of the allies' common interests and the problems raised by contestation in relation to the common enemy.

3. Did contestation strategy threaten the allies' common interests, and thereby their alignment?

Beyond threatening cooperation, bargaining and contestation can also lead to rethinking interests or policies underpinning such cooperation. But anticipation of such shifts in interest and policy may prevent contestation by countries determined to continue the alignment. The concern here is whether the allies are committed to continue their alignment in the face of contestation, and, if so, whether that commitment brings efforts to suppress contestation strategies that endanger the alignment.

4. Can contestation itself cause the downfall of alliances? Alternatively, how do alliances withstand contestation?

The strength, or capacity, of alignment can be determined by how allies manage contestation strategies. Contestation may be so corrosive to common objectives as to undermine alignment. Anticipated benefits to alignment may be smaller than the problems associated with tough bargaining, or allies may have low tolerance for diplomatic disputes and tough bargaining even when they expect large benefits from their alliance, perhaps because of their large initial trust of each other. Such alignments would have a lower capacity. Alternatively, alignments may withstand contestation. Large anticipated gains from alliance may overshadow difficulties associated with disputes. Even when the anticipated benefits of alignment are relatively small, contestation may be understood as normal and surmountable. If so, their alignment may be said to have a high capacity.

IV. CASE PROFILES

The six cases selected for analysis are listed in table 4.3. Space permits only brief outlines of the cases, which have been selected because they embody different partners and different alignment issues. Since the main concern here is not historical description but explanation, richness in historical source material has been sacrificed in favor of a small number of authoritative and insider accounts; in one instance, only a single source has been used.

Case 1: United States–Soviet Union (1941–1945)[51]

The interests of the United States and the Soviet Union converged following the German invasion of the Soviet Union in June 1941. Shortly after the invasion, President Franklin Roosevelt sent Harry Hopkins to Moscow to confirm American willingness to assist Russia, whose only leverage with the United States was its determination to fight Germany. "As a negotiating experience," Joseph G. Whelan writes, "the Hopkins mission was unique. The United States had all the bargaining chips, but it did not bargain: it asked for nothing, only a shopping list. The sole U.S. objective was to keep Soviet Russia in the war, and it was willing to pay the price without asking for anything more than what the Soviets might have been only willing to pay; namely, to fight the Germans. . . . Soviet-American interests coalesced in absolute terms, having the effect of leveling the inequities in bargaining."[52]

President Roosevelt sought to build trust between the United States and the Soviet Union for this purpose, despite past ideological differences.[53] Absence of such trust on the Soviet side, however, ironically required the Americans to bargain in a manner they did not anticipate. As John Deane, who headed the wartime U.S. Military Mission to the Soviet Union, put it, "Every effort to collaborate was a negotiation which had to be bargained out." The continuing challenge for the Americans was to find agreed-upon detailed ways to implement cooperation with the Soviet Union on such issues as information about the Soviet utilization of lend-lease shipments, use of Soviet bases for

Table 4.3. Six Cases Selected for Analysis

1. United States–Soviet Union (1941–1945)
2. United States–Great Britain–Soviet Union (1945–1946)
3. United States–Great Britain (1962)
4. Great Britain–Malta (1970–1972)
5. United States–Israel (1975)
6. United States–Japan (1993–1995)

bombing operations, repatriation of liberated American prisoners of war, and advance planning for Soviet war-making against Japan.

Cooperation on all these matters was poor. The Soviet Union rejected commitments that would constrain it once the war ended. Moreover, its political system did not encourage interaction between the two countries below the highest official levels. Subordinate Russian officials were not able to take responsibility for even routine issues raised by the Americans, and, as a result, these issues could not be resolved. The Americans ultimately found it more effective to act alone than to seek explicit agreement from the Soviet Union to cooperate. The United States was not opposed to bargaining, but negotiation had become too slow and cumbersome for American war-making interests.

Case 2: United States–Britain–Soviet Union (1945–1946)[54]

In early 1945, as the Soviet Army moved toward Germany from the east, and American and British armies advanced toward Germany in the west, the American government decided to seek an agreement in principle on the post-war status of Eastern European countries newly liberated by the Russians from Nazi rule. This agreement, the "Declaration of Liberation in Europe," reached at the Big Three Conference at Yalta in February 1945, included "mutual agreement to concert during the temporary period of instability in liberated Europe the policies of their three Governments in assisting the peoples liberated from the domination of Nazi satellite states of Europe to solve by democratic means their pressing political and economic problems," to help form "interim governmental authorities broadly representative of all democratic elements in the population," and to hold free elections.[55]

Supporting this diplomatic approach, first, was that the United States lacked the will or capability to impede the Soviet military advance.[56] "Under these circumstances," Mark Etheridge and Cyril Black write, referring to Soviet political superiority in the areas liberated by its army, "any specific and detailed agreement might have tended to work to the Russian advantage in the Balkans, as the terms of armistice agreements with the Axis satellite states had already demonstrated."[57] Second, detailed negotiation would have been too time-consuming, and the Soviets in any case could have moved on their own to exert control in Eastern Europe, as they did in Yugoslavia earlier.[58] Third, agreement in principle preserved the great power concert, to which the Americans attached continuing importance, for completing the war against Germany and for shifting forces to the Far East to fight Japan, while still using the concert as leverage to hold the Soviet Union accountable for its political behavior in Eastern Europe.

Fourth, the agreement in principle distracted from an important concession by the United States, never clarified to the American people, over the composition of the postwar regime in Poland. In detailed Yalta discussion about Poland, which far exceeded discussion of the agreement in principle,[59] Josef Stalin opposed a British demand for a "fully representative" Polish government to consist primarily of noncommunist Poles. President Roosevelt mediated a compromise by which the Polish communist faction was to be reorganized with noncommunist elements, but no mention was made of a "fully representative" government.

Agreement in principle could not be used as leverage in relation to the Soviet Union, and it made breaking the alliance more difficult when a dispute later arose over Soviet support for the communist (Lublin) faction as the nucleus of the new Polish regime. As one Roosevelt advisor noted, the Soviets "could stretch [the agreement in principle] all the way from Yalta to Washington without ever technically breaking it."[60] Nevertheless, after Roosevelt died and Stalin ignored the agreement in principle, President Truman in April 1945 condemned Soviet behavior toward Poland in the strongest terms. Threatening the Soviet foreign minister with a break in the alliance in April 1945, he insisted that a new and "genuinely representative" Polish government be formed.[61] American officials had reassessed the need for Soviet intervention in the Far East, concluding that even if Russia halted its war effort, no harm would be done to American war prospects.[62] The Americans did not wish to break the wartime alliance, but they worried about Soviet opportunistic behavior toward states weakened in the war against Germany and Japan, and they employed the Yalta agreements as a lever to limit Soviet power.

In the end, Soviet power prevailed in Poland: communists were retained as a nucleus of a postwar Polish government with noncommunist elements. The British were more anxious than the Americans on this question because of steady American force withdrawal following the end of the war in Europe,[63] but the Big Three alignment prevailed until the end of the war in Asia in August 1945.

Case 3: United States–Great Britain (1962)[64]

The Anglo-American alliance was based on what has been termed "foundations of felt need," including shared global interests, which grew in strength following the Second World War. The United States and Great Britain were said to "never [have] had external ties so variegated and so tight—and so sustained—as those to one another" in this period.[65] In March 1960, the British prime minister, Harold Macmillan, met with President Eisenhower at Camp David and received American assurance that the United States would develop a bomber-carried air-to-surface missile, called Skybolt by the U.S. Air Force, with which the British intended to double the life of the Royal Air Force Bomber Command as a strategic deterrent. It was understood that if the United States found the missile feasible to deploy, it would furnish it to the RAF. (At that time the U.S. Air Force sought the missile, while the secretary of defense doubted whether its technical requirements could be achieved or whether the United States would ultimately seek to deploy it.) Macmillan offered the United States a naval base at Holy Loch in Scotland in exchange for Skybolt development.

The "spirit of Camp David" was invoked to symbolize the close relationship associated with the bomber and naval base deal, but in 1962, after the secretary of defense's staff questioned the value of the missile's development to suppress Soviet air defense, the United States decided to cancel the Skybolt system on budgetary grounds. The United States underestimated the problems this cancellation would cause the British: both a higher price for Skybolt and the threat to British strategic independence and to Anglo-American interdependence if the system were not deployed. For their part, the British government did not propose any alternative when advised by the Americans of their problem with that system.

In this instance, American and British leaders gave insufficient attention to implementing the convergent interests of their two countries. Neither side anticipated the needs of the other or the other's likely reactions to its own decisions. Each side was also reticent toward the other, as policymakers feared that because of their political vulnerability at home, as Richard Neustadt put it, "any word to friends across the ocean, may come back to other ears at home." Because of common interests and close acquaintance, neither side considered that its behavior might harm the other nor was either side motivated to check its views of the other even as inaccurate views risked the political support each sought from the other for its political goals. "Misperceptions," Neustadt writes, "make for crisis in proportion to the intimacy of relations. . . . [A]cquaintance has wrapped up in it a faulty sense of competence, hence misplaced confidence. Instead of countering inaccuracy this contributes to it."[66]

As a public crisis emerged, compromise was forged at a two-day Anglo-American summit conference at Nassau in December 1962. It was decided that the British would receive Polaris missiles from the United States and would build the submarines and their missile warheads. The Polaris system was to be controlled by NATO under an integrated command to which the

United States would also contribute, but the British, intent on having an *independent* deterrent, would be permitted to withdraw the system from NATO control in the event of an emergency.[67]

Case 4: Great Britain–Malta (1970–1972)[68]

Malta, which obtained its formal independence from Great Britain in 1964, thereafter provided facilities for a British and NATO naval and air base and remained heavily dependent on British financial assistance. The two countries' convergent interests lay in common opposition to the Soviet Union, with Malta embedded in NATO defense strategy. However, the new Maltese leader, Dom Mintoff, who by 1971 had grown close diplomatically to Colonel Qaddafy of Libya, raised the possibility of depending on economic support from Libya and the Soviet Union, placing the convergence of interests with Great Britain in question.

Known for unpredictability and rashness, Mintoff abrogated in 1971 the Anglo-Malta base agreement that was due to run until 1974 and demanded, as a condition for its renewal, that Britain pay much higher rent and that other NATO members using Malta's port contribute to the rent. He also declared that American vessels would not for the moment be welcome in Malta's port, thereby engaging the attention of American policymakers. In his bargaining with the British, he used American and Italian officials, who were more committed to continuation of the base facilities than were the British; and also the Libyan and Soviet connections, though aware that neither Libya nor the Soviet Union could provide economic resources to match Britain's rent payment.

The British sought to undermine Mintoff's public support by lessening their financial assistance to Malta, thereby contributing to Maltese unemployment. Showing their growing disinterest in the island, they stretched out the renewal negotiations and ultimately halted the introduction of fresh English troops into Malta. By March 1972, when an agreement on renewing the British base was reached, all but thirty of the British forces had been evacuated and fifty thousand tons of equipment had been withdrawn.[69] Mintoff, who counted on Britain's NATO allies to keep the British presence, argued that "only if we risk all" could Malta gain its needed resources. He succeeded with this tactic. "Dom Mintoff has persuaded enough people in the military and national security bureaucracies of the United States and Italy that he might not agree to a settlement acceptable to Great Britain, and that he just might open the Maltese gates to the Russians," writes Howard Wriggins, adding that "if all states dealt with each other in this way, a viable comity of nations would be impossible to maintain."[70]

Case 5: United States–Israel (1975)[71]

Since the 1967 Six-Day War, Israeli and American interests converged on blunting Soviet influence in the Mideast, neutralizing Soviet military assistance to Israel's Arab neighbors. In the 1973 Yom Kippur War, American military assistance enabled Israel to repel invasion from Egypt and Syria. The United States capitalized on tenuous cease-fire lines on Egyptian and Syrian fronts to press for step-by-step Israeli territorial disengagement in exchange for assurances by Egypt and Syria that would improve Israeli security. American shuttle diplomacy led to the Sinai I agreement, which included an initial small Israeli withdrawal from the Suez Canal, and a small disengagement on the Syrian front (May 1974), designed to serve as the basis for further disengagement agreements on those fronts later. However, in a second American effort at Israeli disengagement in the Sinai early in 1975, Israel refused to accommodate. Returning in late March 1975 from a two-week period of shuttle diplomacy between Israel and Egypt, Secretary of State Henry Kissinger informed President Gerald Ford that the deadlock with Israel was "devastating. . . . I have never seen such cold-blooded playing with the American national interest. . . . What they have done is destroy us. . . . Step-by-step is dead."[72]

The Americans began a publicized reassessment of relations with Israel that contained three elements: (1) a request that American federal agencies end "special relationships" with their Israeli counterparts and that some sophisticated American military assistance to Israel be held up, (2) a decision to accept a showdown in Congress that was expected to resist, on Israel's initiative, the administration's executive initiatives, and (3) a willingness to consider a more ambitious comprehensive initiative for Arab-Israeli peace as a threat to influence the Israelis in the event that another interim agreement were not reached. American officials considered pushing such an initiative, supported by a slowdown in military assistance, despite the likelihood of Israeli and congressional opposition.

Ultimately, American officials decided against prioritizing the ambitious plan and its linkage to military assistance, instead aiming at an interim agreement, postponing the push for a comprehensive settlement and a confrontation with Congress until after the 1976 election. The second interim agreement between Israel and Egypt (Sinai II) was concluded in September 1975; the Israelis disengaged further in the Sinai on the basis of (1) Egyptian agreement to a buffer zone around key Sinai military passes, in which American civilian personnel could monitor a prospective Egyptian invasion effort, and (2) what has been termed "a very impressive list of American commitments" to the Israelis, including a military and economic assistance package and agreement not to negotiate with the Palestine Liberation Organization until it recognized the State of Israel.[73]

Case 6: United States–Japan (1993–1995)[74]

American and Japanese interests converged in opposition to Soviet and Chinese influence in East Asia. But the convergence supported American bargaining for relative advantage in the 1990s, stimulated by a $50 billion adverse trade deficit with Japan. Spurred on by the influence of American domestic insurance and manufacturing interests, which yearned to expand their international trade and to overcome nontariff barriers (chiefly Japanese domestic preference rules) to enter the Japanese market, the United States sought a larger market share in Japan for American products. In ensuing redistributive "managed trade" negotiations, Japanese concessions to American firms diminished market share for powerful Japanese firms. The strategy was backed by the threat of American trade sanctions.

In this episode, the United States expanded its diplomacy into "domestic" Japanese economic policy-making that had earlier been diplomatically out of bounds. "When American foreign policy becomes economic policy," Thomas L. Friedman wrote in 1994 about this episode, "the work of diplomats doesn't stop at another country's borders. To the contrary. It starts there and moves inward. Economic diplomacy requires the United States to get involved in the plumbing and wiring of other nations' internal affairs more deeply than ever before."[75] As he notes, the United States wished to "deliberately cause a political crisis between the two [allied] countries so the leadership [in the target country] felt compelled to force changes on the conservative bureaucrats who have a viselike grip on the country's affairs."[76] As a result, Japan agreed to make a "highly significant" reduction in its current-account trade surplus with the United States "over the medium term," and "objective criteria" were used to measure progress in each market sector.

V. CASE COMPARISONS

We now use our common questions as benchmarks to identify similarities and differences among our cases.

1. What motivated the convergence of allies' interests, and how urgent was that motivation? Did the allies reflect the same urgency about their common interests?

Convergence of interest was strongest in our Soviet-American cases, whose alignments were based on the mutual need to defeat Germany and Japan militarily. Even after Soviet forces repelled the German invasion of the Soviet Union, the war question was urgent and contributed to strong Soviet-American solidarity. (Although the Americans fought almost entirely alone against Japan, the United States accepted the need for Soviet cooperation to gain Japanese surrender.) To be sure, the basis for this convergence weakened in the later stage of the European war, as Soviet forces liberated Eastern Europe from Nazi German domination; the Soviets (and the British) showed more urgency over the status of liberated peoples than did the United States.[77] However, as long as the war against the Axis powers lasted, Soviet-American interests converged and alliance unity remained strong.

In our other four cases, in which a strong third-power threat was missing, alliance solidarity diminished because of differences over particular issues. The United States, wishing to capitalize on momentum associated with its role as a mediator following the conclusion of the Yom Kippur War, desired Israeli agreement to a second Sinai redeployment, but the Israelis rejected military accommodation. The United States and Great Britain had different levels of urgency over the British demand for an air-delivered ballistic missile, as the British expected to receive a Skybolt system that the United States had canceled. And the United States and Japanese reflected different levels of urgency in response to the trade imbalance facing the two countries. In the remaining case, alliance solidarity was reduced because interest convergence was of little consequence to either ally: the Maltese government considered alignment with Libya and even the Soviet Union, while the British nearly evacuated their NATO base because of Maltese demands.

2. How efficient was the allies' collaboration? Was that efficiency diminished by contestation and self-interest?

Allied cooperation was severely impaired by contestation in the British-Malta, U.S.-Israel, and the first Soviet-American cases. Alienated by Dom Mintoff's tough bargaining on the Malta base, the British decided not to cooperate with him, and the value of the base was brought into question. Similarly, Israeli refusal to accommodate on Sinai disengagement angered Henry Kissinger, who brought about American rethinking of Israeli-American relations. His initial preference at this stage was to shift diplomatic ground away from "step-by-step" peacemaking in concert with Israel and toward comprehensive Egyptian-Israeli peace independent of Israel. Although U.S. officials eventually rejected this idea, American-Israeli diplomatic cooperation was interrupted for some months. And cooperation was impaired by the Soviet inability to work with the Americans to enhance war-making against the Germans. For example, the Soviets refused to provide bases for American bombing operations against Germany or to repatriate liberated American prisoners of war.

Contestation did not impair alliance cooperation in other cases. In the second Soviet-American case, intensifying disputes about the postliberation regimes in Romania and especially Poland arose following the Yalta conference, but the United States was not prepared to fight militarily to create regimes representative of their peoples in those countries. It put aside its Yalta concession on Poland when it protested Soviet support for the Lublin communist faction, but shortly afterward it acquiesced to the Soviet actions. Substantial American contestation over Poland did not diminish wartime cooperation with the Soviet Union.

American cancellation of the Skybolt system did not impair Anglo-American cooperation, as leaders from the two countries met shortly afterward at Nassau to agree that Americans would supply Polaris submarine missiles to Great Britain. And American cooperation with Japan was unaffected by the American demand that Japan provide a larger market share to American firms in Japan.

3. Did contestation strategy threaten the allies' common interests, and thereby their alignment?

Contestation threatened but did not rupture convergent interests in the second Soviet-American episode, nor did it do so in the U.S.-Israel and British-Malta cases. In these instances, officials considered breaking an alignment over a particular dispute but decided not to do so.

Some American officials concluded that Soviet efforts to install a regime led by the Communist Party in Poland violated the Yalta Declaration on Liberated Peoples, but the Americans did not break their alignment with the Soviet Union on that question. Again, following the Israeli government's rejection of a second step-by-step agreement, Secretary of State Kissinger blamed Israel for the deadlock but refused to accept it. President Gerald Ford ultimately reaccommodated to the step-by-step peacemaking favored by Israel.[78]

When the British decided on their own that retention of the Malta base was no longer in their interest, only American and Italian intervention in support of the Malta base, and Malta's role in NATO's Mediterranean strategy, influenced the British not to pull out of Malta and to reconcile with Mintoff.

Contestation did not threaten common interests in the other cases. U.S. unconditional support of the Soviet Union in its defense against Nazi Germany did not waver with Soviet refusal to actively cooperate with the United States in the war effort. Convergent interests were then maintained despite the decline of alignment efficiency. Convergence was not at issue in the Skybolt or the Japanese market-share cases.

4. Can contestation itself cause the downfall of alliances? Alternatively, how do alliances withstand contestation?

All our cases demonstrated the capacity of alliances to withstand contestation. In the one example of alignment failure, the breakdown of the Soviet-American wartime alliance and the onset of superpower cold war were not caused by a bargaining dispute.

Salience of the common enemy, as in the Soviet-American wartime alignments, is one explanation for the durability of alliances, but it is noteworthy that the Soviet-American alliance outlived the end of the Second World War in August 1945. Following Soviet concessions on Poland in the summer of 1945, the Americans made a large effort (in the Control Council in Berlin, for example) to collaborate with the Soviet Union, rejecting a showdown "until a longer test had been made of Soviet intentions and of the possibility of living with the Russians in Europe and elsewhere without the tension of an unending test of strength."[79] As this indicates, the wartime alliance did not dissolve because of Soviet contestation over European questions but because of American preoccupation with postwar political instability and weakness in such countries as France, Italy, and Greece. As has been indicated, American hostility toward the Soviet Union was fueled by concern that the Soviets could capitalize on postwar problems fostered by the war against Germany and Japan.

When they lacked military urgency to cooperate, our allies found it difficult to disengage from each other. In long-term alignments (U.S.-UK; U.S.-Israel; U.S.-Japan), the intermingling of allied countries' personnel doubtless helped reduce contestation and enlarge policy consensus, encouraging what Roger Fisher and others have characterized as "friendly bargaining."[80] This approach involves "standard moves . . . to make offers and concessions, to trust the other side, to be friendly, and to yield as necessary to avoid confrontation. The friendly negotiating game emphasizes the importance of building and maintaining a relationship. Priority is given to reaching an agreement."[81] Friendly bargaining contributes to "the process of combining divergent viewpoints to reach a common agreement."[82] It would not be expected when, as in the wartime Soviet-American relationship, an aggressive third power unites previously hostile states.

The durability of alliances cannot hide frequent contestation between alliance partners. Leaders acted to protect their alignment by giving contestation

high-level political attention in the second U.S.-Soviet episode and in the
U.S.-Israel, Anglo-American, and Japanese-American cases. Accepting it was
a high priority, they were determined to continue their alignment. In the first
U.S.-Soviet episode, the United States absorbed the difficulties caused by
Soviet contestation, given that the Soviet Union's share of wartime casualties
was so high. The Malta case presents the opposite extreme, as the British
government was inclined to walk away from its Malta commitment.

Contestation in two of our cases originated from domestic sources independent of government, only to be counteracted by action to reinforce the
alliance. One such action defused those interests so they did not endanger the
alignment. The United States accommodated to Israel in 1975 partly to avoid
provoking pro-Israel domestic opposition that would endanger the Republican Party in 1976. A second method to counteract domestic-source contestation is to ensure that it does not interfere with the allies' convergent interests.
The American government's handling of the U.S.-Japanese market-share
controversy ensured that American and Japanese governmental interests
remained convergent despite the disruptive market-share issues.

VI. REVIEWING THE PERSPECTIVES

Recalling our three perspectives, we can see how our cases highlight their
respective strengths and weaknesses.

A. Political Realism

Political realists' concern for collaboration between allies is their most
important contribution to the analysis, as common danger from third states
requires allied states to temper the struggle for power between *themselves*.
Yet implementing community interests will be more difficult to the degree
that states are *generally* governed by strong interstate competition and
rivalry. At the least, engagement of allies in noncompetitive, collaborative
norms, even against a common threat, cannot be taken for granted. Morgenthau himself, impressed with precise burden-sharing within alliances, seemed
to understand this difficulty. Such precision may be required to overcome
prior interstate suspicions, but it also reflects the burden and cost of implementing common interests.

Collaboration was especially difficult when—as in the U.S.-Israel and UK-
Malta cases—cooperative efficiency between allies was undercut and the
community of interests between them was questioned. It was less difficult
when neither of these problems surfaced, as in the U.S.-UK and U.S.-Japan

examples. In the latter instances, the durability of collaboration depended on the allies' expectations about each other. High expectations generally enhance collaboration but also lower the threshold of collaboration difficulty.

B. Liberal Internationalism

The liberal internationalist contributes to this analysis by affirming state independence and the opportunity for contestation. In an international society characterized by widely accepted norms of order, rules, and institutions, the same set of interstate norms prevails for conflict as for accommodation. The diplomatic strategies states employ will help determine whether norms are strengthened or weakened, but so also will the degree to which state interests are harmonious. If bargaining determines common interests, as the liberal suggests, alliances will be challenging. Yet the convergent alliances detailed here were not produced by bargaining. They demonstrate that common interests between states can come about in ways other than bargaining and that, having registered those common interests, allies were determined to sustain them.

The affirmation of alliance in each of these cases—the alliance "cushion," so to speak—is the best evidence that collaboration can trump contestation. But our cases illustrated different pathways toward collaboration. In some, the immediate third-party threat sufficed as a motive. In cases where considerable contestation was employed, crisis management successfully defused it. And in other cases (such as the U.S.-UK and U.S.-Japan examples), the norm of collaboration was unstated but strongly internalized, so it needed only a minimum of diplomatic protection. These bilateral norms are merely add-ons to norms of international society.

C. Applied Diplomacy

The applied diplomacy approach is valued here primarily because it emphasizes a strategy of collaboration rather than contestation. It vindicates the sustaining of alliance but has little regard for strategies intended to maximize national gains, which delay or impede that result.

Our cases suggest that contestation between friendly governments aware of each other's interests can be attractive because of past suspicion and hostility, closed governments, or inflexible security demands. This perspective asks how governments, committed to alliance against a common enemy, overcome tendencies toward contestation.

When faced with such contestation, the stronger ally more often gives way to the weaker one. One reason is that when the third power is an immediate threat to both sides, the stronger side still gains more from the alliance condition even with contestation by the weaker side (as in the second U.S.-Soviet case). But even when that threat is missing, the superior side is usually unwilling to coerce the weaker in a test of strength, either because the alliance does not provide sufficient gain for the stronger to merit such a strategy (as in the UK-Malta case) or because the stronger does not wish to commit its political capital to the effort (as in the U.S.-Israel example). However, one of our cases (the U.S.-Japan market-share conflict) illustrates how the superior side prevailed when the weaker admitted a new agenda issue that caused it to retreat.

VII. CONCLUSIONS

Contestation and negotiation strategies shape diplomatic outcomes. By disentangling these strategies, this chapter has tracked their use by negotiators when allies' interests converge to oppose a third power. It conceptualized contestation as a challenge to alliances in three ways: (1) detracting from alliance cooperation and lessening its effectiveness, (2) challenging the common interests of the allies, and (3) undermining convergent alignment and impeding cooperation entirely. Each of these challenges constitutes a test of the chapter's hypothesis that collaboration is more important than contestation when states align to oppose a mutually threatening third power.

Our conclusions are tabulated in table 4.4.

Taking our third challenge first, we find that in no case did contestation undermine alliance. Pressure to overcome and even ignore contestation is

Table 4.4. Conclusions of Our Cases

Cases	High third-power threat?	Efficiency threatened?	Interest threatened?	High capacity of alliance?
United States–Soviet Union (1)	Yes	Yes	No	Yes
United States–Soviet Union (2)	Yes	No	Yes	Yes
United States–Israel	No	Yes	Yes	Yes
United States–Malta	No	Yes	Yes	Yes
United States–UK	No	No	No	Yes
United States–Japan	No	No	No	Yes

strongest in our cases against a wartime enemy (Germany), but collaborative interests prevail even when third-power concerns are much weaker (as in the U.S.-UK and U.S.-Japan cases). Contestation between allies is diplomatically subordinated to battling the mutual enemy when the latter is of immediate importance. In the absence of immediate third-power concerns, allies defuse contestation collaboratively through diplomatic crisis management, guided by their convergent interests.

Even when not undermining alliance, contestation could have other negative effects, each of which occurred in two of the cases under consideration: (1) contestation challenged allies by limiting cooperation between them and raising doubts about their commonality of interests; (2) contestation challenged allies only in one respect, but not in the other; or (3) contestation did not detract from alliance effectiveness or threaten common interests.

Our two Soviet-American cases in the second of these categories highlighted vital wartime concerns that bolstered the staying power of alliances. Comparing the first and third categories suggests two other contrasting fundamental supports for convergent alliance. In the most challenged cases (category 1), in which the failure to fully cooperate and the weakness in convergent interests persisted in the absence of a war-making opponent, diplomatic effort (in the form of crisis management) was a key link to alliance solidarity and capacity. Without such effort, the alliance outlook would have been poor. Allies in our least challenged cases (category 3), in which alliance efficiency was undiminished and convergent interests unquestioned, did not depend on crisis management, although they did not lack crisis management potential. They enjoyed a cooperative cushion based on their common interests, and those interests rather than the potential for diplomatic intervention underpinned their solidarity.

NOTES

1. Adam Watson, *Diplomacy* (Philadelphia PA: ISHI Publications, 1986), 20.

2. Frederic S. Pearson and J. Martin Rochester, *International Relations: The Global Condition in the Late Twentieth Century*, 3rd ed. (New York: McGraw-Hill, 1992), 244.

3. Paul Gordon Lauren, Gordon A. Craig, and Alexander L. George, *Force and Statecraft*, 4th ed. (New York: Oxford University Press, 2007), 153–54; emphasis in original.

4. In what follows, "contestation" and "bargaining" are used interchangeably as strategies to maximize gains; "negotiation" and "collaboration" are used interchangeably to describe strategies aiming at mutual gains. Dean G. Pruitt also makes this distinction; see his essay, "Strategy in Negotiation," in *International Negotiation: Analysis, Approaches, Issues*, ed. Victor A. Kremenyuk (San Francisco: Jossey-Bass, 1991), 78–89. Many do not follow this distinction. Some use "negotiation" to include zero-sum issues. Others

employ "bargaining" to include all forms of diplomatic intercourse. Wherever possible, citations by analysts who do not employ the distinction made here will be translated into that distinction.

5. For discussion of diplomatic strategies, see I. William Zartman, "The Analysis of Negotiation," in *The 50% Solution*, ed. I. William Zartman (New York: Anchor, 1976), 1–41; I. William Zartman; "The Political Analysis of Negotiation: How Who Gets What and When," *World Politics* 26 (April 1974): 385–99; I. William Zartman and Maureen R. Berman, *The Practical Negotiator* (New Haven: Yale University Press, 1982), 42–86; Fen Osler Hampson, *Multilateral Negotiations* (Baltimore, MD: Johns Hopkins University Press, 1995), 23–51; Brian C. Rathbun, *Diplomacy's Value* (Ithaca, NY: Cornell University Press, 2014); Fred Charles Iklé, *How Nations Negotiate* (New York: Praeger, 1964); Roger Fisher et al., *Coping with International Conflict* (Upper Saddle River, NJ: Prentice Hall, 1997); Otomar J. Bartos and Paul Wehr, *Using Conflict Theory* (Cambridge: Cambridge University Press, 2002); I. William Zartman, "The Structure of Negotiation," in Kremenyuk, *International Negotiation*, 65–77; Victor A. Kremenyuk, "The Emerging System of International Negotiation," in Kremenyuk, *International Negotiation*, 22–39; Pruitt, "Strategy in Negotiation"; Jack Sawyer and Harold Guetzkow, "Bargaining and Negotiation in International Relations," in *International Behavior: A Social-Psychological Analysis*, ed. Herbert C. Kelman (New York: Holt, Rinehart and Winston, 1965), 464–520; Daniel Druckman and Christopher Mitchell, eds., "Flexibility in International Negotiation and Mediation," special volume of *Annals of the American Academy of Political and Social Science* 542 (November 1995); Daniel Druckman and Robert Mahoney, "Processes and Consequences of International Negotiations," *Journal of Social Issues* 33 (1977): 60–87; and Richard N. Rosecrance, "Diplomacy," in *International Encyclopedia of the Social Sciences*, ed. David L. Sills, vol. 4 (New York: Macmillan and Free Press, 1968), 187–91.

6. Zartman, "Structure of Negotiation," 68.

7. Zartman, "Analysis of Negotiation," 18.

8. Sawyer and Guetzkow, "Bargaining and Negotiation in International Relations," 471–72.

9. Alexander L. George, "Case Studies and Theory Development: The Method of Structured, Focused Comparison," in *Diplomacy: New Approaches in History, Theory, and Policy*, ed. Paul Gordon Lauren (New York: Free Press, 1979), 43–68.

10. Hans J. Morgenthau conceptualizes alliance as a legal step by which states "add to their own power the power of other nations, or . . . withhold the power of other nations from the adversary." *Politics among Nations*, 4th ed. (New York: Knopf, 1967), 175. He goes on to say that "while a typical alliance is directed against a specific nation or group of nations, the enemy of the Anglo-American community of interests could in the nature of things not be specified beforehand, since whoever threatens the European balance of power is the enemy" (176). On alliances, see Jack S. Levy, "Alliance Formation and War Behavior: An Analysis of the Great Powers, 1495–1975," *Journal of Conflict Resolution* 25 (1981): 581–613; Douglas M. Gibler and John A. Vasquez, "Uncovering the Dangerous Alliances, 1495–1980," *International Studies Quarterly* 42 (December 1998), 785–807; Alastair Smith, "Alliance Formation and War," *International Studies Quarterly* 39 (December 1995): 405–26; and Francis A. Beer, ed., *Alliances: Latent War Communities in the Contemporary World* (New York: Holt, Rinehart & Winston, 1970).

11. This distinction builds on Morgenthau's discussion of alliances. Although he writes that "an alliance requires of necessity a community of interests for its foundation," he later distinguishes between alliances serving identical interests and alliances serving complementary interests. In the latter, alliance serves different but compatible primary interests of their members, raising a question of whether a community of interests exists between them. *Politics among Nations*, 176–77.

12. According to one study, negotiation focuses on "the expansion of the realm of the possible in international conflict." Fisher et al., *Coping with International Conflict*, 13. Harold and Margaret Sprout discuss how techniques available to states, including diplomatic negotiation, enhance opportunities or create limitations in what a state is able to accomplish in world affairs. See Harold Sprout and Margaret Sprout, *The Ecological Perspective on Human Affairs* (Princeton: Princeton University Press, 1965), 83ff.

13. Zartman, "Political Analysis," 392.

14. The point might apply most strongly to states that become allies only after a lengthy period of hostile relations.

15. Alan Coddington, *Theories of the Bargaining Process*, cited in Zartman, "Political Analysis," 393.

16. One concise study of eighteenth-century power politics notes how states "changed sides without the guidance of any but the meanest of principles." Lauren, Craig, and George, *Force and Statecraft*, 19.

17. A standard diplomatic history of the nineteenth century reveals many abortive proposals for alliance. See, for example, A. J. P. Taylor, *The Struggle for Mastery in Europe: 1848–1918* (Oxford: Clarendon, 1957), 348 and 353.

18. Sawyer and Guetzkow, "Bargaining and Negotiation in International Relations," 503.

19. Zartman and Berman, *Practical Negotiator*, 33.

20. Zartman, "Analysis of Negotiation," 36.

21. Ibid., 28.

22. Sawyer and Guetzkow, "Bargaining and Negotiation in International Relations," 469.

23. Hedley Bull has written that "common interests have first to be identified by a process of bargaining before any question of maximization of them can arise." *The Anarchical Society* (New York: Columbia University Press, 1977), 177. By "bargaining," Bull seems to mean the setting of a diplomatic agenda.

24. Taylor, *Struggle for Mastery in Europe*, 345.

25. Ibid., 331, 336.

26. Ibid., 336.

27. Ibid., 344.

28. Ibid., 339.

29. Henry A. Kissinger, *White House Years* (Boston: Little, Brown, 1979), 171.

30. Ibid., 178.

31. Ibid., 182.

32. Ibid., 176.

33. China demanded that the United States recognize the government on the mainland as "the sole legitimate government in China" and that Taiwan should be "restored to the motherland." Kissinger refused to take a position on recognition but finessed the issue to

say "the political evolution is likely to be in the direction . . . indicated." Elaine Sciolino, "Records Dispute Kissinger on His '71 Visit to China," *New York Times*, 28 February 2002.

34. Morgenthau, *Politics among Nations*, 135, 532.

35. Ibid., 136.

36. "Negotiation," wrote Henry Kissinger, is "an admission of finite power." *World Restored* (New York: Grosset & Dunlap, 1964), 43.

37. Robert Keohane and Joseph S. Nye Jr., *Power and Interdependence* (Boston: Little, Brown, 1977), 11.

38. Discussing great power resistance to Napoleon, Kissinger writes that "the 'rules' of Cabinet diplomacy according to which the maximum bargain had to be struck in the hour of greatest need, combined to cause Prussia to delay its final commitment [to the anti-Napoleon alliance]." *World Restored*, 15.

39. Morgenthau, *Politics among Nations*, 176–77. Morgenthau was evidently referring here to alignments with convergent and not complementary interests. See endnote 11. Annette Baker Fox suggests that specificity is often the "touchstone" to determine how seriously actors view each other. *The Politics of Attraction: Four Middle Powers and the United States* (New York: Columbia University Press, 1976), 7.

40. Watson, *Diplomacy*, 13.

41. Ibid., 2. Edward Morse maintains that "one principal characteristic of foreign policies under modernized conditions is that they approach the pole of cooperation rather than the pole of conflict." *Modernization and Transformation in International Relations* (New York: Free Press, 1976), included in *International Relations Theory: Realism, Pluralism, Globalism*, by Paul R. Viotti and Mark V. Kauppi (New York: Macmillan, 1987), 341.

42. Watson, *Diplomacy*, 33; emphasis in original.

43. Bull, *Anarchical Society*, 175.

44. Ibid., 176–77.

45. Watson, *Diplomacy*, 62–64. Much of the current literature on alliances theorizes about their link to war. See Smith, "Alliance Formation and War"; Levy, "Alliance Formation and War Behavior"; and Gibler and Vasquez, "Uncovering the Dangerous Alliances."

46. Druckman and Mahoney, "Process and Consequences of International Negotiations," 70. See also Zartman and Berman, *Practical Negotiator*, 42–86; Kremenyuk, "Emerging System of International Negotiation," 22–39.

47. Zartman, "Political Analysis," 388.

48. Zartman and Berman, *Practical Negotiator*, 13.

49. Sawyer and Guetzkow, "Bargaining and Negotiation in International Relations," 467.

50. Fisher, *Coping with International Conflict*, 47.

51. See John R. Deane, *Strange Alliance* (New York: Viking, 1947); and Joseph G. Whelan, *Soviet Diplomacy and Negotiating Behavior: Emerging New Context for U.S. Diplomacy*, vol. 1, prepared for the Committee on Foreign Affairs, U.S. House of Representatives, House Document 96–238 (Washington, DC: U.S. Government Printing Office, 1979).

52. Whelan, Soviet Diplomacy and Negotiating Behavior, 99.

53. Ibid., 174.

54. See W. W. Rostow, *The United States in the World Arena* (New York: Harper &

Row, 1960), 89ff.; Forrest C. Pogue, "The Struggle for a New Order," in *The Meaning of Yalta*, ed. John L. Snell (Baton Rouge: Louisiana State University Press, 1956), 3–36; Melvyn P. Leffler, "Adherence to Agreements: Yalta and the Experiences of the Early Cold War," *International Security* 11 (Summer 1986): 88–123; and Mark Etheridge and Cyril Black, "Negotiating on the Balkans, 1945–1947," in *Negotiating with the Russians*, ed. Raymond Dennett and Joseph E. Johnson (Boston: World Peace Foundation, 1951), 171–206.

55. The declaration is reproduced in Rostow, *United States in the World Arena*, 109.

56. As Melvyn Leffler has noted, "Nothing Roosevelt said or did at Yalta suggested that he had much concern for developments in Eastern Europe except insofar as they might influence the political climate in the United States." "Adherence to Agreements," 99.

57. Etheridge and Black, "Negotiating on the Balkans," 179.

58. Iklé, *How Nations Negotiate*, 9. The advantage to the Soviet Union of precise agreements at this stage was illustrated by the more detailed recommendations made by the United States, Britain, and the Soviet Union at the February 1945 Yalta conference with regard to Yugoslavia, in which the prewar Yugoslav parliament members were asked to enter the postwar Yugoslav Parliament controlled by wartime partisans. Etheridge and Black, "Negotiating on the Balkans," 180.

59. Leffler points out that the Declaration of Liberation in Europe "never received much attention at Yalta" ("Adherence to Agreements," 99).

60. William D. Leahy, cited in ibid., 96. "The ambiguity of the Yalta agreement," Fred Iklé notes, "inhibited the American government from opposing the Soviet take-over in Poland more forcefully." *How Nations Negotiate*, 11.

61. Leffler, "Adherence to Agreements," 97.

62. Ibid., 117.

63. Rostow, *United States in the World Arena*, 114–15.

64. See Richard E. Neustadt, *Alliance Politics* (New York: Columbia University Press, 1970).

65. Ibid., 4.

66. Ibid., 72.

67. Ibid., 53.

68. See W. Howard Wriggins, "Up for Auction: Malta Bargains with Great Britain, 1971," in Zartman, *50% Solution*, 208–234.

69. Ibid., 231.

70. Ibid., 228–29, 233.

71. See Galen Jackson, "The Showdown that Wasn't: U.S.-Israeli Relations and American Domestic Politics, 1973–75," *International Security* 39 (Spring, 2015): 130–69; and Harold H. Saunders and Cecilia Albin, *Sinai II: The Politics of International Mediation*, *Pew Case Studies in International Affairs*, no. 421 (Washington: Institute for the Study of Diplomacy, Georgetown University, 1991).

72. Ibid., 144.

73. William Quandt, cited in ibid., 162.

74. This case profile was prepared from a file of news clippings from the *New York Times* in my possession. For an earlier discussion of this case see Barry H. Steiner, "Diplomacy as Independent and Dependent Variable," *International Negotiation* 6 (2001): 86–88.

75. Thomas L. Friedman, "Diplomacy Is Minding Other Nations' Business," *New York Times*, 30 January 1994.

76. Ibid.

77. Rostow, *United States in the World Arena*, 111. Melvyn Leffler wrote that both Soviet and American officials "tend[ed] to act opportunistically yet demand punctilious behavior from their adversaries" ("Adherence to Agreements," 90).

78. The administration was apparently activated by domestic concerns and was unwilling to act in a manner that would have required a major effort to gain Jewish support in the forthcoming 1976 American presidential campaign. Jackson, "Showdown that Wasn't," 160.

79. Rostow, *United States in World Affairs*, 116–17.

80. On transgovernmental activity, see Anne-Marie Slaughter, "The Real New World Order," *Foreign Affairs* 75 (September/October 1997): 183–97. Zbigniew Brezezinski has argued, on the other hand, that close, intimate relations between allies need not require interchange of personnel. See, on this view, Watson, *Diplomacy*, 145.

81. Fisher et al., *Coping with International Conflict*, 136ff. Fisher and his colleagues argue that "being nice is no answer" on the grounds that it risks creating a "sloppy agreement" and that "a hard game dominates a soft one." Alliance intimacy may lead allies to treat contestation as impolite, or, to the contrary, strengthen their ability as allies to express and absorb it.

82. Zartman, "Political Analysis," 386. Zartman also critiques the "friendly bargaining" approach.

5

Diplomacy as Independent and Dependent Variable

To theorize is to relate cause, treated as an independent variable, to effect, the dependent variable.[1] Doing so allows for making inferences beyond the data that the analyst employs.[2] It also identifies both what the analyst wishes to explain (the dependent variable) and the explanation (the independent variable). Theoretical work can be designed for explanation—probing and understanding puzzles—or for improving policy. When explanation is the objective, the main purpose is to assist the search for associations between cause and effect, and the two must be conceptualized as distinct and separable. "It is the legitimacy of the search for, not the fact of, association between [independent and dependent] variations," James N. Rosenau writes, "that renders foreign policy phenomena internally coherent."[3] When policy critique is the object of analysis, however, cause and effect can become rival interpretations of a given set of developments, and thus be more closely associated. For example, a specific policy decision can be examined alternatively as a causal, independent effort or as an effect of political pressures and constraints.

This chapter provides a comprehensive understanding of diplomatic conflict management both as independent (initiatory) and as dependent (responsive) variable. The analysis is intended to cumulate prior studies of diplomatic cases and issues and to carefully weigh the role of statecraft—whether it affects the international environment, implements prior decisions, or responds to nondiplomatic influences.

Within the scholarly community, realists are most preoccupied with diplomatic cause and effect because they view diplomacy as central for international order. Their writing is useful and important for the diplomatic theorist, but it needs to be broadened. First, the realist emphasis on the decline of classic diplomatic practice has led to a bias in favor of diplomacy as causal action and a neglect of diplomatic adaptation to growing constraints on diplomatic behavior. Second, the deductive realist paradigm reinforces this same bias, as the analyst focuses on a distinctive causal element and demonstrates that its effects outweigh that of other variables.[4]

By comparison, inductive analysis specifies study of the relationship between causal and responsive variables but is not defined by an a priori array of variables. It requires more arbitrary limitation of case scenario, more detailed specification of variables, and more attention to variability in the data than does its deductive counterpart.[5] The focused case comparison method employed in this study, with appropriate specification of case types, can probe either causal, independent behavior or dependent effects, *whatever the conceptualization of cause and effect.* Alexander George notes that use of this method permits features of particular cases to be described "as a particular value of a variable that is part of a theoretical framework of independent, intervening, and dependent variables."[6]

Our understanding of the explanatory purpose for theorizing is anchored in the work of James N. Rosenau, who long ago insisted on a scientific foundation for the study of world politics. Distinguishing between "initiatory," "implementive," and "responsive" variables, he argues that the analyst needs to focus on "a specific context—that of whether variations in the initiatory and implementive stages can be related to variations in the responsive stage. . . . None of the three stages has any meaning for [the analyst] by itself."[7] The "initiatory" stage of interaction consists of "activities, conditions, and influences through which the stimuli of the initiatory stage are translated into purposeful actions directed at modifying objects in the external environment." The "implementive" stage translates stimuli from the initiatory stage into purposeful actions seeking to modify objects outside the initiator's own state. The "responsive" stage consists of "activities, conditions, and influences that comprise the reactions of the objectives of the modification attempts."[8]

Our discussion of the policy improvement theory builds on the ideas of Roger Fisher, who contrasts actual failed policy with more useful and available policy alternatives. Fisher argues that interstate conflict became intractable not primarily from the lack of substantive options, "but in the failure to design, negotiate, and pursue a process that moves us forward from where we are now to where we would like to be."[9] Promoting desired policy movement requires a plan to persuade some individual to make a new decision enhancing joint conflict management. The conflict management effort entails causal action to persuade a target party, but also attention to constraints impeding a favorable response from the target and an alternative decision by the initiator.

This chapter first probes the explanatory mode of theorizing cause and effect. It distinguishes in this mode three versions of diplomatic causal analysis and, with respect to the study of diplomatic effect, action from outcome. Following this, independent and dependent analysis is discussed with reference to improving policy. A study by I. William Zartman that critiques American failures in the 1990s to maximize diplomatic potential in small-state civil war is used to illustrate this approach.[10] A concluding section summarizes what has been learned.

I. THE REFLECTIVE APPROACH: CAUSAL, INDEPENDENT ACTION

According to Arthur Danto, a cause must make a difference.[11] John Lewis Gaddis writes, "Causes always have contexts, and to know the former we must understand the latter."[12] He defines context as "the dependency of sufficient causes upon necessary causes"; sufficient, or exceptional actions, such as a fall that occurs from a misstep on a mountain, and necessary or general actions, such as the existence of the mountain and gravity, produce tragic results with relatively little action. "While context," he writes, "does not directly *cause* what happens, it can certainly determine consequences."[13] Harold and Margaret Sprout maintain that independent variables consist of the attributes of interacting actors and the condition of the environment in which they interact.[14]

We narrow our discussion to three environmental contexts that define diplomatic statecraft as a causal element. In one context, states confronting each other share an interest in seeking to manage their conflict short of war. They employ diplomatic norms and procedures to assist them. In this context, cause is associated with *intentionality* and *purposefulness*, in which diplomats opposed to each other employ a large and uphill effort toward an agreed-upon objective. A second context, more turbulent than the first, highlights how disproportionate effects occur from modest causal action. Diplomatic norms and procedures are weak or missing, and diplomatic commitment makes conflict management uncertain. The causal element in this context is defined by *impact* or *consequence*. In a third context, causal action occurs when states use a special set of situational opportunities to leverage stalemate or deadlock experienced by others. The causal element is then *policy success*.

A. Intentionality

Statecraft, understood by the realists as highly competitive, can have causal effects through the sustained effort required to pursue a specific purpose. Such effort depends on the judgment that an objective can be attained by influencing others who have a different point of view. The mode for obtaining the objective will be determined by how negotiating parties interact; the parties share an interest in managing their differences, and the interaction between the parties opens up a process by which the management can occur. The large effort required is understood not just in terms of finding agreement, but also in relation to comparably influential forces that, left unopposed, would stymie agreement.[15]

Hans J. Morgenthau, writing of diplomacy as intention, characterizes it as a master element of national power that provides direction to integrate other power elements "into an integrated whole . . . awaken[ing] their slumbering potentialities by giving them the breath of actual power."[16] Peaceful management of conflict, rather than conflict resolution, supports such direction.[17] Intentionality can also be understood in terms of risk and danger. The larger the risks and dangers of a diplomatic breakdown, the more understandable is a process to peacefully manage the crisis no matter the opposed pressures for war. Martin Wight writes of "the task of diplomacy to circumvent the occasions of war, and to extend the series of circumvented occasions; to drive the automobile of state along a one-way track, against head-on traffic, past infinitely recurring precipices."[18] A similar point is made by Gordon A. Craig and Alexander L. George in describing crisis management during contemporary Soviet-American cold war. "If catastrophe is to be avoided," they write in regard to this problem, "decision makers in a crisis must be capable of functioning at a very high level."[19] Superpower agreement about the critical importance of that objective, and that objective alone, assisted in avoiding catastrophe. Fearing that any clash of superpower forces could escalate, the United States and the Soviet Union "gave highest priority to managing effectively the confrontations and crises" between them.[20]

Intentionality can have causal effect without being dramatic. For example, the Congress of Berlin of 1878, cited by Morgenthau as "the outstanding example of a successful war-preventing diplomacy in modern times," successfully managed Anglo-Russian territorial disputes in the Balkans brought about by the weakening authority of the Ottoman Empire.[21] Its significance is measured by opposed war-promoting developments, including long-standing Anglo-Russian suspicions in the Balkan area. The British prime minister, Lord Salisbury, who had only a few months to intervene in the 1878 episode, did not draw attention to his contribution, and his biographer cites the unspectacular character of Salisbury's diplomatic work: "Long-prepared and concentrated purpose was of the essence of his policy."[22]

Wight, praising "the capacity of modifying objectives in mid-negotiation," argues that agreement at this congress was greatly assisted by Salisbury's farsightedness.[23] "The capacity to adapt oneself to change is the minimum diplomatic requirement," he writes. "A higher achievement is to anticipate change, to see the dirty weather ahead and avoid it or outflank it. It was the essence of the great Lord Salisbury's diplomatic philosophy."[24] These views bolster the independent significance of diplomatic norms and protocol. "Diplomatic theory presents the role of the 'ideal ambassador,'" writes Hedley Bull, "in terms of adherence to canons of rationality" in acting in a consistent and goal-minded fashion.[25]

B. Impact

A second understanding of causality, linking actions to particular effects, views intentions as inadequate for international stability. Robert Jervis maintains that most contemporary crises occur because of a faulty understanding of the opponent's intentions.[26] If so, the intentions of crisis antagonists will be in question when they confront each other. Furthermore, if military forces are widely understood to be vulnerable to attack, diplomats will have a more difficult time restraining force use. Thomas C. Schelling has famously studied the scenario in which "the urge to preempt . . . could become a dominant motive if the character of military forces endowed haste and initiative with a decisive advantage."[27]

The character of the diplomatic environment can itself add to the danger of war. First, the weakness or absence of diplomatic norms can shift the causal focus away from intentions and toward effects. If adversaries cannot communicate diplomatically, they may understand each other's behavior in prudential terms and act to guard against the most threatening scenario, however improbable it may be. Second, too much diplomatic opposition, encouraging hard bargaining and opportunism, can increase the danger of hostilities. Thomas C. Schelling views states as "continually engaged in demonstrations of resolve, tests of nerve, and explorations for understandings and misunderstandings . . . through a diplomatic process of commitment that is itself unpredictable. . . . The resulting international relations often have the character of a competition in risk-taking, characterized not so much by tests of force as by tests of nerve."[28] Even small issues could occasion the search for relative advantage, as hard bargaining by one antagonist provides an incentive to its adversary to act in similar fashion.[29] The outbreak of the First World War in 1914 showed that diplomats can be too unyielding, thus impeding bargaining and negotiation, when allies are too wedded to each other.[30]

C. Policy Success

"For the Machiavellian," Wight writes, "the only test is success."[31] Action framed for success is conditioned on circumstances that increase the probability of success; diplomats preoccupied with implementing policy capitalize on situational opportunities, such as an existing balance of power, as a source of leverage. "Opportunity," according to Zartman, "is defined as a moment in the conflict or collapse when the external party can get the conflicting parties' attention to constructive measures. [It] is a moment when external entry into the conflict or collapse is justified by either an accepted occasion for a response to an event or by the intervener's ability to produce an attractive way out of a present or prospective difficulty."[32] The primary antagonists' inability to satisfactorily manage conflict on their own is the source of the third party's power potential. "The wider object of diplomacy," as Wight spells out this approach, "is to establish balanced antagonisms, controlled international tensions, so as to gain the maximum influence with the minimum obligation."[33] An equilibrium in which adversaries are relatively equal in strength provides an opportunity for an outside party to decisively gain policy success. When it does so, the opportunistic behavior has causal effect.

This usually requires bold action, as when American military intervention in 1995 in the civil war in Bosnia-Herzegovina broke a deadlock between Croat, Muslim, and Serb warring factions, forcing them to negotiate a diplomatic settlement. Each faction was impelled to cooperate by its fear of being excluded from a settlement. A key characteristic of this intervention, which reversed a three-year-old American policy of not using force in the civil war, was the diplomatic independence granted to Richard Holbrooke, the American assistant secretary of state for European and Canadian affairs. Holbrooke led the warring factions to believe he controlled a NATO-endorsed American bombing campaign directed against the Bosnian Serbs, who had blockaded Bosnia-Herzegovina's capital, Sarajevo. According to one appraisal, "Holbrooke operated with an unusual degree of freedom for a government negotiator." "There are very, very few traditional foreign service officers who would have dared to go off the reservation the way he did," a member of his negotiating team reflected later. "They would have felt they couldn't make any decision without checking back, because if the decision was wrong, then they would have to take the blame."[34]

The conflict in Bosnia-Herzegovina compromised the position of the major powers but leveraged American military involvement. UN peacekeeping forces in Sarajevo, consisting mainly of British and French contingents, were targeted by Bosnian Serb forces surrounding the city. In late May 1995, Bosnian Serbs took peacekeepers hostage, and they increased shelling on the peacekeepers. A majority of the British cabinet favored withdrawing its contingents, and the French government decided its forces would also be withdrawn if this occurred unless the United States intervened militarily.[35] The United States ultimately acted to avoid a UN force withdrawal.[36] President Bill Clinton earlier decided American troops would be used to support UN force withdrawal, and a military plan was created for that contingency. "To assist in the U.N.'s withdrawal," Holbrooke wrote later, "which would be followed by an even greater disaster, made no sense at all. Using American ground troops to fight the war was equally out of the question. Something had to be done or else a Serb victory, and additional ethnic cleansing, were inevitable. It was a terrible set of choices, but there was no way Washington could avoid involvement much longer."[37]

Table 5.1 summarizes these three conceptualizations of diplomatic causal behavior.

II. THE REFLECTIVE APPROACH: DIPLOMACY AS EFFECT

Diplomacy as effect portrays diplomatic action as constrained by, depending on, or responding to outside influences. Because these influences are politically opposed to diplomatists' preferences, they diminish the probability of

Table 5.1. Typology of Causal Behavior

Type	Key characteristics	Key attributes	Impediment
1. Intention, Purpose	Uses diplomatic norms	Anticipating problems	"Uphill" effort
	Adversaries share objectives	Will to accommodate	
2. Impact	Weakness/absence of norms	Test of opposed wills	Difficulty of controlling risk
	Faulty understanding of state intentions	Will to prevail	
3. Success	Leverage misfortune of other states	Opportunism	Reversing primary antagonist stalemate

acting on those preferences.[38] Realists have notably highlighted and faulted this dependence. For example, Craig and George maintain that a "diplomatic revolution," dating from the late nineteenth century, eroded the homogeneity of diplomats and norms that allowed the flexible pursuit of balance-of-power politics and the defusing of interstate crises.[39] They attribute this development to many sources, including technology, transportation, and war; special interest groups; and the rise of new ideologies and nationalism. Newer weapons became available for rapid, immediate, and devastating use, publics were impatient with diplomatic details, and ideologies contributed to endless debates.

Political realists have especially stressed diplomatic timidity in the face of mobilized public opinion. "The retribution that public feeling could wreak upon statesmen and diplomats seeking to deal with complicated international problems in accordance with the rules of *raison d'etat* or national interest was . . . real and intimidating," Craig and George write about the interwar period, and officials were unwilling to challenge it.[40] Referring to the superpower cold war, Morgenthau asserts, "The mistaken identification of press, radio, polls, and Congress with public opinion has had a distorting as well as paralyzing influence upon American foreign policy."[41] He cites as an example how the Truman administration, "frightened by a public opinion that is in good measure but a figment of a politician's imagination . . . has suspended diplomacy altogether [with the Soviet Union] rather than face with courage and determination the accusation of appeasement, or of worse, by demagogues who represent only a small minority of the American people."[42]

Deploring diplomatic constraints, realists have underestimated diplomats' ability to adapt to them—that is, to adhere to diplomatic objectives and norms *even as constraints remain in effect*. In addition, realists, focusing on diplomatic *action* (or its absence), have neglected dependent diplomacy in diplomatic *outcomes*. As Harold and Margaret Sprout note, "*Actions* (decisions, policies, strategies) and *results* (states of affairs, patterns of relationship) are the *dependent variables* (phenomena to be explained or predicted)."[43] The operational diplomatic environment and diplomatic action are narrowed or blocked by particular aspects of the environment that diplomats choose not to affect or fail to affect.

The following spells out these critiques.

A. Diplomatic Action

Probing diplomatists' willingness and ability to adapt to political constraints, we argue that diplomatic adaptation is more likely to be spurred by vital interests than by nonvital ones. Taking public opinion as a constraint representative of the diplomatic revolution and commitment to diplomatic norms as an indication of adaptation to those constraints, we control for the difference between the pursuit of vital and nonvital objectives.

American reaction to emplacement of Soviet missiles in Cuba in 1962 is taken as an example of the pursuit of vital interests, and American preventive diplomacy toward small-state civil strife in the 1990s is used to illustrate less-than-vital objectives. In the Cuban case, ample adaptation to domestic public opinion occurred as crisis avoidance and then crisis management efforts (conforming to the character of the Soviet-American relationship). In the preventive diplomacy example, diplomatic adaptation was largely missing.

1. Vital Interests

Repeated Soviet-American cold war confrontations created a mutual awareness of confrontation dangers. As one analysis puts it, "Every major crisis . . . was coupled with the fear that *any* shooting war between American and Soviet forces, no matter at how modest a level initially, could escalate completely out of control."[44] To avoid crises, the superpowers emphasized diplomatic interaction and communication that encouraged their belief that they understood each other's intentions. According to Alexander George, superpower diplomatic contacts provided "rules of prudence . . . tacit understandings and shared expectations that can be inferred from patterns of behavior" that supported a crisis management "tacit regime."[45] Dean Rusk writes that many of his discussions with the Soviet officials as secretary of state "were what I called 'pointless talks' . . . not to resolve a particular problem or reach a specific goal but to create a broader basis for understanding each other's societies. . . . [O]ver the years I came to know my Soviet counterparts rather well."[46] The subsequent "back channel" between Secretary of State Henry Kissinger and Soviet ambassador Anatoly Dobrynin doubtless served the same purpose.[47]

Yet each crisis created the need for more adaptation in the form of crisis management. Understandings and expectations did not prevent superpower confrontations; in fact, ironically, as a safety net they may have contributed to competitive behavior and to its crisis consequences.[48] George, noting superpower inability to avoid crisis, later commented that "the initiation of a controlled crisis seem[ed] to offer an opportunity for achieving foreign policy goals," and that each superpower seemed attracted to pursue one-sided opportunities "*until the threat of a dangerous confrontation appear[ed] to be imminent.*"[49]

Diplomatic revolution intensified requirements for crisis avoidance and crisis management. Crisis avoidance action took place as a prelude to the Cuban missile crisis. During a midterm American election campaign, Republican senator Kenneth Keating charged in August and September 1962 that the Soviet Union had begun constructing offensive nuclear missile bases in Cuba.[50] Dobrynin, responding to an American request for clarification, informed Attorney General Robert Kennedy that the Soviet Union would not create any problems for the American government during the election campaign. President Kennedy thereupon issued a statement distinguishing between offensive and defensive weaponry, defining offensive weaponry as "offensive ground-to-ground missiles" and warning about the consequences of introducing offensive weaponry in Cuba. These moves, writes Graham Allison, "seem like a textbook case of responsible diplomacy. The United States formulated a policy stating precisely 'what strategic transformations we [were] prepared to resist.' The Soviet Union acknowledged these vital interests and announced a strategy that entailed no basic conflict. This would also seem to be a model case of communication, or signaling, between the superpowers."[51]

Following discovery of the Soviet offensive missiles in Cuba, American officials rejected a purely diplomatic response, believing it could be interpreted as too weak and also could provide Soviet leaders an opportunity to stall until the missiles were made operational.[52] Prominent American officials, including Secretary of Defense Robert M. McNamara, who, viewing the crisis as a "domestic *political* problem" because "we said we'd *act*," advocated attacking the missiles as well as invading Cuba.[53] They were motivated in part by the political concerns of holding together American alliances, "*properly* conditioning [Soviet Premier Nikita] Khrushchev for our future moves," and dealing with the American public.[54] Still, diplomatic adaptation was visible in the American view that the United States should make it as "easy as possible" for Khrushchev to back down, that he should be given a warning prior to air strikes, and that a delayed or imminent trade of Soviet Cuban missiles and the comparable American Jupiter missiles in Turkey be offered, aiming at a "least effort" agreement.[55]

2. Nonvital Interests

While vital interests tend to support stronger efforts at diplomatic adjustments to neutralize constraints, nonvital interests, in which the priority for action is smaller, do not. Constraints are therefore more likely to be accommodated when vital interests are not at stake. An example is afforded by the weakness of American preventive diplomacy in the 1990s, weakness linked to congressional attitudes.

Clinton administration officials believed they had declining authority over diplomatic policy in relation to Congress, viewing congressional assertiveness as an "underlying structural development" that could not be influenced by the executive branch.[56] They sought to avoid confrontation with Congress over these issues, saving political capital for arguably more significant domestic initiatives.[57] "When the Democrats controlled both branches of government in 1993–94," Ivo Daalder writes, "sixty percent of the contested votes on national security issues that the Clinton administration lost concerned peacekeeping and intervention issues. The reason for this is the end of the Cold War, which brought an end to the consensus that had existed on security issues in the U.S. body politic, elevated the importance of domestic and economic issues, and stimulated partisanship."[58]

The problem was compounded when American peacekeepers in Somalia were attacked and killed in October 1993. After this event, Americans were reluctant to participate UN peacekeeping operations (as articulated in Presidential Decision Directive 25, which was finalized in 1994) on the assumption that such operations were *inherently* costly and risky. Daalder notes that in order to take account of political opposition at home, the directive reflected "an appreciation of the constraints any policy on intervention in internal conflicts would inevitably face."[59] Preoccupation with domestic opposition persisted into the late 1990s. When in May 1998 the State Department argued for air strikes against Serbia over Serb atrocities in Kosovo, the American national security advisor challenged the proposal: "Are we going to bomb on Kosovo?" he asked, "Can I explain that to Congress? They'll kill us."[60]

Intervention in small-state civil strife was less constrained early in the conflict cycle, and American officials had an incentive to act earlier, avoiding opposition based on the cost and risks of intervening in polarized small-state conflict. According to this view, the primary American mistake was to postpone intervention because such a delay made engagement more vulnerable to domestic opposition.

In Africa, for example, the Clinton administration pursued goals in Africa that were minimally costly to the United States, and, thus, "as the potential costs and risks of the engagement rose and as congress resisted U.S. commitments . . . the Clinton reaction in the post-Somali period was generally prudent and circumspect. This caution has been similarly evident in . . . peace implementation."[61] The United States adjusted by turning away from direct to indirect mediation, working with other state and nonstate actors.[62]

B. Operational Milieu

Understanding results as a dependent variable accounts for the difference between actual and predicted results based on some assumed decision.[63] The analyst's interest is how the environment affects that outcome outside the awareness or the control of those making the decision. We limit our discussion here to elements of the postdecision environment not known to decisionmakers when they acted. Officials' inability to accurately perceive elements of the postdecision environment may lead to policy failure.

The diplomatic revolution, though not linked by Craig and George to policy results, can explain such policy failures. To spell out how the operational environment is a significant dependent variable, we need only demonstrate that the diplomatic revolution can be consequential for the negotiating process if decisions fail to anticipate it. A classic essay by I. William Zartman that deals with crises as a phase "of a general process of ripening and unripening" of disputes makes these elements clear.[64] Zartman explains that the diplomatic revolution may be neglected, and policy failure may occur, because officials of different states learn about their environment in different ways and at different rates.[65]

At least four elements associated with the diplomatic revolution can spell the difference in negotiating success or failure: (1) domestic political parties and interest groups as constraints on governments; (2) the depreciation of rules and regime; (3) the rising heterogeneity of diplomats; and (4) heightened nationalistic attitudes.

1. Parties and Interest Groups as Constraints

According to Craig and George, "emergence of mass political parties and of special interest groups . . . made it more difficult for governments to pursue coherent and consistent policies."[66] Referring to the process by which a state can break out of a negotiating stalemate, Zartman writes, "Even when dealing with two sovereign states, the institutional spokesmen may be so constrained by a hostile or divided domestic setting that they become unable to enter into the give and take that diplomacy requires. In such a case . . . it becomes necessary for the opponent to enter the other party's domestic politics . . . [to give] careful consideration of the way in which each party's moves are viewed by and affect the political actors on the other side."[67] We have seen how the United States became enmeshed in Japanese domestic politics when successfully pushing for greater Japanese openness to American businesses seeking to compete in the Japanese market.[68] By contrast, the inability or unwillingness of an initiating country to participate in a target state's turbulent domestic politics can cause negotiating failure.[69]

2. Depreciation of Regimes

"As the new technologies of war became more difficult to control," Craig and George argue, "diplomats and statesmen lost faith in the norms, procedures and modalities that had maintained the flexibility and viability of the balance-of-power system."[70] Regimes—understood as sets of norms and institutions—are thus more subject to being challenged as a result of the diplomatic revolution.[71] Zartman points out that while conflicts arising in a regime are generally handled by institutions when the parties' power relations do not change, shifts in the parties' relative power necessitate adjusting regimes. For example, negotiations over the reversion of the Panama Canal ultimately took account of Panama's growing power relative to the United States and thereby enabled the canal negotiations to succeed.[72] By contrast, negotiations over retention of the British base in Malta, discussed earlier, were nearly torpedoed when Dom Mintoff sought a new base regime and the British, apparently complacent about their superior power in relation to Malta, failed to anticipate the Mintoff challenge.[73]

3. Reduced Diplomatic Homogeneity

According to Craig and George, "As the international community became more conflict-prone, the homogeneity of the diplomatic community deteriorated."[74] If homogeneous diplomats enhance understanding and communication between states, then a decline in such understanding and communication would be associated with diplomatic crises, which reflect difficulties in correctly interpreting foreign state intentions. As noted earlier in this chapter, the frequency of crisis in postwar Soviet-American relations can be taken as evidence that the superpowers' appreciation of each other's intentions was often inadequate. In this respect, even extraordinary efforts by superpower diplomats to understand each other's intentions provide a false sense of security if they result in too much mutual trust. Diplomats who confidently estimate adversary restraint—and are proven incorrect, as in the Cuban missile crisis—may be neglecting the diplomatic revolution if they assume state homogeneity.[75]

Zartman points out that crises have some useful consequences in a negotiating process. They block some solutions to a dispute and some efforts to escalate out of it, and they promote ripeness of dispute settlement by increasing diplomatic frustrations. But breakdowns in mutual understanding do not ordinarily contribute to dispute settlement. To limit the effect of such breakdowns, Zartman argues that "conflict management efforts should begin when crises break out (if not before)."[76] Yet crisis produced by faulty or flawed understanding would likely impede such management efforts.

4. Rising Nationalism

Craig and George note in their portrait of the diplomatic revolution that "extreme forms of nationalism tended to increase international friction and dispute."[77] Nationalism, fostering popular identity with a government seeking support over a dispute, will often be significant in prolonging, deepening, and extending deadlock—when, as Zartman notes, "parties are so absorbed by the conflict or so locked in the crisis that they cannot seize the moment or the outcome without the help of a mediator."[78] Mass opinion makes bargaining more urgent, as when "rising threat of a Panamanian mob veto on Canal operations pressed the acuity of the Panamanian problem."[79] Even when a mediator attempts to generate an understanding between primary antagonists that the antagonists cannot provide on their own, nationalistic attitudes bolstered by governments can make it unwelcome. Here again, the diplomatic revolution can be decisive for diplomatic results: initiatives to mediate or otherwise push negotiations for dispute settlement that do not anticipate nationalistic resistance, especially in long-lasting deadlock, risk being imperiled by that resistance.

III. POLICY CRITIQUE: CAUSE AND EFFECT

We next employ I. William Zartman's critique of American preventive diplomacy to understand cause and effect as policy critique. Zartman's analysis, like Roger Fisher's, proceeds on normative and empirical levels. On the normative, corrective level, Zartman measures and reconstructs American preventive diplomacy potential in six cases emerging in the 1990s. He estimates what the United States could have done in these examples, using what he terms "standard elements of diplomacy," to assist small-state antagonists to negotiate an end to their conflict. Consistent with international norms, he argues, the United States should have intervened in a large number of problematic civil war situations—at "a moment in the [civil] conflict or collapse when the external party can get the conflicting parties' attention to constructive measures"—to push conflict management and alternatives to violence.[80] American diplomatists had the opportunity, he believes, to succeed without incurring excessive costs or commitments. Zartman also describes the persistently ineffective, actual American diplomacy in these cases, which fell short of normative and utilitarian standards. The failures led him to characterize the United States as a "cowardly lion."

Zartman does not provide a general explanation for the policy failures, but his normative and empirical analyses can yield alternative explanations. On the normative level, his analysis is diplomatically causal because it is predicated on presumed effectiveness. But policy failure at the empirical level can be understood differently. If American domestic politics constrained and narrowed feasible responses, then the empirical policy failure is an example of diplomacy as effect. The entrenched outlooks of politically powerful domestic doctors serve as the causal variable, and the weakened will to intervene in intrastate war is the dependent variable. Table 5.2 compares these two conceptions.

We test this distinction using two of Zartman's own cases in *Cowardly Lions*.

A. Yugoslavia

Civil insurrection and warfare were prominent features of Yugoslavia in the 1990s, following the death of dictator Josef Tito in 1988 and the emergence of Serb nationalist leadership in Belgrade. Despite outside state efforts to keep Yugoslavia whole, the provinces of Slovenia and Croatia separated from Yugoslavia in 1991. In 1992, Bosnia-Herzegovina decided through a referendum to separate. In response, the Serb-dominated Yugoslav army in the north and east, and the Croatian army in the south and west, confronted Bosnia-Herzogovina. The largely unarmed Bosnian government requested United Nations assistance to protect its own authority and its mostly Muslim population against those onslaughts. In 1995, NATO and Bosnia-Croat military action forced Belgrade to end its military assistance to Serb opponents of the Bosnia regime. In 1996, in a separate action, Kosovars rebelled against the Belgrade government. NATO, responding to Serb military retaliation, launched air attacks against Yugoslavia in 1999 and forced Belgrade to relinquish control over Kosovo.

Zartman identifies five missed preventive diplomacy (PD) opportunities over Yugoslavia from 1989 to 1998: First, in 1989 and 1990, the United States, together with the European Community, should have sponsored a conference to keep Yugoslavia whole. Second, in March through June 1991, the United States should have provided support for Yugoslav transition and state-building. Third, from February 1992 through January 1993, the United States should have conditioned recognition of Bosnia-Herzegovina independence on creating stable institutional arrangements for the new country. Fourth, in September through December 1996, the United States should have intervened in Kosovo to prevent the Belgrade government from suppressing the Kosovars. And, fifth, in October 1998 the United States should have intervened to bring about transitional status negotiations over Kosovo.

All of these missed opportunities required backing PD initiatives with

Table 5.2. Comparing Independent and Dependent Approaches to Policy

Conceptualization	Causal variable	Operationalization	Dependent variable	Expected results
Diplomacy as independent variable (Zartman conception)	Will to intervene in local conflict	Actual: Relatively low will (low priority, low risk propensity) OR Hypothetical: High will (higher priority and higher risk propensity)	Influence on parties to local conflict	"Cowardly Lions": Larger incidence of failed conflict management OR Greater likelihood of successful conflict management
Diplomacy as dependent variable	Entrenched congressional and military outlooks	Leaders and diplomats unwilling to challenge these outlooks	Will to intervene in local conflict	"Cowardly Lions": Larger incidence of failed conflict management

credible threats, especially the threat of force. In regard to the first opportunity, Zartman notes there was "no positive [U.S. and EC] policy for deterring [Yugoslav provincial] separation and preserving unity without force," and no American preparedness for holding Yugoslavia together by force.[81]

Discussing the second opportunity, Zartman dwells on the need for credible carrots and sticks to dissuade Slovenia and Croatia from seceding from Yugoslavia, and specifically the need to use the framework of the Commission on Security and Cooperation in Europe (CSCE) for this purpose. "Croatia and Slovenia could be put on notice that they would be held responsible for triggering the anticipated violence," he writes. "The CSCE itself had no military or economic leverage, but its members did, and they were free to apply incentives and disincentives on their own in support of CSCE goals and actions." This was not done.[82]

Zartman emphasizes inadequate military enforcement of mediating goals most strongly in connection with the third opportunity. The best-known mediation effort was the joint UN and EC initiative led by Cyrus Vance and David Owen in which a single demilitarized Bosnian state would be divided into ten provinces, each with a multiethnic government. "The onus for the failure of the Vance-Owen plan," Zartman writes, "belongs at the feet of Clinton and the new administration, who refused to give it assent. . . . [T]he heart of the problem was domestic: Clinton had a distaste for force and was simply not strong enough internally or politically to override the Pentagon's opposition to the commitment of U.S. military forces."[83]

In regard to the fourth opportunity, Zartman notes the failure of the Western powers to convey to Serbian leader Slobodan Milosevic that Europe and the United States meant what they said about responding to Serb atrocities in Kosovo, reaffirming President George H. W. Bush's 1992 statement that war in Kosovo would threaten American national interests. And in regard to the final opportunity, Zartman emphasizes the absence of enforcement capability to verify Kosovar-Serb agreement for Serb withdrawal from Kosovo. "NATO fell into its own trap," he writes, "believing that it could dictate to a dictator and forgetting that it had taught him in the previous years that bombing threats were empty or at least subject to long delays."[84]

Our tentative conclusion is that Zartman's examples fit dependent diplomacy. They suggest, in short, that "cowardly lions" in these cases depended on a domestic American political structure that was largely unwilling to employ the threat and use of force required to enable preventive diplomacy to succeed. Zartman's analysis cites the importance of the threat or use of military capabilities, and the resulting significance of the attitudes of the American military leadership. Zartman also notes how the mediating diplomacy of ambiguity and timidity fostered perceptions by the local Yugoslav antagonists that they could solve their conflict in their own way, without outside interference.[85] Although more study should be done to fully establish the linkage, the Yugoslavia case is consistent with a pattern in which the attitudes of the military establishment, and deference of political leaders to them, rule out the more assertive PD that Zartman prescribes.

B. Liberia

Liberia's traditionally close relationship with the United States was taxed during the increasingly autocratic regime of Samuel K. Doe, who began ruling the country in 1980. In 1985, Liberia defaulted on its debts and was declared ineligible for International Monetary Fund assistance; election tampering that year provided Doe a tiny majority of the votes. When Charles Taylor, a former high official in the Doe government, led a rebellion against the government in 1989, member states of the Economic Community of West African States (ECOWAS) intervened to protect Doe and, after his murder in 1990, protected the interim government they established. The efforts of ECOWAS to reconcile Taylor's faction with the interim government were frustrated until 1992, when former Doe followers rebelled. Negotiations to accommodate the political contenders failed, and four years of intense civil war ensued. Elections were held in 1997, and Taylor, who had threatened to renew violence if he did not win, was elected. However, civil war had spilled over to neighboring Sierra Leone, financed by Sierra Leone's diamonds and Liberia's timber. An agreement between the two countries in 1998 was unable to control Liberian state collapse.

Zartman discusses five missed opportunities for Liberia: First, in October 1985 the United States should have worked to decertify the fraudulent Liberian election and end the regime of President Samuel Doe. Second, in June 1990 the United States should have used an opportunity to send Doe into exile while forces led by Charles Taylor held off attack against Monrovia. Third, from April to July 1992 the United States should have supported the Carter Center's involvement to strengthen one of the more promising cease-fires in the civil war before rival buildups occurred in neighboring Sierra Leone aimed at a military showdown in Liberia. Fourth, in July 1993 mediation sponsored by the Carter Center and the UN could have strengthened a Liberian cease-fire, had the UN approved a larger number of peacekeepers for the country. And, fifth, from July through October 1998, a group monitoring the border between Sierra Leone and Liberia should have been strengthened to interrupt the flow of arms and diamonds to Taylor's group.

Zartman's narrative about Liberia, which focuses mainly on the United States, contrasts with his narrative about Yugoslavia in two ways. First,

American diplomacy to remove Doe and stop the civil war had much less to do with credible threats of force and military display than did diplomacy toward Yugoslavia. The primary option envisioned by Assistant Secretary of State for Africa Herman Cohen in 1990, for example, was that Cohen would travel to Monrovia and personally obtain Doe's abdication. In 1998, the American government agreed to provide financial aid to support the border monitoring group, which would have made possible larger and more effective troops levels, but then failed to provide that aid. In these respects, relatively modest involvement could have made a major difference in the development of local conflict. The scope of the involvement was apparently not the major issue for the United States, but rather whether the United States should intervene at all.[86]

Second, the American government took an executive decision in 1990—what Cohen has characterized as a "White House stop order"—that American interests did not warrant intervention.[87] It decided to avoid even relatively low-level American intervention in Liberia by determining American interests on the basis of larger priorities, without respect for institutional pressures or for the availability of capabilities to fulfill those interests.[88]

The mediation problem was different in the two cases. The issue in Yugoslavia was whether state institutions would cohere and their integrity would be protected, on the one hand, or whether secession would occur, on the other. Integrity required constructing stronger statewide institutions, or at least providing some federal solution in which ethnic autonomy could be preserved if the state were kept whole. The mediating question in Liberia was less complex and more traditional. Choosing the state leader and the problem of political succession were at issue, not state integrity; the leverage and creativity required to cope with this issue were smaller than in the Yugoslav case, in which institutions could not cope with ethnic antagonists and therefore needed to be created or recreated.

The Liberia case material is consistent with causal, independent diplomacy. It illustrates how the independent approach would seem to have greater explanatory power when (1) relatively small-scale capabilities are needed to successfully mediate, so those who control offers and threats that support mediation are less influential relative to diplomatic officials, leaders, and their calculations, and (2) mobilizing mediating capabilities depends on situational thinking and substantive policy arguments rather than on policy structure, and is therefore more subject to shifts in circumstance and in argument. By contrast, the dependent approach seems more valuable—as in Yugoslavia—when (1) foreign policy stakes and mediation requirements are considerable and those controlling the specific capabilities required to mediate become key determiners of the success or failure of outside mediation, and (2) domestic interference with mediation initiatives is likely to be long-term because it is structural.

Table 5.3 summarizes differences between the Yugoslav and Liberian cases discussed in this section.

IV. CONCLUSIONS

Cause-and-effect analysis is required to cumulate case-based insights in diplomatic conflict management and to anchor efforts to generalize about diplomatic behavior. It introduces greater complexity into theorizing and suggests new lines of inquiry.

This chapter has aimed at conceptual clarity and at identifying analytical choices for weighing cause-and-effect relationships. The starting point has been realist insights about diplomatic statecraft. The realist bias for causal analysis of such statecraft is rejected here: that diplomacy is impacted by other developments should not be taken to mean that the quality of such diplomacy is inevitably worse. The potential for diplomatic adaptation to those developments, in which existing policy objectives continue to be pursued in spite of them, must always be considered. This potential, which is neglected by the realists, appears linked to the importance of the objective that is sought. When state interests are vital, adaptation deepens commitment to diplomatic norms.[89] In addition, contrary to the realists, diplomacy as effect should not be limited to action or decision; new lines of inquiry are opened when diplomatic action is distinguished from diplomatic outcome.

We distinguish between explanatory and policy improvement purposes for theorizing. In the former, diplomatic causal linkage can be defined in terms

Table 5.3. Contrasting Mediation in Yugoslavia and Liberia

	Yugoslavia	Liberia
Key mediation issues:	1. Challenge of state integrity 2. State building	1. Choice of ruler 2. Political succession
Major diplomatic impediment:	Intervention without enforcement	"White House Stop Order"
Consequences:	1. Hollow diplomacy 2. Diplomatic ambiguity	1. Reduced mediation initiative 2. Deadlock encourages rivalries and spoiler groups

of intention, impact, or leverage. For each of these definitions, obstacles to successful outcomes are the objects of diplomacy and require consideration. The "uphill" character of causal diplomacy reflects the often formidable character of these obstacles. When diplomacy succeeds, obstacles may be overcome fully or in part to achieve a policy objective, such as war prevention. Alternatively, failure to achieve or sustain an objective such as peace diplomatically must be explained in terms of why the obstacles to agreement were so formidable.

Each of our definitions of causal diplomatic linkage highlights a distinct impact of diplomatic statecraft on international conflict. Defining successful independent exercise of diplomacy as impact draws attention to overcoming obstacles when interstate conflict is entrenched and norms of world politics are relatively weak. When independent diplomacy is understood in terms of intentionality, undramatic but steady, purposeful action overcomes obstacles. The third causal framework, policy success, highlights how diplomatic promise is enhanced by the adversities of target states, and that hurting stalemate, while not planned for, can work as a capability multiplier for a state that capitalizes on it.[90]

For causal analysis, crisis politics can explain the relative strengths of diplomatic undertakings and war-contributing tendencies, which would be apparent from the outcome of the crisis. Alternatively, analysis of diplomacy as effect can compare why and how diplomats at times adapted to a given element of the diplomatic revolution, such as political ideology or public opinion, but at other times did not. Or it might use cases of negotiating failure to explain how perceptual barriers in the operational milieu accounted for those failures.

When implemented for policy critique and improvement, the primary concern in cause-and-effect analysis is to enhance diplomatic success. Cause and effect then become competing concerns in a case-based debate about policy choices. It is appropriate for policy planning, which identifies the strengths and weaknesses of a given course of action as a prelude to policy decision. And it is central to the study of policy failures that aims at policy improvement or new policy departures.

NOTES

1. "Cause" and "independent variable" are used in this chapter interchangeably, as are "effect" and "dependent variable."

2. Gary King, Robert O. Keohane, and Sidney Verba, *Designing Social Inquiry* (Princeton: Princeton University Press, 1994), 8.

3. James N. Rosenau, "Comparative Foreign Policy: Fad, Fantasy, or Field?," in

The Scientific Study of Foreign Policy, by James N. Rosenau (New York: Free Press, 1971), 82.

4. The paradigm shapes the analyst's expectations about relationships, enabling the analyst, according to James N. Rosenau and Mary Durfee, "to think theoretically [by] presum[ing] that there is a cause for every effect even though one does not seek to explain every effect." *Thinking Theory Thoroughly*, 2nd ed. (Boulder, CO: Westview, 2000), 229. By contrast, a version of the liberal paradigm that highlights how domestic politics increasingly constrains diplomatic initiative is more compatible with the study of diplomacy as effect. See ibid., 41–43.

5. Illustrating the modesty of the inductive method, chapter 3 took the unfamiliar context of the absence of diplomatic communication, while chapter 4 was limited to instances in which states aligned against a common adversary.

6. Alexander L. George, "Case Studies and Theory Development: The Method of Structured, Focused Comparison," in *Diplomacy: New Approaches in History, Theory and Policy*, ed. Paul Gordon Lauren (New York: Free Press, 1979), 47.

7. Rosenau, "Comparative Foreign Policy," 82–83. Intermediate and implementive variables are omitted from this essay to simplify the analysis.

8. Ibid., 80–81. Rosenau divided each category of variables between those internal to the actor and those external to it. Substantive diplomatic statecraft is contained in each of his interaction variables. Among the initiatory variables, for example, diplomatic incidents could precipitate official government actions. Intervening variables include "any and all of the resources, techniques, and actions that may affect the way in which decisions designed to preserve or modify circumstances in the international system are carried out." Diplomatic procedures and capabilities are among such resources, techniques, and actions. And dependent or responsive variables include "readiness of another actor to enter into and/or conclude negotiations" (ibid.).

9. Roger Fisher, Elizabeth Kopelman, and Andrea Kupfer Schneider, *Beyond Machiavelli* (Cambridge, MA: Harvard University Press, 1994), 5. See also Roger Fisher, Andrea Kupfer Schneider, Elizabeth Borgwardt, and Brian Ganson, *Coping with International Conflict* (Upper Saddle River, NJ: Prentice Hall, 1997).

10. I. William Zartman, *Cowardly Lions* (Boulder, CO: Lynne Rienner, 2005).

11. Arthur C. Danto, *Analytical Philosophy of History* (Cambridge: Cambridge University Press, 1965), 245.

12. John Lewis Gaddis, *The Landscape of History* (New York: Oxford University Press, 2002), 97.

13. Ibid.; emphasis in original.

14. Harold Sprout and Margaret Sprout, *Toward a Politics of the Planet Earth* (New York: Van Nostrand Reinhold, 1971), 190.

15. The most prominent recent example of this form of causal action has been the 2015 Joint Comprehensive Plan of Action to control Iran's nuclear capability.

16. Hans J. Morgenthau, *Politics among Nations*, 4th ed. (New York: Knopf, 1967), 135.

17. Fisher, Kopelman, and Schneider, *Beyond Machiavelli*, 4.

18. Martin Wight, *Power Politics*, ed. Hedley Bull and Carsten Holbraad (New York: Holmes & Meier, 1978), 137. In this sense, causal undertakings are produced by value decisions. For analysis of a value decision for war, see Glenn D. Paige, *The Korean Decision* (New York: Free Press, 1968).

19. Gordan A. Craig and Alexander L. George, *Force and Statecraft*, 3rd ed. (New York: Oxford University Press, 1995), 227.

20. Ibid., 105. On superpower norms see also Alexander George, "U.S.-Soviet Efforts to Cooperate in Crisis Management and Crisis Avoidance," in *U.S.-Soviet Security Cooperation*, ed. Alexander L. George, Philip J. Farley, and Alexander Dallin (New York: Oxford University Press, 1988), 583–85.

21. Morgenthau, *Politics among Nations*, 549.

22. Cited in Martin Wight, *International Theory*, ed. Gabriele Wight and Brian Porter (New York: Holmes & Meier, 1991), 190. Salisbury's biographer also noted that "[Salisbury's] own conception of a perfect diplomacy was always of one whose victories come without observation" (ibid.).

23. Ibid., 189.

24. Ibid., 190.

25. Hedley Bull, *The Anarchical Society* (New York: Columbia University Press, 1977), 170.

26. Robert Jervis, *The Logic of Images in International Relations* (Princeton: Princeton University Press, 1970), 95.

27. Thomas C. Schelling, *Arms and Influence* (New Haven, CT: Yale University Press, 1966), 227.

28. Ibid., 93–94.

29. For an illustration of this phenomenon during the superpower Cold War, see Philip E. Mosely, "Some Soviet Techniques of Negotiation," in *The Kremlin and World Politics: Studies in Soviet Policy and Action*, by Philip Mosely (New York: Vintage, 1960), 21–22.

30. Kenneth N. Waltz, *Theory of International Politics* (Reading, MA: Addison-Wesley, 1979), 167.

31. Wight, *International Theory*, 193.

32. Zartman, *Cowardly Lions*, 13.

33. Wight, *International Theory*, 193.

34. Susan Rosegrant and Michael D. Watkins, "Getting to Dayton: Negotiating an End to the War in Bosnia," in *Perspectives on American Foreign Policy*, ed. Bruce W. Jentleson (New York: Norton, 2000), 219. Holbrooke's actions in this instance fit Charles de Gaulle's view that "future power can be successfully used like present power if this done with boldness, imagination and utter intrepidity." Wight, *International Theory*, 193.

35. Richard Holbrooke, *To End a War* (New York: Random House, 1998), 64–65.

36. Ibid., 66–67.

37. Ibid., 66.

38. On constraints narrowing policy choices, see Bruce Russett and Harvey Starr, *World Politics: The Menu for Choice*, 5th ed. (New York: W. H. Freeman, 1996), 161ff.

39. Craig and George, *Force and Statecraft*, 286.

40. Ibid., 54. A later edition of this study made the same point regarding superpower cold war. See Paul Gordon Lauren, Gordon A. Craig, and Alexander L. George, *Force and Statecraft*, 4th ed. (New York: Oxford University Press, 2007), 91.

41. Hans J. Morgenthau, *In Defense of the National Interest* (New York: Knopf, 1952), 232. For an analysis of the impact of public opinion upon diplomacy that gives extended attention to Morgenthau's writings, see chapter 8, below.

42. Ibid., 233.

43. Sprout and Sprout, *Toward a Politics of the Planet Earth*, 190.

44. Lauren, Craig, and George, *Force and Statecraft*, 95.

45. George, "U.S.-Soviet Efforts to Cooperate," 585.

46. Dean Rusk, *As I Saw It* (New York: Penguin, 1990), 357.

47. Henry A. Kissinger, *White House Years* (Boston: Little, Brown, 1979), passim.

48. On common understandings as a safety net, see Harold H. Saunders, "Regulating Soviet-US Competition and Cooperation in the Arab-Israeli Arena, 1967–86," in George, Farley, and Dallin, *U.S.-Soviet Security Cooperation*, 575.

49. George, "U.S.-Soviet Efforts to Cooperate," 581, 591; emphasis in original.

50. Sheldon M. Stern, *The Week the World Stood Still* (Stanford: Stanford University Press, 2005), 20.

51. Graham T. Allison, *Essence of Decision* (Boston: Little, Brown, 1971), 42. For diplomatic conflict management in the Cuban crisis, see also Raymond L. Garthoff, *Reflections on the Cuban Missile Crisis*, rev. ed. (Washington, DC: Brookings Institution Press, 1989), 97ff.

52. Glenn H. Snyder and Paul Diesing, *Conflict among Nations* (Princeton: Princeton University Press, 1977), 568.

53. Stern, *Week the World Stood Still*, 52; emphasis in original.

54. Ibid., 56; emphasis in original. They also desired to neutralize the Soviet missiles before they became operational and to prevent additional missiles from entering Cuba.

55. Ibid., 57, 60, 187.

56. Ivo H. Daalder, "The United States and Military Intervention in Internal Conflict," in *The International Dimensions of Internal Conflict*, ed. Michael E. Brown (Cambridge, MA: MIT Press, 1996), 477.

57. Ibid., 484.

58. Ibid., 477.

59. Ibid., 481.

60. Eric Moskowitz and Jeffrey S. Lantis, "Conflict in the Balkans," in *Fateful Decisions: Inside the National Security Council*, ed. Karl F. Inderfurth and Loch K. Johnson (New York: Oxford University Press, 2004), 256.

61. Donald Rothchild, "The United States and Africa: Power with Limited Influence," in *Eagle Rules? Foreign Policy and American Primacy in the Twenty-First Century*, ed. Robert J. Lieber (Upper Saddle River, NJ: Prentice Hall, 2002), 230.

62. Ibid., 234.

63. This section is heavily indebted to Sprout and Sprout, *Toward a Politics of the Planet Earth*, 194ff.

64. I. William Zartman, "Alternative Attempts at Crisis Management: Concepts and Processes," in *New Issues in International Crisis Management*, ed. Gilbert Winham (Boulder, CO: Westview, 1998), 213. Zartman notes that "a ripe moment may . . . be characterized as a mutually hurting stalemate with a way out" (ibid.).

65. Ibid., 210.

66. Craig and George, *Force and Statecraft*, 286.

67. Zartman, "Alternative Attempts at Crisis Management," 214.

68. See chapter 4.

69. Glenn Snyder and Paul Diesing maintain that "governments generally do not do well in analyzing each other's internal politics in crises, and indeed it is inherently difficult." *Conflict among Nations*, 523.

70. Craig and George, *Force and Statecraft*, 286.

71. Stephen D. Krasner, ed., *International Regimes* (Ithaca: Cornell University Press, 1983).

72. Zartman, "Alternative Attempts at Crisis Management," 211–12.

73. See chapter 4.

74. Craig and George, *Force and Statecraft*, 286.

75. Albert Wohlstetter and Roberta Wohlstetter, "Controlling the Risks in Cuba," *Adelphi Paper*, no. 17 (London: Institute of Strategic Studies, April 1965).

76. Zartman, "Alternative Attempts at Crisis Management," 222.

77. Craig and George, *Force and Statecraft*, 286.

78. Zartman, "Alternative Attempts at Crisis Management," 218.

79. Ibid., 211.

80. Zartman, *Cowardly Lions*, 13–14.

81. Ibid., 146.

82. Ibid., 154–55.

83. Ibid., 163. "In part because of the military's opposition," Daalder has written, referring to intervention in small state conflict, "Clinton ruled out the use of U.S. ground troops for any purpose other than enforcing a peace agreement or helping to evacuate UN peacekeepers." Daalder, "United States and Military Intervention in Internal Conflict," 474. This Pentagon attitude was already present in the 1980s. See Craig and George, *Force and Statecraft*, 265–68.

84. Ibid., 171.

85. Ibid., 147. "The ambiguity," he writes, "had the effect of giving the green light to all parties to pursue their unilateral objective."

86. For example, Brent Scowcroft, then the president's national security advisor, believed that American intervention would require permanent American forces in Monrovia. Zartman, *Cowardly Lions*, 58.

87. Herman J. Cohen, *Intervening in Africa* (New York: St. Martin's, 2000), 162.

88. Cohen notes that American Department of Defense assets in Liberia were totally neglected in the decision to avoid mediation (ibid., 161).

89. Adaptation may not always be diplomatic; pursuit of a diplomatic objective may be protected by a nondiplomatic adaptation. For example, the United States, responding to political constraint, took action against Iran that might not have been taken in the absence of the nuclear agreement: in response to Iranian ballistic missile tests, which flaunted a UN Security Council resolution prohibiting them, the United States is reported to have imposed sanctions against Iran "as a carefully calibrated answer to critics, from Capitol Hill to Saudi Arabia, who have argued in recent months that President Obama is willing to overlook almost any Iranian transgression in order to avoid derailing the [Iran] nuclear deal he pursued for so many years." Helene Cooper and David E. Sanger, "Iran's Missile Tests Remind the U.S. That Tensions Have Not Ended," *New York Times*, 31 December 2015.

90. For a study of how mediation overcomes opposition and capitalizes upon the adversity of antagonists, see chapter 6.

6

Diplomatic Mediation as an Independent Variable

By probing cases of mediation success, this chapter investigates third-party mediation as an illustration of diplomacy that has a causal and therefore independent impact on international affairs.[1] The analysis emphasizes the complications making third-party mediation an "uphill" challenge rather than attempting to explain successful mediation, which would necessitate evaluating examples of unsuccessful as well as successful mediation.[2]

The six cases studied here, involving mediation in three interstate and three intrastate disputes, illustrate intractable conflict that resists diplomatic solutions and the use of war as a method for coping with disputes.[3] They collectively illustrate how, when impediments to mediation are considerable and when the anticipated costs and risks of third-party mediation are not clearly outweighed by foreseeable benefits, the mediator nevertheless can illustrate how diplomacy has an independent effect.[4] The particular interest here is to compare pathways that lead to that effect. A major purpose is to force consideration of diverse pathways to mediation success, using the same set of questions addressed to each of the cases.[5]

The chapter also tests the widespread belief that defusing internal conflict by diplomatic negotiation is much more difficult than is defusing conflict between states.[6] This view, while supported by recent experience demonstrating the difficulties of mediating intractable intrastate conflict, needs to be reconsidered. While much third-party mediation in recent years has been directed to intractable intrastate conflict, that tendency represents a shift. Third-party mediation was primarily directed for much of international history to disputes between states, but because of recent experience such disputes have been relegated to the periphery of dispute analysis. Yet, like their intrastate counterparts, interstate conflicts can be intractable, and theoretical work can legitimately compare aspects of both. The present research gives equal weight to both dispute types, not to explain why one type is preponderant at any given time but rather to reveal patterns by which a particular outcome occurs.[7]

Intrastate cases generally turn out to be more problematic for mediation and require greater activism by the mediator, but the differences between the intrastate and interstate mediating experiences are not as great as expected. Differences between our interstate and intrastate mediation cases are displayed in five empirical categories, but only three of these appear to account for the added difficulty of mediating intrastate conflicts.

After a discussion of the significance of comparing interstate and intrastate mediation cases and the complications encountered in doing so, profiles of six cases are presented. The cases are then compared, and, based on the comparisons, the view that intrastate conflicts are more difficult to mediate than their interstate counterparts is reconsidered.

I. THE SIGNIFICANCE OF COMPARING INTERSTATE AND INTRASTATE MEDIATION CASES

From one angle, the low rate of success in mediating disputes *between states*, rather than the lower rate of mediation success in intrastate cases, should be of primary analytical interest. One study notes that of 382 cases of mediation in intractable interstate conflict, more than 50 percent were unsuccessful, the parties continuing their earlier confrontational relationship.[8] But a significantly higher proportion of interstate wars than intrastate ones are resolved by negotiation, and a significantly higher proportion of intrastate hostilities result in the surrender or elimination of one side than is the case in interstate wars. The major interest here is to seek out especially difficult mediating cases and establish the consequences of different levels of mediating difficulty, holding successful outcome constant. Given this interest, the primary question must be whether interstate or intrastate type affects the *added relative difficulty* of the mediation process.

Mediators in intrastate cases are at a relative disadvantage, when, according to I. William Zartman, "the mediator is basically illegitimate and usually unwanted. If both the parties saw that they needed help out of their mess, the mediator's job would be greatly facilitated, but this is rarely the case. More than other parties to the negotiation process, a mediator must build leverage, [but mediators] are . . . caught in a vicious circle. Their leverage depends largely on finding an attractive solution, and their conveying a solution depends on their leverage."[9] By contrast, the mediator in interstate cases is often close to one side of a conflict and seeks to improve ties with the other; the latter is attracted by the prospect that the mediator may be in a position to deliver its ally to a peaceful settlement.[10] Mediation strategies and tactics would logically vary in the two instances.

Conceptually, distinguishing between the negotiability of interstate as against intrastate disputes is problematic when the relative capabilities of parties to conflict are taken into account. To be sure, the balance of the capabilities of the antagonists can be linked to negotiability. For example, the emergence of a mutual hurting stalemate (MHS) between the parties to conflict, "a moment when the upper hand slips and the lower hand rises, both parties moving toward equality, with both movements carrying pain for the parties," can enhance successful interstate and intrastate mediation.[11] An MHS can strengthen mediation when the parties cannot act on their own.[12]

While this suggests that conflicts are more negotiable when the parties are relatively equal in strength, in internal war the parties are inherently unequal. "Asymmetry [between the parties]," argues Zartman, "means that the most propitious conditions for resolving conflict are difficult to obtain."[13] The special importance of asymmetry in intrastate conflict hinges on the fact that such conflict matches government support by trained and equipped military establishments against political challengers with significantly smaller military capability. When domestic conflict leads to civil war, the unequal military strengths of government and challenger presumably diminish the chances that the two sides will accept a military deadlock, an indispensable condition for successful third-party mediation. On the other hand, the unequal strengths commonly lead the weaker side to be much more favorable to third-party mediation than is the superior antagonist.[14]

Often, the antagonists in interstate hostilities are not equally strong either, so it is not readily clear why the asymmetry should make intrastate wars more difficult to mediate than interstate ones. On the other hand, symmetry between the opponents can also be problematic for third-party mediation. In their important study of negotiation participants' power and negotiating outcomes, Zartman and Jeffrey Rubin confirm that "perceptions of equal power among negotiators tend to result in more effective negotiation than unequal power."[15] However, they say this generalization does not apply in intractable conflict. "When negotiators are competitive in [motivational orientation] and equal in power," they write, "all hell breaks loose! . . . [W]hen states in conflict tend to be competitive, equal power may be expected to be the least productive condition for negotiation."[16]

This development may be linked to what Zartman elsewhere has referred to as "a soft stalemate that is stable and self-serving (known as the S^5 situation), with a painful but bearable effect," in which equal capabilities and the high motivation of the parties account for the stalemate.[17] It suggests, however, that even when asymmetry is deflated as an explanation for the greater difficulty of intrastate as against interstate conflict, shifts in the antagonists' military strength—however indispensable for the mutual hurting stalemate condition—are not easily translated into greater mediating efficacy.

We need to consider, then, whether negotiating success is accounted for by the MHS. A mutually hurting stalemate may assist mediation differently in the interstate and intrastate cases, or, alternatively, it may aid mediation uniformly. This study investigates the impact of power balances and intractability, attending to how the capability balance between the antagonists affects the mediation outlook in each case. Examining these on a case-by-case basis, and comparing the results, the study may gain greater clarity about the impact of third-party mediation on the primary antagonists, and more specifically about how the antagonists' capabilities affect that impact.

II. THE CASES

As indicated, this study is limited to three interstate and three intrastate cases. The three interstate cases studied here are (1) the Russo-Japanese conflict, 1894–1905, mediated by American president Theodore Roosevelt; (2) the Israeli-Egyptian and Israeli-Syrian conflicts, 1967–1975, mediated by American secretary of state Henry Kissinger; and (3) conflict between India and Pakistan, 1965–1966, mediated by Soviet prime minister Alexei Kosygin. The three intrastate cases are (1) the conflict in Zimbabwe-Rhodesia, 1965–1979, mediated by British foreign minister Peter Lord Carrington; (2) the Muslim-Serb and Croat-Serb conflicts in Bosnia-Herzegovina, 1992–1995, mediated by Assistant Secretary of State for European and Canadian Affairs Richard Holbrooke; and (3) the SWAPO–South African conflict in Namibia, 1981–1989, mediated by Assistant Secretary of State for African Affairs Chester Crocker.

Each of these cases illustrates parties unable on their own to manage their conflict. The examples force consideration of alternative pathways—challenges and adaptations to circumstances—that ultimately produce successful mediation outcomes. Common questions are asked of each of the cases to highlight the potential for alternative pathways (see table 6.1). This contributes to empirically suggestive generalizations and facilitates more focused study later. Treating each case as "deviant" to force displays of diversity is justified by the present weakness of theory, and particularly by the

Table 6.1.   Common Questions Asked of the Six Cases

1. What were the most important sources of intractability between the antagonists? Was war one of these sources?
2. What conditions favored a negotiated settlement? Did the antagonists perceive that obtaining a settlement was urgent?
3. What interests impelled the mediator to intervene in the conflict?
4. What was the mediator's strategy in working toward a settlement?
5. What specific issues in the conflict received most of the mediator's attention, and why?
6. How large was the mediator's leverage on the antagonists, and what were the sources of this leverage?
7. What developments most aided the success of the mediation?
8. What developments most interfered with the mediator's efforts and threatened to derail them?

presumption that mediation is more difficult in intrastate than in interstate conflict.[18] The resulting detailed comparisons can test arguments and sharpen questions, conceptions, and associations in ways a larger case sample cannot. A limited sample, on the other hand, cannot be used to confirm either preponderant trends or representative diversity in the universe of mediation. Only a fuller case sample, which would be much less rich than the case material adduced here to understand mediating difficulty, could probe the frequency of successful outcomes in interstate and in intrastate cases.

1. Russo-Japanese Conflict (1894–1905)[19]

By the mid-1890s, Japan viewed the steady expansion of Russian influence into Manchuria and Korea as a threat to its independence and survival. Though they were not in conflict about specific territorial objectives, neither Russia nor Japan could allow Korea or Manchuria to fall into the hands of the other. Japan especially opposed Russian expansion into Korea, an unstable country absorbed entirely into the Russian sphere of influence by 1894, because of Korea's proximity to the Japanese home islands.

The intractableness of the Russo-Japanese conflict was the major reason Japan went to war against Russia in 1904. In extensive Russo-Japanese discussions, the security aspirations of both countries could not be reconciled without one side retreating. The Russians viewed the growth of the Far East Russian railway network as ensuring the success of their expansion and thus had little incentive to negotiate or to reassure Japan about Russian intentions. This expansion objective grew out of a competition for power of many domestic Russian factions, which did not acknowledge opposing Japanese interests. Finally, influential military parties on both sides feared the military strength of the other side.

The Russo-Japanese conflict became much more manageable as the result of war. The Japanese decision to make war was predicated, in fact, on the assumption that Japan would receive international assistance to end the war. Having aimed diplomatically at the opportunity to challenge Russia militarily without interference from other major states, Japanese leaders had the United States in mind as a mediator prior to going to war, and actively sought American mediation following victories over Russia at Mukden in March 1905 and two months later in a decisive naval battle at Tsushima Island. Japan occupied the Russian island of Sakhalin in July 1905 primarily to compel the Russians to make peace. While its military victories ensured the containment of Russian influence, continued warfare on the mainland favored Russia: while Japanese Army matériel and manpower was limited, the Russian ability to transport reinforcements into Manchuria steadily grew. On the Russian side, revolution and naval mutiny in 1905 raised doubts about the political reliability of Russian forces.

President Theodore Roosevelt, responding favorably to the formal May 1905 Japanese overture for mediation, sought "balanced antagonism" between Russia and Japan on the Far East mainland, an interest that led him to support, prior to the start of peace talks in the summer of 1905, a compromise peace entailing Japanese freedom of action in Korea and substantial Russian interests in Manchuria. Roosevelt also showed what John A. White has characterized as "his strong partisanship toward Japan as well as . . . frank acceptance of a major role in the Far East for a victorious Japan," an attitude that shaped his strategy of mediation.[20] While Roosevelt did not attend the peace conference in Portsmouth, New Hampshire—instead making himself available to break deadlocks that arose—he worked behind the scenes far more closely with the Japanese than with the Russians, and Japan provided every opportunity for him to do so. Upon its decision to go to war, Japan sent a former Harvard University classmate and friend of Roosevelt as a special representative to the United States specifically to cultivate American goodwill toward Japan. American goodwill was forthcoming: after the Russian emperor appeared to be reneging on a commitment to enter peace talks, Roosevelt suggested that Japan seize Sakhalin as a coercive step. He supported the Japanese preference for dealing initially with the easier questions at the conference, and he had arranged that Japan would be cleared of any responsibility if the talks broke down.

The most controversial issues at the conference—the Russian demand that Japan leave Sakhalin and the Japanese demand for a Russian war indemnity—both resulted from military action (one more contentious issue, the origin of the war, was sidestepped, as the two sides had agreed not to discuss it). Japanese negotiators were instructed to seek their objectives on these two issues as circumstances permitted, but their Russian counterparts were prepared to break off the talks if the Japanese insisted on them. Ultimately, both were dropped from the Portsmouth agreement. In the final confrontation over these issues, Roosevelt, who favored dropping both, worked for peace by strongly challenging the indemnity demand and helping to persuade Japan not to insist on it.

Roosevelt lacked the power to enforce his views on the indemnity and Sakhalin questions. His leverage largely came from the will to peace of the two belligerents—and especially the Japanese desire for peace, because, though militarily victorious, Japan sought most to end the war. This intention followed from the initial Japanese war strategy; inasmuch as the Japanese strategy depended on Roosevelt's assistance to end the war, his partisanship increased his influence potential with the Japanese government when the success of the talks was at stake. But that influence also depended on Japan's adherence to its strategy: had Japan insisted on the indemnity or on territorial acquisitions, Roosevelt would not have been able to save the talks.

Roosevelt's mediation was aided by the Russian willingness to base peace terms on the actual achievements of Japanese military forces, which allowed for (1) Russian concessions to Japan in Korea and Manchuria and for (2) each belligerent to demonstrate to the other that it had a margin of security that would prevent the other from asserting a hegemonic role in the Far East. It was also aided by Japanese leaders' awareness that Japan had reached its upper limit of striking power in Manchuria and should end the war before its serious weaknesses became known to the Russians. A mutual hurting stalemate existed in this case, as the side that had suffered military adversity was confident of its military potential, while the belligerent that had prevailed thus far was insecure. On the other hand, mediation was most challenged by the Russian refusal to compromise on the indemnity and Sakhalin questions, requiring Japan, then militarily superior, to give way.

2. Israeli-Egyptian and Israeli-Syrian Conflict (1967–1975)[21]

The 1967 Six-Day War, which ended with Israel in full military control of Egyptian territory in the Sinai Peninsula and of Syrian territory in the Golan Heights, added to the intractability of Israeli-Arab conflict dating back to 1948. Israel believed it needed to occupy Egyptian and Syrian territory to secure its own borders. Following the war, Egypt and Syria were vitally committed to recovering their territory, but Israel, having difficulty in determining its antagonists' intentions, was uncertain whether they were prepared to accept Israel's existence. Israel pointed to Egyptian leader Anwar Sadat's use of the phrase "the legitimate rights of the Palestinians," after he assumed power in 1971, as indicating his support of the Palestinian terrorist campaign to liquidate the State of Israel. On both military fronts, a security dilemma prevailed because of the advantage of striking first (as Israel did in 1967) and because of the difficulties of distinguishing defensive from offensive force buildups. With American peacemaking initiatives deadlocked, intensive shelling took place between Israeli and Egyptian forces on opposite sides of the Suez Canal in 1970 and 1971, and in October 1973 Egypt and Syria forced the territorial issue by coordinating and launching a limited war against Israel. Their offensives were initially successful but were subsequently contained and reversed; after an initial cease-fire agreement on October 22 broke down, Israel gained more Syrian territory than it had in 1967, surrounded the invading Egyptian Third Army in the Sinai, and crossed the Suez Canal in the direction of Cairo.

Unlike the 1967 war, the October 1973 war enhanced the potential for negotiation. Sadat, whose country had long been allied with the Soviet Union, decided in planning that war to shift ties to the United States afterward, using American support to offset Israel's military dominance over Egypt and to translate Egyptian war-making into political gains from Israel. His decision removed the Soviet Union as a counterweight to the United States in the Middle East and made it possible for U.S. secretary of state Henry Kissinger to mediate between Egypt and Israel and between Syria and Israel without Soviet interference. Moreover, isolation of the Egyptian Third Army behind Israeli lines created an Egyptian need for prompt American diplomatic intervention, and Sadat's earlier strategic decision to switch alliance partners—a decision that had been communicated to the United States—made it possible for Kissinger to respond quickly to that need. Two agreements for Israeli force pullbacks in the Sinai, in January 1974 and September 1975, and one on the Syrian front, in May 1974, were brought about by Kissinger. Demilitarized and force limitation zones included in these agreements had been suggested earlier by Israeli defense minister Moshe Dayan and communicated to Sadat by a UN-appointed mediator prior to the 1973 war.

While the October war was being fought, the United States decided on active mediation and worked to foster military stalemate between the parties that, Kissinger believed, would enhance the chances of mediation success. Mediation was intended to increase American influence in the region at the expense of the Soviet Union and to terminate an oil embargo from Arab countries to the United States that had been initiated to bring pressure on Israel to make concessions on borders to Egypt and Syria. Forging for the

first time an Arab policy, and maintaining close relations particularly with
Sadat, Kissinger stressed the Egyptian and Syrian need to deal with the
United States diplomatically because of the close American-Israeli relationship. He also provided negotiating advice to the Israelis, at first telling them
not to concede too fast, so as not to appear weak to the Arabs, and then, when
his mediation seemed deadlocked, urging them to be more forthcoming. He
cultivated a crisis management role as indispensable for building confidence
between the parties about each other and about the prospect of agreement,
stressing the disutility to both sides of mediation failure. He never clarified
the ultimate American aims in border and force demarcation discussions,
stressing process over substance.

The most urgent issues tackled by Kissinger arose out of the shift in military momentum in the October war: (1) the rectification of borders on the
Sinai and Syrian fronts and (2) disengagement of forces on those fronts to
diminish mutual fears of attack. Kissinger obtained in the first disengagement
agreement still larger Israeli force pullbacks than were initially sought by
Egypt and Syria, so as to make the case that Egypt and Syria stood to gain
more by negotiation than by war. He used relatively small, partial agreements
to reassure the Israelis about Arab intentions and to enhance his potential to
negotiate follow-on agreements. When the adversaries' conflicting positions
subsequently hardened, as over Israel's demand for an Egyptian pledge of
nonbelligerency as a condition for the second Israeli Sinai force pullback,
Kissinger, shuttling frequently between the parties, formulated his own proposals, often posing ideas from one side to the other as his own.

Because of incompatible Israeli and Arab positions, Kissinger needed to
impose agreement on the parties, primarily by highlighting and increasing
the dependence of the parties on the United States. This dependence was
greater for Israel, the most resistant to American influence and to force concessions. When Israel held out for Egyptian nonbelligerency and for Egyptian
fulfillment of a large number of preliminary Israeli demands before discussing a second withdrawal line, Kissinger suspended negotiations and spoke of
a need to reassess the American-Israeli relationship. Ultimately, however,
that relationship was strengthened still further by new American security
assurances and aid to Israel, which a previously deadlocked and uncooperative Israeli government found sufficiently attractive to approve the second
Sinai force agreement. Though Egypt and Syria did not have the same close
relationship to the United States, they became strategic partners with the
United States because they decided that it was expedient for them to do so.

Kissinger's mediation was most importantly assisted by military stalemate
between the parties. All three antagonists viewed Israeli forces as superior to

their Arab counterparts and not subject to military defeat. But, while Egyptian and Syrian forces could be militarily defeated by Israel, the October war showed that the two countries could still impose extreme costs by making war against Israel and that their defeat did not enhance Israel's long-term security.

American linkages to the hostile parties indirectly transformed the relationship between them and overcame their entrenched and irreconcilable positions. The mutual insecurity resulting from longtime Israel-Arab antagonism, the volatile character of that antagonism, and the difficulty in Israel's case of overcoming stalemated political leadership were the major obstacles to mediation success.

3. Pakistan-India Conflict (1965–1966)[22]

Since 1947, when Kashmir was divided between India and Pakistan, Pakistan has claimed all of it on behalf of the territory's Muslim majority, while India, rejecting majority rule, argued that Kashmir's religious composition was irrelevant and that India's foundation would be undermined if Muslims dictated the territory's future. Kashmir was also contested geopolitically between Pakistan and India and between India and China.

Intractable conflict over Kashmir was demonstrated by five rounds of Pakistan-India talks over Kashmir between December 1962 and May 1963, sponsored by the United States and Great Britain and ending in deadlock. The United States worried that India-Pakistan hostility would make containing Communist Chinese expansion more difficult; Pakistan, closely aligned with the United States, supported outside involvement in the Kashmir question, while India generally opposed it.

Determined to force India to make concessions on Kashmir, Pakistan decided in 1965 on a policy of "leaning on India." It endeavored to improve relations with China and with the Soviet Union to offset weakening American support for Pakistan; the visit of Pakistani president Ayub Khan to the Soviet Union in April 1965 has been termed a "landmark" in Soviet-Pakistani relations, contrasting sharply with the American cancellation of Ayub's visit to the United States earlier in the year.[23] Pakistan also conducted in January 1965 a limited military probe in the Rann of Kutch, territory outside of Kashmir disputed by Pakistan and India, and in August 1965 it implemented a plan to foment and capitalize on a Muslim rebellion in the Indian-controlled portion of Kashmir Valley, utilizing soldiers trained in Pakistani military camps, before India could respond militarily.

These moves responded to Indian steps between December 1964 and

March 1965 integrating Indian Kashmir with the rest of India, accommodating the Indian Hindu nationalist agenda but stimulating Muslim unrest in
Indian-controlled Kashmir. India suspected that Pakistan and China had
become secretly aligned and thus became hypervigilant about Pakistan and
Kashmir. Rising oppositional domestic politics in both countries added to the
political pressure to make relative gains over Kashmir.

The Pakistani covert action did not produce a Muslim uprising but instead
brought a three-week war in which neither side obtained a clear-cut military
victory. Regular Pakistani forces crossed into Indian-controlled Kashmir,
threatening Indian land access into Kashmir. Indian forces, which fought
more effectively than anticipated by Pakistan and had the upper hand militarily, subsequently crossed into the Pakistani province of Lahore, controlling
a salient near Lahore city. An imperfectly observed standstill cease-fire was
secured on August 5, 1965, by the UN secretary-general, U Thant. The UN
Security Council appealed for a full military withdrawal by both sides, but
the antagonists remained in their advanced military positions.

The Soviet Union, supported by the United States, offered during the war
to provide "good offices" to bring the fighting to an end. It was motivated to
forestall Chinese intervention and to replace the Western powers as stabiliz-
ing elements in South Asia. In December 1965 the antagonists accepted the
Soviet offer, agreeing to attend talks the following month in Tashkent under
the auspices of the Soviet prime minister Alexei Kosygin.

At Tashkent, Kosygin sought agreement without particular concern about
its substance. Engaged in conveying the views of each side to the other and in
bridging viewpoints, he stressed addressing lesser Pakistani-Indian disputes
rather than major ones, in order to build confidence. This approach downplayed Kashmir, which Pakistan hoped to highlight and India did not wish to
discuss. A formal agenda was avoided; Pakistan was prevailed upon not to
let Kashmir dominate the conference, while India agreed to allow the issue to
be raised. However, the bitter Kashmir deadlock, and the absence of ongoing
mediation that dealt with the broader India-Pakistan issues, made it difficult
for the parties to concede on anything.

Disengagement of forces to prewar lines (including the infiltrators into
Indian Kashmir that Pakistan did not concede) and an India-proposed two-
power no-war pact received the most attention. India initially insisted on the
pact as a prerequisite for withdrawing from Pakistani territory, while Pakistan
linked it to a full Kashmir settlement. Kosygin seems to have concluded that
the Kashmir withdrawal and the no-war pact issues could not reinforce each
other and were mutually limiting. Only a minimal agreement of mutual depri-
vation could be ultimately obtained. India's demand for the peace pact as
compensation for military withdrawal was resolved in the end by referring in

the conference declaration to Pakistan's commitment, as a member of the United Nations, to the UN Charter's prescriptions for the peaceful resolution of disputes. Agreement by both sides to "withdrawal of all armed personnel" to prewar lines allowed India to argue that the Pakistani infiltrators were included.

Kosygin did not offer material incentives to the antagonists to agree, and his leverage on the antagonists was small. He stressed the difficulties either side would bear in the case of the talks' failure. He indicated to India that the Soviet Union would not impede an adverse reaction at the UN if India did not withdraw from forward positions in Pakistan. To the hard-line Pakistani foreign minister, he explained that Soviet officials opposed either side gaining more from the talks than war-making had achieved.

Contributing to mediation success in this case was the Pakistani president's personal rapport with Kosygin and, to a lesser extent, with his Indian counterpart, Lal Shastri. Success was also assisted by Kosygin's tactic of insulating the negotiations against failure by drastically limiting the substance of the agreement, especially in connection with the Kashmir issue, and persistently cajoling the parties at the end to agree. Finally, mediation was aided by the support given to it, and to full military withdrawal by the antagonists, by Western powers and the UN.

The most important impediment to the mediator's efforts was the increased intransigence of the parties resulting from the hostilities, as each side demanded that its political goals—for Pakistan, Indian concession on its part of Kashmir, and for India, Pakistani agreement to avoid war over Kashmir—be implemented despite the war's failure to produce a clear winner. The antagonists' objectives over Kashmir remained as irreconcilable as in the past, yet the parties could agree only by explicitly depriving themselves of fully achieving their objectives. In this mediation, characterized as "a frightening cliff-hanger that dealt effectively with the most urgent problems it faced," the parties were required to put their larger objectives to the side in order to provide for their immediate need, a cease-fire with full military withdrawals to the prewar boundaries.[24]

4. Conflict in Zimbabwe-Rhodesia (1965–1979)[25]

Intractability in Zimbabwe-Rhodesia was due to the intensification and the internationalization of civil war in the country, and to the zero-sum question of who would rule there. After the minority Rhodesian white community unilaterally declared independence from England in 1965, two competing black guerrilla organizations, the Zimbabwean African National Union (ZANU), based in Mozambique, and the Zimbabwe African People's Union

(ZAPU), based in Zambia, emerged to oppose it. Two years later, ZAPU and ZANU, supported by their patron states as well as by international sanctions against the white Rhodesian regime, formed the Patriotic Front coalition to oppose it.

The white regime, supported heavily by South Africa, thereafter conceded the principle of majority rule by blacks while denying it in practice, insisting the white minority be given a disproportionate number of representatives in the national legislature as well as a veto over legislation. This arrangement underpinned the so-called internal settlement of March 1976, which provided for a government by coalition until elections were held. Determined to avoid any compromise with the Patriotic Front, the Rhodesian regime launched raids against the guerrillas in Zambia and Mozambique. The regime hoped the raids would, by spurring aid to the guerrillas from Communist bloc countries, provoke South Africa and the United States to enter the war on the side of the regime, forestalling full majority rule. A Cuban plan to assist the Patriotic Front in 1979 would likely have brought about the escalation sought by the Rhodesian regime, but Zambia and Mozambique, which controlled the flow of weapons to guerrillas inside Rhodesia, did not approve it. Failed mediation efforts between 1974 and 1978 added to pessimism about a negotiated settlement, and the guerrillas themselves believed their military victory was inevitable.

Following the election in April 1979 of a black coalition leader, Bishop Abel Muzorewa, as Rhodesian prime minister and the election of an African parliamentary majority, the Rhodesian government, by then exhausted by the effects of war, requested recognition from the newly elected Conservative government in Great Britain headed by Margaret Thatcher. The British government held off on recognition, proposing instead a conference in which the Patriotic Front and the Rhodesian regime would work to end Rhodesia's civil war. The British proposal replaced escalation plans as the immediate focus of the local adversaries. Zambia and Mozambique, reeling from the high cost of the war, supported the British initiative and threatened to shut down the guerrilla organizations within their countries. A ZANU decision to escalate was made contingent on the failure of the British-sponsored conference. The Rhodesian regime, strengthened by the possibility that failed negotiations would lead to British recognition, elected to bargain from a position of strength.

The British government approached Rhodesia not as a vital question but as an irritant to relations with important allied states—the United States, European allies, and the Commonwealth—on which a great deal of diplomatic effort had already been expended. Recognition of the Muzorewa government, in British foreign minister Lord Carrington's view, would merely have intensified conflict with allied states, and peacemaking was not likely to endure without the participation of the Patriotic Front. The latter's participation would facilitate, as Carrington saw it, "the widest possible international recognition" of a settlement, and the British sought and received approval of their strategy at a Commonwealth conference in Lusaka, Zambia, in August 1979.[26] In the ensuing Lancaster House conference in London, from September to December 1979, only the Rhodesian parties and the British government participated.

The Lancaster House conference was controlled by Carrington, who held the only working document and insisted on considering, step by step, three baskets of issues: (1) a new Rhodesian constitution removing the white minority's veto but protecting whites through a bill of rights and legislative representation, (2) a transition to the new system to be handled over two months by existing Rhodesian military and police forces, in which Muzorewa would step down as prime minister and a British-appointed governor would ensure new elections to decide on a successor, and (3) a two-stage cease-fire, deploying white regime forces to their main bases and then gathering Patriotic Front forces at assembly points monitored by Commonwealth peacekeepers. Rather than highlighting at the outset the ultimate shape of the peacemaking framework, Carrington constructed the framework inductively part by part, emphasizing the discussions as the last opportunity to avoid a larger war and acting as crisis manager and arbitrator by making his own proposals to overcome deadlocks.

Carrington's chief source of leverage at the conference was his threat to recognize the Rhodesian internal settlement if the Patriotic Front factions chose not to participate or walked out. Inasmuch as the Rhodesian whites and Muzorewa believed that the Thatcher government would carry out whatever it promised, they accepted British proposals at every stage in the belief that Britain could supply Rhodesia peacefully what it could not obtain militarily. A second source of leverage, as issues became more difficult at successive stages and the Patriotic Front delegation became more recalcitrant, was the momentum built up in the conference negotiating process, which discouraged defection by leaders of the front. Members of the Patriotic Front, who believed that momentum in the civil war favored them and who suspected that Britain was secretly allied with the white-dominated regime, nevertheless stood to gain most from a peaceful settlement. In the end, Robert Mugabe, the ZANU leader, was elected prime minister of Zimbabwe-Rhodesia in a landslide victory.

Aiding Carrington's mediation was the widespread awareness that the most likely alternative to peacemaking was an unwanted dramatic escalation in the civil war. Zambia and Mozambique most emphasized at the Lusaka meeting the disutility of the escalatory option, and negotiating success at Lancaster House added to the disutility of escalation for all parties. Another development contributing to mediation success was the unwillingness of any of the participating factions to be blamed for wrecking the conference. Finally, Carrington strengthened the mediation by first choosing to deal with the constitution question, affirming the issue of majority rule as the major source of Rhodesian tension and dividing the Rhodesian whites from Muzorewa on the question of whether to accept it.

The most difficult problems for the mediation were persisting volatile military conditions and substantial South African involvement in the civil war. Internal conflict in Rhodesia made it possible for either side to gain military victory, which increased the reluctance of the adversaries to endorse accommodation. In November 1979, Rhodesian forces destroyed the last rail bridge linking Zambia with the outside world, eliciting a Carrington ultimatum for a Rhodesian halt to cross-border operations in Zambia and an end to Patriotic Force movements from Zambia to Rhodesia. South Africa, stubbornly opposed to the assumption of power by the Patriotic Front in Rhodesia, disengaged from the country more quietly than most expected, apparently because it anticipated that Muzorewa would win the ensuing Rhodesian election.

5. Muslim-Serb and Croat-Serb Conflict in Bosnia-Herzegovina (1992–1995)[27]

Following the death in 1980 of Yugoslav president Joseph Broz Tito, mutually suspicious ethnic groups in Bosnia-Herzegovina, becoming stronger as the centralized government in Yugoslavia weakened, found it impossible to coexist as they had in the past. An ethnic contest for influence emerged in Bosnia-Herzegovina after a March 1992 election approved separating from Yugoslavia and declaring independence. When the Muslim-dominated provincial government in Bosnia-Herzegovina shortly afterward declared independence, Serb and Croat populations—31 percent and 17 percent of the province's population, respectively—refused to accept the result, and the new state was invaded from Bosnia-Serb strongholds in the east (supported by the Yugoslav military), and from Croatia in the west and south.

Lacking an army, the Bosnia-Herzegovina regime totally depended on foreign assistance, which it requested, to repel the invaders. As UN peacekeepers and massive supplies of humanitarian aid arrived to protect and sustain the Bosnian population, Serb militias very quickly isolated Sarajevo, the capital of the new state; killed and expelled hundreds of thousands of civilians; and cooperated with Croat paramilitary forces in an effort to partition the new country. Serb militias at the height of their power controlled 70 percent of Bosnia-Herzegovina territory, while the Muslims held only 10 percent, and truces negotiated by UN military officials in the Sarajevo area were regularly broken by militarily superior Serb gunners.

Institutions such as the UN and the European Union sought to apply international norms to mediate between the antagonists, but they rejected mediation. At the outset, numerous, poorly coordinated mediation initiatives failed to prevent civil war. Later, mediation was better coordinated but hamstrung by the effects of war and by differences between the major powers. The UN primarily sought to protect populations from the effects of war, which required a cease-fire agreement. The EU's priority was to use regional conflict management machinery to defuse the conflict. A joint UN-EU proposal for a single demilitarized Bosnian state divided into ten provinces, each with a multiethnic government, was deadlocked, while the Muslim regime sought a military option enabling it to gain better results than international mediation offered. The Americans violated a UN-mandated arms embargo by providing covert military assistance to the Muslims and Croats, distancing themselves from the Russians, who supported the Serbs, and from the British and French, whose troops formed the backbone of the UN peacekeeping force and who worried about the vulnerability of their cadres. A so-called Contact Group of major powers took over mediation responsibilities in the spring of 1994 but was stymied by internal divisions.

By 1994, the United States, only belatedly a key mediator, upgraded its priority for peace in Bosnia-Herzegovina. The United States was determined to overcome major-state disunity and bring about an effective collective major-state response to Serb truce violations, making it no longer possible for Serb forces to act against Muslim areas with impunity. By mid-1995, nearly a year after having been placed in charge of U.S. State Department handling of the negotiations, Richard Holbrooke successfully pushed to employ NATO to enforce UN resolutions in Bosnia-Herzegovina. When evidence pointed to Bosnian Serb responsibility for a mortar shell that landed in a Sarajevo marketplace in late August 1995, killing thirty-seven and wounding more than eighty, NATO launched its first massive and sustained bombing campaign against Bosnian Serb targets. The bombing led to a cease-fire in October 1995 and a peace conference in Dayton, Ohio, shortly afterward.

Because of the adversaries' recalcitrance, Holbrooke's strategy required hands-on shuttle diplomacy as well as speed. He offered territory to the Muslims and Croats, who were winning battles against the Serbs in western Bosnia by 1995. Holbrooke coached the Muslims and Croats on territorial objectives, advising them to quickly seize territory not otherwise available in a peace treaty, with the exception of the major town of Banja Luka, the taking of which could have upset the delicate Muslim-Croat alliance. Holbrooke's diplomacy depended on the bombing campaign to coerce Bosnian Serb retreat from Sarajevo, where the Muslims could not challenge the Serbs. The bombing was a fading opportunity, destined to stop when the NATO target list was exhausted.

Holbrooke defined three main issues for peace negotiations, each associated with peace-building for an independent Bosnia-Herzegovina state: (1) a governmental structure for an intact Bosnia-Herzegovina, (2) autonomous zones within Bosnia-Herzegovina for Serb and Croat populations, and (3) a cease-fire. The Muslims conceded on autonomous zones, while the Croats and Serbs conceded a unitary Bosnia-Herzegovina state. Capitalizing on Muslim and Croat military momentum, the Americans tackled the cease-fire question last. Two meetings of Balkan country foreign ministers ratified a declaration of principles about the three issues, leaving detailed agreement about political structure (including a constitution and elections) and autonomous zones (the map) for the Dayton conference.

Neither the Bosnian Serbs nor the Muslims accepted that a hurting stalemate existed. Holbrooke's leverage over the Serbs was primarily the increasing military pressure on Serb forces in the west and the NATO bombing campaign, as the Serb's superior military position eroded. The leverage primarily affected Yugoslav president Slobodan Milosevic, who controlled the interests of the Bosnian Serbs. Holbrooke's leverage over the Muslims, who wished to capitalize on their military success to gain a full military victory, was that if they fought on—as the Americans had earlier encouraged them to do—they would be excluded from peacemaking, their international stature would diminish, and their interests in peace-building would be neglected. The United States was thus in a position, with Milosevic's support, to further manipulate the military balance between the adversaries to ensure that military victory was not available to either side.

The parties' war-weariness was not strong enough to ensure negotiating success. Equally important were the NATO force option, Milosevic's initiative to speak for the Bosnian Serbs, and Holbrooke's strengths as a mediator. Holbrooke was largely free from constraints on his behavior, either from Washington or from the Contact Group, although he represented their interests. His insistence on pressing the adversaries to make the necessary accommodations prevailed over the reluctance of the adversaries to do so.

6. SWAPO–South Africa Conflict in Namibia (1981–1989)[28]

In the early 1960s, the South West Africa People's Organization (SWAPO) launched a war to liberate South West Africa (later called Namibia) from the

Republic of South Africa, a former League of Nations mandatory power that, continuing its occupation in that territory in defiance of the United Nations, eventually sought to impose an apartheid-based political system there. By 1981, the bush war between SWAPO and South Africa had become regional, with SWAPO conducting raids into Namibia from bases in neighboring Angola, and South Africa (militarily much the stronger) seeking to destroy SWAPO as a guerrilla force by driving it as deep into Angola as possible. Regular Cuban troops, introduced in 1976 to protect the newly established Marxist Angolan regime against South African raids, clashed with South African forces. Namibian conflict was also shaped by persisting civil war in southern Angola, prompting South Africa to move military units into Angola. SWAPO depended on the patronage of the Marxist Angolan regime, and South Africa became allies with UNITA, the Marxist regime's main challenger. The Soviet Union—making use of regular Cuban troops as proxies—was linked to the Angola regime, while the United States was aligned with South Africa and UNITA. In addition, the earlier election of a radical black regime in Zimbabwe stiffened South African resistance to compromise on Namibia.

Neither side demonstrated sufficient military strength to defeat the other, although neither acknowledged that fact. Five Western members of the UN Security Council converted themselves in 1977 into a diplomatic "Contact Group" to negotiate Namibian independence from South Africa. Their settlement proposal, which broadly defined the major political and military issues and was supported in principle by the major antagonists, was approved in April 1978 as UN Security Council Resolution 435.

Consistent with the foreign policy orientation of the Ronald Reagan administration, the United States primarily sought mediation to exclude the Soviet Union from South African peacemaking and to weaken the Soviet allies—the Angola regime, Cuba, and SWAPO—in the peacemaking process. This made the United States more dependent on, and more willing to placate, its often swaggering and unilaterally acting South African ally. Led by Chester Crocker, the American assistant secretary of state for African affairs, it forged a regional approach linking Namibian conflict resolution to management of the Angolan civil war, and particularly to the removal of Cuban troops from Angola. In contrast to the earlier American use of the same linkage to block Namibian independence, this new approach bolstered credibility for American mediation with the South Africans and with UNITA. The approach was based on the view that (1) the prospects for reconciliation and negotiation of political change *within* countries in the region was directly affected by the security climate *between* them and that (2) Angola questions would not go away if Namibia questions were settled on their own. Most

Contact Group members, on the other hand, felt linkage would impede a Namibian settlement.

Crocker initially used credibility on Namibia issues to provide leverage on Angola questions. The mediation was projected to consist of three phases: (1) obtaining agreement between South Africa and frontline African states on constitutional principles for Namibia, (2) addressing the tasks and structure of the UN Transition Assistance Group (UNTAG) provided for in Resolution 435, and (3) gaining South African commitment to a "date certain" to implement Resolution 435, coordinating South African withdrawal from Namibia with the withdrawal of Cuban forces from Angola and with the arrival of UNTAG in Namibia.

Crocker gave very little attention to the first and second phases, which were settled relatively quickly at a summer 1982 conference in New York, called by the United States, attended by six frontline African states, the Contact Group, the UN Secretariat, and the primary antagonists: SWAPO and South Africa. Detailed constitution-writing was postponed, but the Namibian political parties were asked to draft agreed-upon constitutional principles; these were transmitted in a letter from the Contact Group governments in July 1982 to the UN secretary-general. On phase 2 issues, the frontline states accepted responsibility for SWAPO behavior, and they and SWAPO agreed that UN teams controlled by UNTAG would monitor SWAPO bases in Angola and Zambia. South Africa accepted an upper limit of seventy-five hundred UNTAG personnel.

Crocker's prominence as mediator increased as the Contact Group faded after 1982 and as he and his team dealt entirely with Angolan issues, including the linkage between Cuba and South Africa. Diplomacy then slowed and became more plodding, as the United States sought from Angola a Cuban withdrawal schedule, comparable to a timetable for South African withdrawal, worked out in 1978. Only in 1984 did Angola provide such a schedule and concede linkage, but its proposal, 67 percent Cuban withdrawal over three years and a permanent residual force, was far from South Africa's demand of full Cuban withdrawal in twelve weeks. Persevering, the United States feared that a breakdown of negotiations would imperil Resolution 435 as a mediating standard and justify a South African military solution.

The United States had few tangible assets to exert over the primary antagonists, no basis for projecting American power in the conflict area, and no control over timing and deadlines. Its primary threat was the threat to cease mediation. It enlarged its influence by cultivating the primary antagonists' perception of American credibility; by giving attention to both Namibian and Angolan agendas, showing the motivation and knowledge to appear indispensable to the opponents; and by building on the legacy of the earlier Carter administration in Resolution 435.

Assisting the American mediators was that South Africa, the strongest military power in the region, depended on the United States to gain withdrawal of the Cuban forces from Angola. Although the mediation did not take place within the UN, the mediation was assisted by UN legitimation of the negotiating agenda (in the first two phases) and by the role of UN personnel in verifying Cuban and South African force withdrawals. The UN representative for Namibia successfully managed a potentially incendiary incident in April 1989 in which large numbers of heavily armed SWAPO personnel crossed into Namibia from Angola and confronted Namibian police. Finally, the Cuban leader Fidel Castro aided mediation in 1988 when, following a disastrous defeat for Angolan forces when the South African military intervened deeply into Angola in the summer and fall of 1987, he sent fifteen thousand additional Cuban troops to southern Angola to confront South Africa, thereby reinforcing the American strategy of linking a Namibian settlement with military conditions in Angola. As Crocker put it, "Two forces of moderate size [Cuban and South African] tested and checked each other for nine months. . . . The two forces endured a nasty and prolonged engagement in horrible conditions."[29]

Interfering with American mediation were the incentives to the militarily superior South Africans to strike out against their adversaries; covert American military assistance to UNITA following the repeal of the Clark Amendment, which prohibited covert military assistance, in 1985; and the stress on the illegitimacy of apartheid in South Africa by American interest groups, which led Congress to enact economic sanctions against South Africa, lessening American leverage over the South Africans.

III. COMPARATIVE ANALYSIS

If mediating intrastate conflict in our cases is more difficult than mediating interstate disputes, it should be evident in one or more of five aspects of the case data: (1) causes and impact of intractability, (2) mediator motives, (3) mediator agenda, (4) mediator leverage over the adversaries, and (5) ripeness and mediation timing. We now probe these aspects.

1. Causes and Impact of Intractability

Intractability was diplomatic in character in the interstate cases and was an important cause of hostilities because one of the antagonists found the intractability unsustainable. In the intrastate cases, by contrast, war between the primary antagonists was the most important source of intractability.

Our war initiators in the interstate cases sought novel diplomatic align-ments that would allow them to wage war at a time of their choosing. Japan was determined to avoid being confronted by a coalition of major powers such as those that defended China after the Japanese victory over China in 1895. Egypt expelled Soviet advisors that could have impeded the decision to go to war in 1973. Pakistan distanced itself from the United States, a traditional ally, and sought support from the Soviet Union and China to pur-sue the newer Pakistani policy of "leaning on India" that prior American mediation efforts opposed. In each of these cases, the war initiator sought diplomatic assistance in advance, primarily through outside mediation, to ratify the results of anticipated military success. Mediation was necessary because the war initiators lacked their own means of ensuring concessions by their opponents. Without it, the diplomatic potential associated with Japa-nese and Arab military successes, and planned Pakistani military activity, would have been lost.

Interstate war sometimes eases intractability and sometimes deepens it. Japan recognized that time favored Russia's ability to reverse Japan's military successes; at the same time, Russian losses made Russian leaders more respectful of Japanese military power. The widespread perception of greater military equality in these circumstances was conducive to negotiation of a new diplomatic framework. The Israeli understanding that Egypt could, despite its military inferiority, make gains against Israel on the battlefield also eased intractability, as the United States took a committed position in protecting the antagonists from each other. By contrast, war-making in the Kashmir case did not ease intractability, as neither side was restrained diplo-matically by military stalemate and both made clear they would not be coerced by such a stalemate to retreat from their Kashmir positions.

Adversaries in the intrastate cases gave no prewar diplomatic attention to their differences because they did not support each other's legitimacy and instead sought to weaken or eradicate each other through military action. The white minority in Rhodesia, led by Ian Smith, was determined to rule on its own after declaring independence from British rule and rejected any consid-eration of black African interests. Violent ZANU and ZAPU resistance to white minority rule developed because resisters lacked any alternative modes of conveying their demands. Serb and Croat resistance to the Muslim-dominated regime in Bosnia-Herzegovina flowed from unconditional opposi-tion to the independence of Bosnia-Herzegovina from Yugoslavia. Supported by their respective state allies, Bosnian Serbs and Bosnian Croats from the outset sought to partition the new state. In the Namibia case, South Africa sought to destroy SWAPO as a political and military force.

Since intractability presumes long-term diplomatic frustration, it cannot be said that intractability existed prior to the outbreak of civil war in these instances. The conflicts became intractable in practice only after war began: war effects added to mediation difficulties by making the adversaries more determined to fight indefinitely toward military victory and to avoid diplomatic accommodation.

2. Mediator Motives

Mediators in the interstate cases were heavily guided by power politics, while in the intrastate cases they aimed to increase major-state collaboration. In the Russo-Japanese case, Roosevelt sought to gain a regional balance between Japan and Russia and to blunt the expansionist interests of both. Such a balance would help secure his country, which then lacked the military strength to contain either one. In the Arab-Israeli case, Kissinger viewed his mediation of Arab-Israeli differences as part of an American search for strategic advantage in relation to the Soviet Union, which the United States sought to exclude from an active diplomatic role in the Mideast, contrary to agreed-upon principles guiding superpower behavior. And in the Kashmir case, the Soviet Union sought to ensure that Communist China would not intervene in the Indian-Pakistani conflict.

In the intrastate cases, major-state collaboration contributed to mediating success in each case. Prior to the mediation efforts detailed here, the Rhodesian and Bosnia-Herzegovinian wars exacted huge diplomatic effort by Great Britain and the United States, respectively, for which relatively little accrued in national power; Carrington and Holbrooke as mediators sought to defuse war issues as diplomatic questions and, by doing so, to enhance the potential for major-state cooperation on other questions. Carrington was supported by the United States, and Holbrooke by NATO members of the Contact Group for Bosnia-Herzegovina. UN Security Council Resolution 435, resulting from major power collaboration, legitimated outside mediation in the Namibia case.

On the other hand, Contact Group intervention in the Namibia case weakened as major power collaboration was undermined by American interest in linking conflict management in Namibia and Angola. American interest in enhancing its power relative to the Soviet Union and its allies, a key objective from the start, became still more significant, suggesting that Namibia is, in this respect, a hybrid case. A second blurred pattern is suggested by the Kashmir case, in which American support of Soviet mediation—notable in an era of superpower competition—presumably had much to do with Soviet success in gaining mutual Pakistani and Indian military withdrawals; the

United States (as elsewhere) had the ability to block Soviet initiatives had it wished to do so.

3. Mediator's Agenda

Interstate cases raised fewer and less challenging issues for the mediators than did intrastate cases. Mediating issues are shaped in interstate cases by war results. The mediator ordinarily rejects providing an antagonist what has not been earned in war, but the less that is earned, the smaller the room for mediating maneuvers. Japan won major gains through military action and had little difficulty preserving them by conceding on less critical questions. The two issues in the Russo-Japanese peace negotiations on which Roosevelt was required to intervene were not only less important to Japan than to Russia but also less important to Japan than vital Japanese war-making territorial goals that Russia was prepared to concede based on Japanese military successes. Vital Japanese goals in Korea and Manchuria, moreover, would probably not have been realized in the Portsmouth peace talks had Japan insisted on Sakhalin and on the indemnity. Japan's interests in protecting war gains coincided with Japanese concessions on the two issues, the course of action Roosevelt strongly recommended.

Military gains were far smaller for the war initiator in the other two interstate cases. Israel, unlike Russia in the earlier case, was being asked to make significant territorial concessions even as it was under no military pressure to do so. Not surprisingly, it sought security assurances that Egypt and Syria were not prepared to give, and in the second Sinai disengagement agreement, the United States needed to satisfy Israeli security interests in a different way by strengthening its security assurances to Israel. Israel's security needs also required limiting the security dilemma associated with Israeli and Arab forces on the Sinai and Golan fronts. In addition, the disengagement agreement contained a transitional element in which Egypt and Syria would be diplomatically recognized as having equal military stature with Israel despite their relative military inferiority. Diplomatic recognition of parity between Egyptian and Syrian military strength, on the one hand, and Israeli military capabilities, on the other, dictated a preoccupation with detailed force limitations on both sides. Finally, military gains were least impressive in the Kashmir war, and a major challenge for Kosygin was to rule out demands over Kashmir that were not validated by military fortunes. Indian-Pakistani military parity provided a basis for ending the war but not for making progress on Kashmir. Agreement in that instance was limited to the disengagement of forces and the Indian demand for a peace pact.

In addition to force limitation questions, our intrastate mediations raised state-building issues that were constitutional and political: (1) By what authority would rulers exercise power over the territory in which civil war had occurred? (2) What procedures would be instituted to determine which group or individuals would rule? (3) Would nonruling groups and individuals have been given reliable assurances that their needs and interests would be protected? And (4) how would groups that had fought against each other transition to a framework in which they would compete for power peacefully?

In Rhodesia, Carrington was required to gain approval of a constitution for a unitary state in which all candidates would compete for power in a central government. All the competing factions accepted the principle of democratic rule as the organizing concept of peace arrangements. In the Namibia case, Crocker was little concerned about constitutional or transitional issues for the new state, as those issues were effectively handled in a July 1982 conference under the auspices of the Contact Group. At that conference, the guidelines of UN Security Council Resolution 435 prevailed, and Crocker abandoned the American proposal that a constitution for Namibia be drafted before holding elections. Crocker's main agenda item was the interstate issue associated with the American regional approach to Namibia: the link between Cuban forces in Angola and South African forces in Namibia.

Constitutional and political issues proved more complex and difficult in ethnically divided Bosnia-Herzegovina than in Rhodesia or Namibia. Holbrooke in Bosnia-Herzegovina had to balance competing federal and provincial imperatives: (1) the territorial needs of Serb and Croat minorities in Bosnia-Herzegovina, with each minority group seeking to carve provincial boundaries to facilitate political expression by majorities it controlled in particular localities and regions, and (2) an integrated Bosnian state in which Muslim, Serb, and Croat factions would share power in a central government—an objective that Serbs and Croats had gone to war in 1992 to prevent. In this case, negotiating controversy extended to the organizing concept as well as the details. A formally integrated Bosnia-Herzegovina state, based on the principle of interethnic cooperation, was ultimately accepted by the adversaries only on the condition that much of the effective authority over the new state's inhabitants would be exercised at the provincial level, where significant cooperation between ethnic groups was highly improbable at best.

4. Mediator's Leverage

In each of our interstate cases, the mediator's leverage over the antagonists increased as the initiator of hostilities forged a special relationship with the then-prospective mediator. This self-interested strategy also enhanced the opposing antagonist's receptivity to mediation. No comparable leverage existed in the intrastate cases, in which the antagonists were generally resistant to mediation.

Japan's invitation to Roosevelt to mediate between Japan and Russia increased American influence potential in the regional conflict by (1) creating a presumption that Japan would be receptive to Roosevelt's suggestions in the event of Russo-Japanese deadlock, and (2) implying for Russia that the United States could stimulate Japanese cooperation in the same circumstances. Inasmuch as neither of the parties was recalcitrant, Roosevelt could mediate effectively by exercising good offices between the antagonists: he did not define the issues, invent solutions, threaten to shift American support between the parties, or offer side payments. Roosevelt's efforts at persuading Japan to drop its indemnity and Sakhalin demands, and his shifting tactics on the Sakhalin issue, were based on the importance for Japan of ending the war.

Sadat's invitation to Kissinger to mediate in the Mideast case similarly enhanced American influence potential, in relation to Egypt (and by extension to Syria), with whom new American ties were being created, and in relation to Israel, which now could accept that its American ally could bring pressure on Israel's Arab adversaries. In this instance, however, good offices would not have sufficed for mediating success because the invitation from one party was counteracted by recalcitrance from Israel and Syria. Because of the recalcitrance, Kissinger was required to invent force and territorial solutions, build agreements inductively step-by-step, and emphasize his own indispensability to the parties as an alternative to mediation failure. As in the Russo-Japanese case, the invitation to mediate by one adversary strengthened the mediator's hand, but the mediator in this instance was also required to take account of the special needs of the other adversary. These entailed providing side benefits to gain Israeli consent to accommodation and inserting American forces into the Sinai to ensure enforcement of the agreement, steps requiring American strategic as well as tactical flexibility.

The link between Pakistani diplomacy and Russian mediation in the Kashmir war is less established, but Ayub's effort to improve relations with the Soviet Union enhanced Soviet mediation potential in relation to Pakistan and India. Ayub may well have used his China link to successfully draw in the Soviets to mediate, and he was likely to focus also on the prospect of mediation to influence India to yield territory in Kashmir, once Pakistan had shown its military superiority over India.

By contrast, our intrastate antagonists lack a special relationship with a prospective mediator. They value allies for their direct support rather than for their mediating potential. Rejecting coexistence with each other, they usually oppose mediation; when one side—usually the weaker—proposed mediation, the other side frequently neutralized it. Muslim rulers in Bosnia-Herzegovina valued the American link primarily for strengthening their military potential and proved, in the end, to be the most unwilling of all the antagonists to make political concessions. The long-lasting American link to South Africa in the Namibia case was primarily based on South African opposition to the Soviets and their allies. Crocker stressed the American need to build up credibility to neutralize South African skepticism about American mediation potential.

Still, in these instances and in the Rhodesian case, American and British mediators, unable to create confidence or trust between the parties, or even substitutes for trust, dwelled on prior linkages of the parties with the mediator. They employed two coercive strategies not utilized in the interstate cases: (1) threatening to exclude the antagonists from a settlement, and (2) threatening and using confrontational force.

In Rhodesia, Carrington's threat to exclude the Patriotic Front if it rejected agreement was an opportunity for the white minority, as the whites had sought British recognition of the internal settlement and were offered this recognition in the event that the Patriotic Front rejected participation. Even though Carrington insisted on undoing the white minority's 1976 unilateral declaration of independence, the white delegation depended heavily on British support, and that dependence was a key element of Carrington's leverage over the whites. Carrington compelled the Patriotic Front and Rhodesian whites to view him as indispensable to gaining a peaceful settlement they believed was preferable to continued civil war.

Holbrooke's strategies in Bosnia-Herzegovina were largely coercive. His tactic of heightening the adversaries' fear of exclusion primarily affected the highly recalcitrant Muslim faction, which suffered the most from the war but which used its military link to the United States to make important military gains in the latter stage of the war. By contrast, American coercion of the Bosnian Serbs was applied through Yugoslav president Milosevic, who took responsibility for gaining Bosnian Serb approval of the Dayton settlement. Coercion was largely missing, on the other hand, in the Namibia case, in which the United States had little ability to threaten the antagonists. This accounts for the plodding American effort to bridge South African and Angolan views about a timetable for South African and Cuban troop withdrawal.

5. Ripeness and Mediation Timing

Mediation was urgent in each of our interstate cases because of the instability of cease-fire agreements worked out earlier by the antagonists. If third-party mediation was not forthcoming, the antagonists, aware of the military instability, were likely to resume hostilities. The urgency in the intrastate cases was quite different. No cease-fires preceded mediation in those cases, as the antagonists continued to fight each other; the urgency instead was the risk of escalating hostilities. The mediator could not build on either a cessation of hostilities or the fear of renewed warfare, but instead needed to enlarge the incentives for competing peacefully so that they became more attractive than continued warfare.

Although Japan surprised Russia with military victories, the new balance between them was not sufficiently painful to either side to rule out further hostilities. Russia could expect to turn the tide with superior overland logistics if Japanese forces advanced against their Russian counterparts in Manchuria, but this was ruled out by diplomatic restraint. Russia was prepared to concede to Japan political influence based on prior Japanese military successes, for which Japan had fought in the first place. Japan could not be confident of continuing military success under those same circumstances, however, and desperately sought to rule out this eventuality. The key to preventing further hostilities was that the parties had no vital or even secondary need for further fighting. Roosevelt's task was the straightforward one of underscoring that no further Russo-Japanese fighting should occur under any circumstances and that no barriers should be placed in the way of overcoming any Portsmouth deadlocks.

The cease-fire lines were unsustainable in the Mideast case because Egyptian and Israeli forces were closely intertwined and the dynamic of the war placed them in an unstable relationship. The Egyptian Third Army, which had crossed the Suez Canal, was surrounded by Israeli forces, and Israeli forces had crossed the Suez in the other direction and were headed toward Cairo. Kissinger's mediation capitalized on the antagonists' awareness of this instability, but inasmuch as the war had turned in favor of Israel, Kissinger was required to dissuade Israel from capitalizing on its military advantage to gain a clear-cut victory. Had Israel done so, American mediation would have been completely undermined. When it did not do so, Kissinger could persuade Egypt and Israel (and Syria) that each antagonist could gain more from a partial pullback of forces, and from mutual agreement to rule out the future use of force, than it could through hostilities.

In the Kashmir case, the antagonists' separate military initiatives each led to some control of the opponent's territory; neither side had demonstrated military superiority over the other, but each had an incentive, in the absence of a mutual pullback of forces, to build on its prior military success. Kosygin's priority as mediator was to counter this incentive, even as the intractable Kashmir dispute was left for diplomatic and military resolution at a later time. He succeeded by discovering some minimum agreement to bring the war officially to an end.

A cease-fire in the intrastate conflicts was the *last* major issue addressed by the mediators, who subordinated war cessation to a framework for a political settlement. War increased intractability in those cases, and hostilities could not be brought to an end until the mediator underscored the promise and prospects of peace. This was partly accomplished by the threat to switch loyalties away from uncooperative antagonists to cooperative ones, increasing the latter's political gains at the expense of the former.

Carrington felt that problems in reaching a cease-fire between Rhodesian factions would be greater than those encountered in discussing the constitution and the transition to a new government, issues focused on earlier at Lancaster House. He reasoned that the momentum from dealing successfully with those other two issues would assist in gaining a cease-fire and that the closer the factions came to completed agreement—permitting them to compete for victory in elections rather than on the battlefield—the less likely they were to break off discussions. Had mediation failed—for example, had one or more factions walked out—or had mediation had not been attempted, the Rhodesian civil war could well have escalated; instead, the lure of election victory proved stronger than the incentive to keep fighting.

Holbrooke similarly placed the cease-fire problem last on his negotiating timetable, partly to provide more time to the Bosnian army to gain more territory from the Serbs, but partly also to use agreement on the other items—a governmental structure for Bosnia-Herzegovina and on autonomous zones—to add incentives for a decision to compete peacefully, even as the factions desired on their own to continue the war. Here again, the fear of being excluded from agreement and from international support became a strong disincentive to reject mediation, as Holbrooke would then have shifted his support to the opposing side.

In the Namibia case, Crocker linked a cease-fire to mutual Cuban and South African withdrawal from Angola. In 1988, when Castro, following confrontation between South African and Cuban forces in Angola in the summer and fall of 1987, added fifteen thousand new Cuban troops to confront South Africa, he increased the danger of the Cuban–South African war, but he also demonstrated how—as the Americans and South Africans had maintained—the Angolan civil war could only be resolved on a regional basis. In this instance, the cease-fire was, in practice, related only a little to developments in Namibia but very much to the risks of force escalation in Angola. Alone among our six cases, the Namibia case illustrated a mutually hurting stalemate in its latest stages, following augmentation of both Cuban and South African forces and skirmishes between the two sides in southeastern Angola beginning late in 1987 and extending into the summer of 1988. These developments, suggesting to the antagonists that Cuban and South

African forces were becoming more nearly equal, strengthened attention to the costs of military stalemate and the risks of further escalation. By doing so, they contributed significantly to Crocker's mediating success.[30]

IV. CONCLUSIONS

Our comparative analysis confirms that distinctions in levels of mediating difficulty do apply to cases of intractable conflict and should be considered when generalizing about pathways to mediation success. The analysis confirms the widespread view that intrastate conflict is more difficult to mediate than its interstate counterpart. But the results also draw attention to the importance of comparing intrastate and interstate cases in successful instances of third-party mediation. Had analysis been limited to more plentiful examples of intrastate conflict alone, we could not know whether the intrastate context specifically, or mediation more generally, better explains difficulties manifested in efforts to mediate intrastate conflict. The conclusion here is that the intrastate context is the more significant of the two.

This chapter has attempted to account for the added difficulty associated with intrastate as against interstate mediation. The results are mixed: (1) three of our analytical categories—the causes and impact of intractability, mediator leverage, and mediation timing—affirm the difference; (2) two categories—mediator motives and mediator agenda—do not; and (3) asymmetrical antagonist military forces challenge mediation of *both* interstate and intrastate disputes. We now examine these results and their implications for managing mediation.

1. Accounting for Mediation Difficulties

Mediation in intrastate conflict is more difficult because of the greater reliance and commitment of the primary antagonists to war as a means of coping with their conflict and the greater resistance of the primary antagonists to the mediator's intervention. Table 6.2 summarizes the differences in the three analytical dimensions that seem to account for the added difficulty of mediation in intrastate, as compared with interstate, conflict.

First, our case comparisons suggest that mediation will be easier when, as in our interstate cases, intractable conflict is primarily diplomatic in origin, and more difficult when, as in the intrastate cases, intractability is mostly brought about by war. In the former, hostilities were recognized by the antagonists as an abnormal condition, and the mediator reinforced that perception.

Table 6.2.   Significant Variability in Mediation Cases

Dimension	Less difficult	More difficult
1. War and intractability	War removes intractability	War adds to intractability
2. Mediator leverage	Invitation to mediate facilitates mediation	No invitation to mediate; mediator must create own stature
3. Ripeness	Cease-fire enhances cooperation on other issues	Peace framework provides incentive for cease-fire

In the latter instances, war became regularized, accepted, and justified by the antagonists, part of a soft stalemate that was painful yet bearable.

Second, we conclude that the mediator's task is easier when one of the antagonists not only depends on a mediator's intervention but predicates its military planning on that intervention, as in our interstate cases. In such cases, the link that one antagonist has with the mediator becomes highly important in attracting that antagonist's opponent to the mediating process. The mediating task is more difficult when, as in the intrastate cases, the antagonists resist mediation in the hope that they can achieve a one-sided solution. The mediator alone must then overcome the antagonists' mutual resistance to mediation.

Third, the mediator's task is easier when mediation can build upon a prior cease-fire, as in the interstate cases, and when the mediator primarily acts to counter the antagonists' incentives to continue a military struggle that is in abeyance. Military force pullbacks can be implemented even when important political questions remain unresolved or deadlocked, as in the Mideast and Kashmir cases. Mediation is more difficult, as reflected in the intrastate conflicts, when stopping hostilities depends on constructing political incentives more attractive than continual fighting. In this instance, the mediator cannot succeed with a partial political solution or with no political solution at all but must inductively construct, step-by-step, a comprehensive peace plan and gain the antagonists' approval of it.

The requirement in intrastate cases of tackling force issues only later in the mediating process rather than initially draws attention to the fact that mutually hurting stalemates are difficult to bring about between antagonists whose hostilities are driven by an unwillingness to compromise. If an MHS were easier to establish, mediators would have incentives to tackle force issues first and political questions only later in the mediating process. In practice, as we will see, asymmetrical forces and soft stalemate seem more significant as barriers to mediation than MHS is as a support for it.

2. Failure to Account for the Difficulty

The differences between intrastate and interstate conflict in mediator motives and mediator agenda found in our cases do not seem to account for the greater difficulty of intrastate as against interstate conflict mediation. Table 6.3 summarizes those differences. We elaborate here on why those differences do not appear significant.

Taking the agenda issue first, we find that although the intrastate cases opened a larger number of contentious disputes than did their interstate counterparts, the number of disputes on the mediator's agenda does not in itself seem linked to mediation difficulty. The Kashmir case shows that a relatively small number of disputes can be very difficult to manage when the parties are deadlocked on matters of vital concern. Many complex issues, such as force limitations addressed in the Mideast case, can be framed as technical rather than political; the antagonists agreed on the central requirement of making it more difficult for either side to renew ground warfare. And where, as in our intrastate cases, many complex issues are treated as political rather than technical, the mediator can initially address less contentious questions and use progress on them to strengthen the prospects for negotiation later on. Even if, in those cases, limitations on the use of force cannot be addressed until political issues are resolved first, coping with the latter can be a means to facilitate progress on the former.

As to the mediator's motives, our initial surmise was that the motive of increasing major-state collaboration would be more of a challenge to mediators and therefore less readily adopted than was the power politics motive because independent-minded major states would not easily cooperate and because the search for international support is ordinarily a nonvital interest. Major power collaboration was especially impaired in the Bosnia case by conflicts of interest. On the other hand, mediators in Rhodesia and in Namibia benefited greatly from a coalition of like-minded states supporting their goals.

Moreover, power and collaboration can assist the cause of the same mediation. Though a strategic rival of the United States, the Soviet Union in the

Table 6.3.   Insignificant Variability in Mediation Cases

Dimension	Less difficult	More difficult
1. Mediator motives	Balance of power/ prudence	Strengthen international legitimacy and norms
2. Mediator agenda	Few issues	Many issues

Kashmir case nevertheless benefited from American support of the Tashkent mediation. Crocker in the Namibia case benefited greatly from major power collaboration in approving UN Security Council Resolution 435, but after the United States insisted on broadening the Namibia negotiations to include regional stability, it was left to manage and mediate the highly contentious issue of the Cuban force in Angola on its own.

The choice between power politics and international collaboration seems less linked to mediation difficulty than to the fact that the major powers are less inclined to mediate alone than they were in the past. Difficulties in assembling an international coalition can be considerable, as shown in the response to the Bosnia-Herzegovina civil war during the 1990s, but these difficulties need to be faced if, as suggested here, major states are individually less disposed than before to intervene in small-state affairs.[31] Short of important geopolitical interests that impel governments to mediate independently, as with the United States in Southern Africa, multilateral mediation is likely to receive more emphasis.

3. Asymmetrical Force Balances as a Mediating Challenge

Asymmetrical forces are potentially problematic for mediation in both intrastate and interstate disputes because they permit the militarily superior antagonist to believe it can dictate a military solution. However, this problem is dampened in intractable interstate disputes. In the Russo-Japanese case, the Japanese were self-restrained, in part because Japanese war aims were limited and in part because the Japanese were aware of the potential military strength Russia could bring to bear on Japan if war continued. Israel, the superior power in the Mideast case, used military superiority as a source of diplomatic leverage in relation to the United States. Kissinger won Israeli force withdrawal by providing special security assurances to Israel, which rendered Israel's military momentum unnecessary. In the Kashmir case, India and Pakistan could have capitalized on their respective military gains to widen the war but chose not to do so.

By contrast, in the intrastate disputes the political challenger was initially weaker than the regime it challenged, strengthening the determination of the latter to impose its own military solution. The forces of the Rhodesia regime were stronger than its challengers; the Serbs, controlling the Yugoslav military, were stronger than the Muslims; and the South Africans were much stronger than SWAPO was. Later, the force balance shifts in favor of the weaker side, either through direct military assistance, such as that provided to Black Rhodesian groups and to the Muslims in Bosnia-Herzegovina, or through the entrance of new belligerents, such as the Cubans in Angola. The immediate result of this shift is the soft, self-serving military stalemate described above by Zartman.[32]

A mediator cannot readily convert this soft stalemate to an MHS but can affect the momentum of hostilities, as with the shift in Bosnia-Herzegovina to favor the Muslim-dominated Sarajevo regime. In the absence of an MHS, the mediator can and must manipulate the symmetrical balance, making it clear to the parties that inflexibility or continued pursuit of military advantages by one side will lead to decisive assistance to its opponent. But what a mediator must do to bring about an MHS in intractable intrastate cases remains unclear; moreover, even if the requirements for doing so were known, they would likely be virtually impossible to fulfill. In the one instance of intrastate MHS documented in this study, its emergence was fortuitous, not directly related to the mediator's actions: an MHS was produced in the Namibia case by a Cuban buildup in Angola that the United States opposed.

4. Managing Added Mediating Requirements in Intrastate Cases

Taking account of the limits on the mediator's ability to bring about an MHS in intractable intrastate cases, we nevertheless conclude that the difference in mediating requirements between interstate and intrastate cases is best conceptualized on an individual level. Whether mediators can surmount the additional problems that emerge seems to depend more on the character, skills, and ingenuity of the mediators than on the structure of the mediating situation. The more inflamed and difficult the mediating context, as in our intrastate cases, the more important is the mediator's manipulation of the conflict situation.[33] The mediator's personal qualities are especially significant when dealing with the power asymmetry between the conflicting parties.

Specifically, we conclude the following:

1. A mediator addressing internal conflict must be more stubborn and inflexible in resisting the rising intractability of internal conflict than is required of a mediator coping with interstate conflict.
2. A mediator in internal conflict must establish leverage without assistance from the antagonists, in contrast to mediators in the interstate cases.
3. Because a mediator in internal conflict cannot depend primarily on an MHS, negotiations on key issues must be managed while a soft stalemate exists between the antagonists, unlike the situation for mediators in interstate cases.

In the less volatile interstate cases, the success of mediation has more to do with mediating context than with the qualities of the mediator. The context for mediation is then less inflamed, and the antagonists are mutually aware of the disutility to them of continued fighting and of the dangers of renewed warfare if mutual force withdrawals do not occur. These conditions apply irrespective of whether the party initiating hostilities achieved its major objectives; if it did not, as in the Pakistani-Indian war, the mediator still has standing because of the prior relationship with one of the antagonists.

NOTES

1. The literature on third-party mediation is very large. See, for example, Saadia Touval and I. William Zartman, eds., *International Mediation in Theory and Practice* (Boulder, CO: Westview, 1985); Daniel Druckman and Christopher Mitchell, eds., "Flexibility in International Negotiation and Mediation," special issue of the *Annals of the American Academy of Political and Social Science* 542 (November 1995); Jacob Bercovitch, ed., *Resolving International Conflicts: The Theory and Practice of Mediation* (Boulder, CO: Lynne Rienner, 1996); I. William Zartman, *Cowardly Lions* (Boulder, CO: Lynne Rienner, 2005); Jacob Bercovitch, *Social Conflicts and Third Parties* (Boulder, CO: Westview, 1984); I. William Zartman, "Dynamics and Constraints in Negotiations in Internal Conflicts," in *Elusive Peace*, ed. I. William Zartman (Washington, DC: Brookings Institution Press, 1995), 3–29; Stephen John Stedman, *Peacemaking in Civil War: International Mediation in Zimbabwe, 1974–1980* (Boulder, CO: Lynne Rienner, 1991); Chester A. Crocker, "The Varieties of Intervention: Conditions for Success," in *Managing Global Chaos*, ed. Chester A. Crocker, Fen Osler Hampson, with Pamela Aall (Washington, DC: United States Institute of Peace Press, 1996), 183–96; Thomas Princen, *Intermediaries in International Conflict* (Princeton: Princeton University Press, 1992); Jacob Bercovitch and Jeffrey Z. Rubin, eds., *Mediation in International Relations: Multiple Approaches* (New York: St. Martin's, 1992); and Jacob Bercovitch, "Mediation in the Most Resistant Cases," in *Grasping the Nettle*, ed. Chester A. Crocker, Fen Osler Hampson, and Pamela Aall (Washington, DC: United States Institute of Peace Press, 2005).

2. "It is the task of diplomacy," Martin Wight wrote, "to circumvent the occasions of war, and to extend the series of circumvented occasions, to drive the automobile of state along a one-way track, against head-on traffic, past infinitely recurring precipices." *Power Politics*, ed. Hedley Bull and Carsten Holbraad (New York: Holmes & Meier, 1978), 137.

3. On intractable conflict, see Chester A. Crocker, Fen Osler Hampson, and Pamela Aall, eds., *Grasping the Nettle* (Washington, DC: United States Institute of Peace Press, 2005).

4. See also Barry H. Steiner, "Diplomacy as Dependent and Independent Variable," *International Negotiation* 6 (2001): 79–104; and Steiner, "Diplomacy and International Theory," *Review of International Studies* 30 (2004): 493–509.

5. Alexander L. George, "Case Studies and Theory Development: The Method of Structured, Focused Comparison," in *Diplomacy: New Approaches in History, Theory, and Policy*, ed. Paul Gordon Lauren (New York: Free Press, 1979), 43–68.

Chapter 6

6. See, for example, Zartman, "Dynamics and Constraints," 3; and Stedman, *Peacemaking in Civil War*, 11ff.

7. George, "Case Studies and Theory Development," 60.

8. Bercovitch, "Mediation in the Most Resistant Cases," 116. See also Bercovitch, *Social Conflicts and Third Parties*, 140.

9. I. William Zartman, "Negotiations and Prenegotiations in Ethnic Conflict: the Beginning, the Middle, and the Ends," in *Conflict and Peacemaking in Multiethnic Societies*, ed. Joseph V. Montville (New York: Lexington, 1991), 530–31. In a subsequent writing, Zartman notes that "a mediator is always regarded as a meddler to some extent, but more than ever when it comes to internal wars." *Cowardly Lions*, 12.

10. Saadia Touval and I. William Zartman, "Conclusion: Mediation in Theory and Practice," in Touval and Zartman, *International Mediation*, 257.

11. I. William Zartman, "Ripeness: The Hurting Stalemate and Beyond," in *International Conflict Resolution after the Cold War*, ed. Paul C. Stern and Daniel Druckman (Washington, DC: National Academy Press, 2000), 228.

12. Zartman, *Cowardly Lions*, 11.

13. Zartman, "Dynamics and Constraints," 8.

14. Ibid., 19.

15. I. William Zartman and Jeffrey Z. Rubin, eds., *Power and Negotiation* (Ann Arbor: University of Michigan Press, 2000), 15.

16. Ibid., 19.

17. Zartman, *Cowardly Lions*, 11.

18. George, "Case Studies and Theory Development," 59. George argues that even unique cases can contribute to theory development and that, in any event, controlled comparison of cases allows for heuristic and plausibility probes (ibid., 47, 52).

19. On this case, see John Albert White, *The Diplomacy of the Russo-Japanese War* (Princeton: Princeton University Press, 1964); and Ian Nish, *The Origins of the Russo-Japanese War* (London: Longman, 1985).

20. White, *Diplomacy of the Russo-Japanese War*, 158.

21. On this case, see William B. Quandt, *Peace Process*, 3rd ed. (Washington, DC: Brookings Institution Press; Berkeley: University of California Press, 2005), chs. 4–5; Harold Saunders and Cecilia Albin, *Sinai II: The Politics of International Mediation*, Pew Case Studies in International Affairs, no. 421 (Washington, DC: Institute for the Study of Diplomacy, Georgetown University, 1991); Michael I. Handel, *The Diplomacy of Surprise: Hitler, Nixon, Sadat* (Cambridge, MA: Harvard University Center for International Affairs, 1981), ch. 5; Amos Perlmutter, "Crisis Management: Kissinger's Middle-East Negotiations (October 1973–June 1974)," *International Studies Quarterly* 19 (September 1974), reprinted in *The Theory and Practice of International Relations*, ed. Fred A. Sondermann, David S. McLellan, and William C. Olson, 5th ed. (Englewood Cliffs, NJ: Prentice-Hall, Inc., 1979), 209–18; and Edward R. F. Sheehan, "Step by Step in the Middle East," *Foreign Policy*, no. 22 (Spring 1976): 3–70.

22. On this case, see Thomas P. Thornton, "The Indo-Pakistani Conflict: Soviet Mediation at Tashkent, 1966," in *International Mediation in Theory and Practice*, ed. Saadia Touval and I. William Zartman (Boulder, CO: Westview, 1985), 141–65; Thomas Thornton and Maxim Bratersky, "India and Pakistan: The Roots of Conflict," in *Cooperative Security*, ed. I. William Zartman and Victor A. Kremenyuk (Syracuse, NY: Syracuse

University Press, 1995), 179–203; Sumit Ganguly, *Conflict Unending* (New York: Columbia University Press, 2001), ch. 2; and Sumantra Bose, *Kashmir* (Cambridge, MA: Harvard University Press, 2003).

23. Thornton, "Indo-Pakistani Conflict," 144.

24. Ibid., 163.

25. On this case, see Stedman, *Peacemaking in Civil War*; Stephen John Stedman, *The Lancaster House Constitutional Conference on Rhodesia*, Pew Case Study in International Affairs, no. 341 (Washington, DC: Institute for the Study of Diplomacy, 1993); Peter Lord Carrington, *Reflecting on Things Past* (New York: Harper & Row, 1988), ch. 13; Stephen Low, "The Zimbabwe Settlement, 1976–1979," in Touval and Zartman, *International Mediation*, 94–109; and Donald Rothchild, "Successful Mediation: Lord Carrington and the Rhodesian Settlement," in Crocker, Hampson, and Aall, *Managing Global Chaos*, 475–86.

26. Carrington, *Reflecting on Things Past*, 288.

27. On this case, see Susan Rosegrant and Michael D. Watkins, "Getting to Dayton: Negotiating an End to the War in Bosnia," in *Perspectives on American Foreign Policy*, ed. Bruce W. Jentleson (New York: Norton, 2000); Richard Holbrooke, *To End a War* (New York: Random House, 1998); and David Owen, *Balkan Odyssey* (New York: Harcourt Brace, 1995).

28. On this case, see Chester A. Crocker, *High Noon in Southern Africa* (New York: Norton, 1992); Robert S. Jaster, "The 1988 Peace Accords and the Future of Southwestern Africa," *Adelphi Paper*, no. 253 (London: International Institute for Strategic Studies, 1990); and Cedric Thornberry, "Namibia," in *The UN Security Council*, ed. David M. Malone (Boulder, CO: Lynne Rienner, 2004), 407–22.

29. Crocker, *High Noon in Southern Africa*, 371.

30. Zartman, "Ripeness: The Hurting Stalemate and Beyond," 233.

31. This has been a continuing theme of William Zartman's work. See his *Ripe for Resolution* (New York: Oxford University Press, 1985), ch. 6; and Zartman, *Cowardly Lions*.

32. See Zartman, *Cowardly Lions*, 11.

33. I am indebted to unpublished work by Jacob Bercovitch and Paul Schroeder for the distinction between individualist and contextual variables.

7

To Arms Control or Not

The preoccupation of states with relative military power, a fundamental feature of international life, is no better illustrated than in interstate arms competition. According to Hans J. Morgenthau, "Competition for armaments reflects, and is an instrument of competition for power . . . [and of] contradictory claims in the contest for power."[1] In three potential ways, arms rivalry tests the commitment of adversary states to their respective relative power aspirations. Initiators of arms rivalry act to improve military power relative to a rival. To attain their desired force ratio, initiators must respond to intervening force deployments by the rival. Finally, the rival may act not only to resist the initiator's weapons deployments but also to create a new force ratio favorable to itself.[2]

Relative advantage, a primary goal in arms competition, is best attained by self-help, autonomy, and flexibility.[3] Yet arms rivals committed to gaining relative advantage over each other are able at times to negotiate limits on force increases or improvements.[4] The search for relative advantage and negotiated limits then coexist. For example, arms negotiation was a continuing preoccupation in the Soviet-American cold war nuclear arms competition, in which two superpowers worked for a more stable and predictable balance of power. It has also been important in a very different arms race, the post–cold war rivalry between the United States and North Korea, in which a superpower sought to prevent a regional power contender from cultivating a nuclear weapons arsenal. At other times, the search for relative advantage has not been accompanied by efforts at arms negotiation. Negotiated cooperation between arms rivals was absent in European nineteenth-century naval competition and also appears to be missing in the contemporary nuclear weapons competition between Pakistan and India.

The difference between arms rivalry with agreement and that without agreement, the primary preoccupation of this chapter, is linked to a major dispute in the literature about whether cooperation has a greater value than armaments. One school of thought contends that cooperation between arms rivals often emanates from a fundamental misunderstanding of the political effects of arms competition; if arms rivalry is dangerous, cooperation is not likely to be forthcoming, while if rivalry is not dangerous, cooperation is irrelevant.[5] Accentuating the requirements of long-term arms competition, it emphasizes the need for autonomous and flexible decision-making and critiques much of the experience of negotiated arms agreement.[6] The opposing school of thought emphasizes the need to enhance cooperation between arms rivals and argues that such cooperation does not inevitably suggest failure to take competitive objectives into account or imply a softening of those objectives.[7] The approach draws attention to the fact that cooperation between arms rivals may be shaped by competitive motives and can enhance the search for relative arms advantage. It also recognizes that such cooperation is likely to be rejected and stymied when it does not contribute to the rivals' perceived relative advantage.

The present analysis seeks to move beyond this debate by comparing arms competition with and without arms cooperation, the first time such a comparison has been made, so far as is known. We also inquire whether case comparison reveals testable generalizations linking the causes of cooperation in arms races with the causes of its absence. Some might argue that, given the rivals' interest in flexibility and autonomy in arms development, the two patterns would not be comparable but would each depend on context and circumstances. Yet a link between the two is logical—that is to say, empirically grounded tendencies and not merely incidental differences in circumstances should affect the behavior of arms rivals in this respect.[8]

Three independent variables, each a candidate for validation, are introduced here as alternative explanations for the difference in cooperative tendencies, the dependent variable in the case analysis. Each of the independent variables and the dependent variable can be linked to arms competition in the post–cold war period. They are applied to two documented historical cases with very contrasting arms control experiences—the nineteenth-century Anglo-French naval competition and the twentieth-century Soviet-American nuclear arms competition—to determine whether the dynamics of one or more of the independent variables are interrelated in the two cases. One of these variables, the rivals' integration of their security and political relationship, does reflect such an interrelationship and thus explains some of the variance in diplomatic management of the two cases. A concluding section applies these conclusions to the American–North Korean and the Pakistani-Indian nuclear weapons competitions of the present day.

I. THE RESEARCH PROBLEM

This chapter tests the importance of the search for advantage against the importance of incentives for cooperation in arms racing. Our primary concern is to explain why arms competitors were concerned with mutual advantage in one of our cases but not in the other. To develop such an explanation, we ask: Why should the arms rivals' search for national advantage be accompanied by the search for mutual advantage?

Our analytical framework contains two key working assumptions. First, consistent with our definition of arms races, we assume that rivals in arms competition are guided primarily by the search for relative advantage. By the nature of their competition, the rivals have no inherent need for mutual arms restraint because their primary objective is to attain more favorable force goals, overcoming their opponents' intervening force accumulation and improvements to obtain them. A second assumption, which allows for but does not mandate negotiated arms restraint, is that the rivals' search for relative advantage is difficult and burdensome, taxing not only their material resources but their definition of force equivalence in relation to each other. In theory, no matter how strongly arms racers seek unilateral advantage over their adversary, they *always* have an incentive to seek such advantage at a lower cost and with the adversary's cooperation. While no racer would wish to unilaterally slacken its arms efforts if the result was added force vulnerability to its opponent's arms increases, agreement for mutual restraint may provide both with more security at less expense.[9]

Our two cases—the Anglo-French and superpower competitions—have been selected because they embody differences in the dependent variable, the propensity of arms competitors to cooperate for mutual advantage. The two are not representative of the universe of arms races, but the contrast between them affords an opportunity to understand patterns that can and should—because of the attractiveness of arms restraint—be applied to any arms race case.[10] That is, even a very small case sample can probe the question of why some arms races can proceed for decades without arms limitation while others seem obsessively directed to that task.

Moreover, the limited case sample adopted here has special value in countering the analyst's tendency to be too wedded to one set of expectations, a point stressed by the most trenchant critics of arms control practice and theory.[11] The Anglo-French case questions the frequency of negotiated arms restraint, as well as the notion that diplomatic arms management is central to arms rivalry. Whatever difficulties and burdens the arms rivals experience, those developments may not lead them toward mutual restraint; instead, force deployments by the opponent—resistance to a rival's relative force objectives—may reinforce the rival's determination to improve its relative power. Because of the strength of that determination, incentives for the rivals to cooperate on force restraint may be overwhelmed by the effort to gain national advantage.

By contrast, the Soviet-American example questions how arms rivals can compete over a long period without negotiated restraints—that is, how cooperation between rivals can be anything but central. Difficulties and burdens of competition may, as in the superpower case, contribute to negotiated arms restraint. Incentives to cope jointly with those difficulties and burdens will remain strong, for example, if one or both rivals conclude that the arms competition leads to economic or political challenges not envisioned at the outset of the competition.

The three independent variables are as follows:

1. *Force equivalence*, a standard by which each racer gauges the military strength of the opponent against its own and aspires to some level of strategic superiority.
2. *Intelligence capabilities*, defined in terms of one racer's ability to distinguish and anticipate force additions or improvements by its adversary.
3. *Security and political interests*, a rival's integration of its arms programs with its broader international diplomatic position.

The three variables are not the only ones that might have been chosen.[12] Nor are the explanations yielded by any or all of them fully adequate for understanding the propensity of arms competitors to negotiate on armaments. Rather, each is a foundation for arms competition as well as arms control, and, taken together, the three can assist in explaining the difference in the diplomatic experience of our two cases.

Each of the variables is logically associated with arms racing.[13] The first and second of these variables have been selected because they are connected to the endeavor of arms competitors to improve their relative power. The first, force equivalence, does not signify equality between the competitors but rather a force objective providing some force advantage that would be lost in the absence of arms competition. The force objective, defined in relative terms, is taken as a standard to evaluate the adequacy of the rival's force exertions and the overall character of the force relationship between the competitors. Aspirations of the arms competitors would be defined in detail in terms of this standard. Perhaps the best known of such force standards was the long-standing British two-power naval standard, according to which Great Britain aspired and worked toward a level of strength equivalent to that of the next two ranking naval powers.[14]

The second variable, intelligence capabilities, is as indispensable for arms agreement as it is for competition in the absence of agreement because reliable information about the rival's current and anticipated force strength is needed to determine the risk of limiting one's own forces at any level. Not only is knowledge of the adversary's force strength a possible substitute for additional forces, but force transparency provides cooperative potential even in the absence of negotiated agreement.[15]

The third variable was chosen to reflect the arms competitors' overall relationship, which is likely to contain political rivalry but also some measure of cooperation.[16] For example, arms racing has been linked to the likelihood of war between the racers; the interest in this variable is whether the competition does in practice increase tensions and, conversely, whether cooperation over armaments can reduce them. An interest in normalizing or improving relations can stimulate cooperation on armaments, but the rivals may not attach high priority to such diplomatic development. Our dependent variable, as indicated, is the propensity of arms rivals to cooperate on armaments. Inasmuch as this is a preliminary study, the variable has been simplified to draw attention to developments most contributing to the contrast between our cases. A fuller study would use a larger case sample and define at least two logical intermediate positions between the opposed tendencies here: (1) acting on informal rather than negotiated arms restraint,[17] and (2) discussing mutual restraint in armaments without success.[18]

II. THREE INDEPENDENT VARIABLES

Each of the independent variables logically contributes to cooperation for arms restraint, as well as to the search for relative advantage. We distinguish between and analyze each of the independent variables to understand when the difficulties of competing lead to negotiated restraint and when those difficulties do not have this effect.

1. Force Equivalence

To realize its force aspirations, each rival must define a force standard relating its perceived actual and potential military strength with those of its opponent.

Since war-making is the primary test of force adequacy, procurement standards should depend on war scenarios and objectives. For example, the great German naval buildup aimed at Great Britain prior to the First World War was predicated on the assumption that Britain, unlike Germany, would be unable to concentrate its large fleet in the North Sea.[19] More often, force standards are political, advertising commitment to rivals or neutralizing political opposition at home. The British two-power standard, for instance, was primarily political. When not incompatible, force equivalences or standards may provide the basis for agreement between the rivals on overall force structures or, more narrowly, on anticipated force installments, enabling them to fulfill force goals more rapidly and with less expense. For example, each rival may assume that it will have a defensive position to contain an offensive-minded competitor. Negotiated arms control agreement is then justified when it bolsters the defender's ability to protect itself and allows the defender to convey its resolve and preparedness.[20] While leaving cities vulnerable to attack, Soviet-American arms agreements were designed to discourage attack by bolstering the capabilities of long-range forces to retaliate once an attack had taken place.

Even when force equivalences are not compatible, in diplomatic negotiation arms rivals may accommodate key actual or potential strengths when neither side believes it can coerce its opponent to accept its ideal standard or even to practice force restraint. Its force aspirations remain, but an arms rival, acting on a determination of force equivalence, agrees to circumscribe an adversary's force options while placing limits on its own. Such agreements are predicated on a determination of relative advantage. According to John Mearsheimer, "States motivated by relative power concerns are likely to forgo large gains in their own power, if such gains give rival states even greater power, for smaller national gains that nevertheless provide them with a power advantage over their rivals."[21] For example, any American proposals in the 1950s and 1960s to disarm obsolescent superpower bomber forces could have capitalized on large American numerical superiority in long-range bombers over the Soviet Union; if implemented, the proposals would have enhanced relative American advantage over the Soviets even as they destroyed more American than Russian planes.[22] The point here is that the search for relative advantage on force equivalences can be compatible with negotiated agreement.

Although negotiated agreement would seem to rule out imposing one side's force goals on the other, agreement can be facilitated by threatening force additions to gain adversary force restraint. Specifically, a rival may commit itself to respond to some adversary force deployment with force programs of its own or may agree to abstain from provocative force programs only if the adversary practices equivalent restraint.[23] While application of these strategies can be nondiplomatic, the interest here is in their ability to contribute to negotiated arms restraint if the competitors—determined to gain relative advantage—also incorporate common interests into an agreement.

Finally, the need for reciprocal strategies will be still larger when force goals are especially demanding and difficult to attain, or when, because of continual and rapid technological innovation in weaponry, developing force equivalences between rival military strengths is unusually difficult. While quantitative additions to forces based on force equivalences may discourage arms negotiations by fostering the view that force aspirations are attainable, technological rivalry in armaments can legitimate such negotiations by bolstering the view that competition is not only stalemated but—assuming continued incompatible force aspirations—destined to end in deadlock. Soviet-American arms limitation talks affirmed, according to Gerard C. Smith, "that the most likely outcome of the strategic technology race was stalemate. . . . Technology had provided no answer to escaping from an escalating competition. That would have to come from international politics whose prime technique is talk."[24]

On the other hand, security competition will prevent both agreement and force restraint if the rivals have divergent notions of force equivalence and each overinvests in offensive or defensive forces to avoid endangering its security. This is particularly problematic when the security dilemma, whereby one side's defensive-minded forces are interpreted by the rival as offensive, is severe.[25] Scares in England associated with offensive-minded French forces recurred in the Anglo-French naval rivalry, and fears about offensive-minded Iranian nuclear forces heavily preoccupy Israel at present. Second, technological rivalry may prevent negotiations by emphasizing not the stalemate in the competition but the uncertain value of deployed forces, which makes it difficult or impossible to develop force equivalences. British battleship building was retarded in the 1880s by concerns over French submarine building. A third reason for the absence of agreement is that the rivals are determined to complete their force programs and lack strategies of reciprocity. As in the German naval buildup before the First World War, highly motivated force development cannot be modified in exchange for equivalent restraint by rivals.

2. Intelligence Capabilities

The racers' national estimative intelligence of each other's military strengths and intent permits them to adopt and act on force equivalences. Asymmetry in national intelligence can be fundamental for achieving force aspirations or for compensating for military inferiority. It is thus critical for gaining relative advantage in arms racing. But improved appreciation of the rivals' capabilities may dampen arms rivalry to the rivals' mutual benefit. For example, arms controllers viewed shifting nuclear weapons technologies in the superpower case as a danger because those shifts introduced uncertainties into force planning and into gauging adversary intentions. The rivals may realize they lack full awareness of their opponents' strength and intentions and thus become hypervigilant. According to Thomas Schelling and Morton Halperin, "The most important circumstance in which both sides might gain from an improvement in intelligence about each other's military strength is that in which information on both sides (or perhaps just on one side) is so poor, and is recognized to be so poor, that there are strong motivations to err on the upward side."[26]

Alternatively, poverty of information may prevail even when the rivals are not aware of it. When rivals think they know the opponent's intentions and capabilities well but do not, they may become complacent, underestimating their opponent.[27] A defensive-minded state that acts to contain an expansion-minded one risks being misperceived when it expands its forces.[28] Its goal is to demonstrate that its force expansion does not affect its defensive intent and therefore that the adversary need not react to the expansion. Though the purpose for the rival's weapons expansion is defensive, its competitor may exaggerate the defender's hostility as the result of that force buildup because it is too confident of its information.[29]

While self-help improvements in intelligence gathering and collection can help remedy exaggerated force estimates by distinguishing offense from defense,[30] arms rivals can also diplomatically share force program information as a means of calming tensions.[31] They can then use this information to respond more accurately and effectively to the opponent's force programs. Both sides gain by better understanding the propensity of their adversaries to react to their force buildups. Competition is then dampened when rivals obtain information about their adversaries' force programs, especially when those force programs advertise intentions. "When offense and defense are distinguishable," Charles Glaser writes, "arms control provides a bilateral option for achieving the same results as a policy of unilateral defense emphasis. . . . Relative to defense emphasis, arms control becomes more attractive as the advantage of offense grows, since defeating the adversary's offense with defense becomes more expensive and at some point exceeds the defender's means."[32]

To be unable to distinguish defensive from offensive intent in arms competition, on the other hand, invites heightened danger of war. "Unless the requirements for offence and defense differ in kind or amount," according to

Robert Jervis, "a status quo power will desire a military posture that resembles that of an aggressor."[33] Racing intensified by the rivals' inability to distinguish offensive from defensive weaponry (a consequence of the security dilemma) and by what Jervis has termed "the unintended and undesired consequences of actions meant to be defensive" adds to the urgency of distinguishing defensive force programs from offensive ones.[34] Exchanging information can permit the rivals to race more safely, lessening fears of each other's offensive intent.

Still, intelligence capabilities and requirements may not stimulate arms restraint. First, the rivals may view their intelligence capabilities as a source of relative advantage that they are unwilling to relinquish or even concede. Those capabilities may add to the vulnerability of a rival's force, especially when it is small or offensive-minded. Upon becoming known to the adversary, those capabilities can intensify arms rivalry because one side's fear of attack may grow even when the other is reassured. Opaque forces, on the other hand, can be a security resource against such capabilities. Second, intelligence capabilities promote arms acceleration but not restraint when the rivals are unable to distinguish offensive from defensive weaponry. And, third, rivals hypervigilant about each other's forces will have difficulty sharing information even when dissatisfied about their knowledge of the rivals' programs. Attaching great significance to small differences in forces, they will be unwilling to let their adversary know how much information they possess.

3. Security and Political Interests

Arms rivals, reacting to each other's weapons deployments, are also interdependent in other ways. Our concern here is whether the larger relationship between the rivals is linked to their arms rivalry and, if so, what the character of that linkage is. A strong link would mean that arms agreement is unlikely when rivals lack the security relationship.

Major powers cooperate in continuing, permanent ways on issues extending far beyond military force procurement. They may actively concert over a specific question for a long period. They may agree to mitigate or prevent military confrontations in specified areas. They may share norms establishing agreed-upon spheres of influence. They may agree to consult in relation to the actions of other states.[35] States treat each other as interdependent in each of these instances. As Alexander George notes in his discussion of the cold war Soviet-American relationship, "Each side realizes that it has to take into account, however imperfectly and at times incorrectly, the impact its own policies and actions are likely to have on the other side."[36] The search for relative advantage is not incompatible with such interdependence and may be facilitated by it. In their larger political relationship, one rival may seek to exercise greater influence than its opponent, or even sideline its opponent completely on a consequential issue.[37] Self-help persists in arms rivalry as well, as negotiated arms control supplements but does not replace national defense measures.[38]

The point is, however, that negotiated arms control reflects an important component of highly valued cooperative security between rivals, whose commitment to political cooperation stimulates diplomatic arms restraint because they believe their cooperative relationship requires it. That is, arms racers accept that competition for relative force advantage in the absence of negotiated agreement would likely undermine cooperation on other issues, while agreed-upon arms control would enhance larger common interests.[39]

On the other hand, understandings between arms rivals on nonmilitary questions may be weak or nonexistent, undermining the incentive for negotiated arms control otherwise provided by such understandings. Traditional realists, who play down interstate norms of cooperation and accentuate the importance of self-help, view arms races as a manifestation of intractable political rivalry—as Michael Krepon puts it his analysis of superpower relations, "political dynamics that lead both sides to compete for at least marginal gains out of fear of consequential losses."[40] However, although the importance of attaining desired force goals is higher in this scenario, the rivals are likely to maintain strong efforts to control their arms competition for two reasons. First, the security dilemma will be more problematic when political understandings are sparse or insignificant, as the rivals would then be less able—for political reasons—to distinguish defensive capabilities and intent from offensive ones. Second, in the absence of broader common interests and agreement between them, the rivals are likely to be more sensitive to the actual and potential security-diminishing consequences of their rivalry.[41]

That is, even when the political stimulant to arms negotiations described above in our first scenario is lacking, arms racers are still likely to cope cooperatively with arms races because common security in armaments then has a different and perhaps even more important role than it would in a well-developed political framework. The rivals' need for common interests in armaments is then arguably greater. When a larger cooperative framework exists, however, broader understandings can be used as a source of agreement, making negotiation over armaments less urgent.

Nevertheless, wider political interests may impede arms restraint. First, geopolitical interests may stimulate defensive-minded and offensive-minded states alike to compete in weaponry, perhaps by enabling rivals to insulate their overall diplomatic relationship from arms race irritation without arms agreement. Second, the volatility of the arms competition is partly due to the competitors' problematic security relationship; for example, arms rivalry tends to accelerate upon the onset of crisis between the competitors.[42] Third, a security relationship, whether problematic or not, may lead arms rivals to insist on autonomy in regulating the size and quality of their military forces. Finally, an improving political relationship between the rivals may not translate into arms restraint, either because the urgency of the competition is then perceived to be relatively low or because the rivals are emboldened to compete vigorously in weaponry. The rivals may accept the cost of arms competition as the price of an improved security relationship, and persisting competition may be more tolerable because of the overall improvement.

Table 7.1 summarizes the arguments justifying and opposing arms restraint for each of our three variables.

III. THE DEPENDENT VARIABLE: DIPLOMATIC ARMS MANAGEMENT

Our dependent variable is the propensity of arms race participants to negotiate diplomatically over weapons that they have accumulated or plan to accumulate. Adam Watson defines diplomacy as "negotiation between political entities which acknowledge each other's independence."[43] Negotiation means formalized discussions over weaponry by diplomatic representatives. A prerequisite for such discussions, according to one analysis, is "an appreciation of the fact that the parties have a shared risk, a mutual desire to avoid the consequences of an enforced threat, and a common interest in solving problems."[44]

One important incentive for such discussions is the perceived link between arms competition and the likelihood of war. While competitive behavior can objectively reduce the likelihood of war or increase it, this analysis uses the preoccupations of the competing states as the primary indicator of the link between competitive arming and the danger of war. If arms competitors are anxious about the tension-increasing aspect of their rivalry, they can address those dangers and act to reduce each other's incentives to attack even as they pursue competitive goals. Doing so logically requires mutual arms restraints and awareness of common interests, which are most important for international stability. Whether they acknowledge this link or not, on the other hand, competitors may rely entirely on self-help, autonomy, and flexibility as instruments of strategic advantage or stability.

Our cold war case highlights the rivals' concern for common interest as well as self-help, while our nineteenth-century case underscores the rivals'

Table 7.1. Three Independent Variables

Variable	Supporting diplomatic arms restraint	Opposing arms restraint
1. Force Equivalence	(1) Regardless of whether force equivalences are compatible, relative power can be improved through force agreement more easily than without it. (2) When force equivalences are incompatible, agreement can be supported by a reciprocity strategy. (3) When competition appears stalemated or force aspirations are demanding, force agreement and reciprocity are especially useful.	(1) Divergent notions of force equivalence are hard to satisfy, especially when the security dilemma is severe. (2) Rapid technological change impedes the development of force equivalence. (3) Rivals are determined to complete force programs.
2. Intelligence Capabilities	(1) Lessening uncertainty about competitors' intent and capabilities promotes agreement by dampening arms rivalry, reducing complacency, and reducing war danger. (2) Sharing information promotes agreement by clarifying competitors' propensities to react to each other's force programs, especially when advantages to offense grows relative to defense.	(1) Intelligence capabilities are viewed as a source of strategic advantage. (2) Information about force capabilities enhances vulnerabilities for an inferior force. (3) National intelligence will not promote restraint if it does not adequately distinguish offensive from defense capabilities. (4) Hypervigilant competitors have difficulty sharing information, attaching large significance to small force asymmetries.
3. Security and Political Interests	(1) When mistrust in racing imperils the competitors' larger relationship, their mutual desire to protect their larger political relationship promotes force agreement. (2) When mistrust is associated with an absence of a larger agreement, arms agreement is promoted by a more problematic security dilemma and by greater sensitivity to the political and economic costs of arms racing.	(1) Geopolitical competition stimulates arms rivalry. (2) Security relationship is changeable, so arms accumulation is volatile; for example, a diplomatic crisis accelerates arms competition. (3) Competitors would rather be free than bound when deciding on force accumulation. (4) Competitors' improved security relationship makes the arms race more tolerable.

priority for self-help and their disregard for common interest. This chapter capitalizes on this difference by employing each case as a deviant example— that is, each case is used to generate questions whose answers must be taken into account when searching for regularities. Because one of our cases reflects arms negotiation and the other does not, the challenge in conceptualizing our dependent variable is to outline why we would expect arms negotiation to take place even when it did not.

From the superpower arms rivalry we ask: Why was the nineteenth-century naval case *not* like the superpower rivalry in reflecting persistent arms negotiation? Reasoning from the superpower arms negotiations, we may hypothesize that arms racers, who have adversarial interests in conflicting force goals, also have convergent and mutual interests over slowing or modifying arms increases that cause them greater insecurity.[45] We would expect the racers to become aware of the convergent interests over time and to act on them.

We would expect diplomatic preoccupation with armaments to take one of two forms. One would be to mutually stem declines in security associated with interactive force increases. The rivals would be most concerned about force increases they perceived as facilitating military advantage in an attack, or as contributing to war if an arms competitor were in doubt about the defensive intentions of its opponent. In short, the competitors would be expected to clarify through discussion and agreement the sources of the so-called security dilemma described above. A second diplomatic preoccupation with armaments would be preventive—to protect accommodation on other vital issues from being disturbed by competitive arms increases. That is, when arms competition is defined as an important diplomatic issue, an objective of the competitors—assuming they are not able to end the arms rivalry—would be to insulate it as a factor in their overall relationship.[46]

From the naval example we ask: Why was superpower nuclear rivalry not like the naval competition? Specifically, why did the preoccupation with relative advantage not prevent the nuclear arms rivals from gaining agreement on common arms concerns—either to address the rivalry itself or to prevent it from affecting accommodation on other questions? According to this understanding, convergent interests do not weigh significantly in the rivals' calculations. Arms races should be characterized as bargaining relationships in which participants contest their balance of forces and seek to maximize their advantages.[47] First, while each might desire force restraint, the rivals may be more determined to push force programs for relative advantage than to limit those of the opponent. Second, arms agreement may not be required to stabilize the balance between the racers. Unilateral defensive action may be as useful as arms agreement for providing military stability between the racers.

Neither is free from the risk that the adversary will misperceive the defensive intent of increased deployments and view them instead as offensive.[48]

Third, the rivals may not act to protect or insulate other accommodation from their arms rivalry, nor see those other issues as linked to arms management. Fourth, substitutes for diplomatic arms restraint in the form of fiscal limitations or changes in weapons technology, which may have been present in the naval competition, may have made diplomatic initiative unnecessary. Finally, the rivals may not perceive arms competition as increasing the likelihood of war but instead are willing to accept their arms conflict, and its security-threatening aspects, as an element of international anarchy and intractableness.[49] In short, bargaining over armaments may be either unfeasible or unnecessary. Taken together, these arguments support the null hypothesis.

IV. THE CASES

We have established that our three causal variables can be logically linked to the choice between self-help and arms restraint in arms competition. Our common questions, each designed to assist the detailed pursuit of the research interests defined here and each emerging from our cases, are designed to permit displays of linkages of this kind as well as of the variances between our cases (see table 7.2).

The superpower case has been thoroughly studied and analyzed, while the Anglo-French case is relatively unknown.[50] We now discuss those cases with reference to these questions.

Table 7.2. Common Questions Asked of Our Two Cases

1. What stimulated the start of the competition? What made it mutual?
2. How did the competition reflect efforts by the rivals to improve their relative military position? What standards of force equivalence did the rivals have to guide their weapons accumulation?
3. Were there important uncertainties in weapons technology that complicated or interfered with prior force goals or standards of force equivalence?
4. Were the rivals significantly impeded in estimating their adversaries' actual and potential military strength, or were those strengths clearly apparent to them?
5. Did the larger security relationship between the competitors affect their rivalry, and, if so, how?
6. What were the sources of arms restraint? Were these sources related to the sources of arms acceleration?

1. The Anglo-French Naval Competition, 1840–1866[51]

France, having traditionally accepted a navy two-thirds the strength of Great Britain, sought naval parity with the British following an Anglo-French diplomatic crisis over Syria in 1840. The French, acting to prevent British naval domination, subsequently increased the number of their seamen to almost equal the British strength, enlarged their naval dockyards, and indicated they would utilize steam propulsion in naval vessels rather than sail, upon which British naval superiority had been based. In 1846 the French Parliament approved a steam fleet construction program. The British Admiralty, seeking to perpetuate British naval domination, responded by rapidly converting line-of-battle and frigate sail-ships to steam from 1846 to 1848, outdistancing the French program.

By 1856 the French stopped laying down new ships of the line, instead converting sail-ships to steam and wooden ships to armor-plated ironclads; the British government stated early in 1859 that France had completed the same number of steam-powered battleships as had England. France, the first to introduce ironclad construction (in 1859), began a large ironclad naval program in 1860, to which the British responded with a large ironclad program of their own in 1861. England continued in this period to build wooden ships fitted with armor plate, proposing as late as 1860 building eight wooden battleships and twelve wooden frigates.

Anglo-French rivalry was stimulated by the widespread British belief that the advent of steam warships enhanced the potential for a French invasion of the unprotected British coast. Three "invasion panics" took place in England: in 1847 and 1848, 1851 to 1853, and 1859 to 1861, bolstered by French steam warship building and the weakness of the British militia. On the other hand, British and French defense expenditures declined from 1847 to 1851, and in 1848 the British Parliament rejected an income tax increase to bolster the militia.

A. Force Equivalence

The French as challengers sought newer steam and ironclad technologies to overpower more plentiful but obsolescent British ships, while the British, seeking to preserve naval supremacy, accepted larger arms burdens in order to be numerically superior in all types of naval vessels, including obsolescent wooden ships. On the other hand, shifts in naval technology complicated efforts to determine force equivalence between older and newer vessels (particularly for the British, with a larger assortment of warships), and it also contributed to renewed competition at each new design plateau, in which each side aimed at numerical superiority. The French enjoyed parity or superiority to England in steam vessels in 1859 and in ironclad numbers from 1859 until 1866, when the competition ended and the British reestablished the three-to-two ratio over France that it enjoyed before 1840. As the competitors aimed at numerical superiority in steam and iron warships, they lacked flexible or negotiable force programs.

B. Intelligence Capabilities

Exchanging information about naval building was little needed, as the French did not hide their naval strength. "It would be just as possible," according to Richard Cobden, a keen observer of this rivalry, "to build a great hotel in secrecy in Paris, as to conceal the process of constructing a ship of war at Toulon or Cherbourg."[52] Fears remained in England, however, about French offensive intentions and French naval budgets. The advent of Louis Napoleon as French ruler in 1851 coincided with reports of "immense" French naval budget increases, and former British foreign minister Lord Palmerston, intent on bolstering the militia, stoked fears that fifty thousand to sixty thousand men could be transported without notice from Cherbourg to England in a single night.

C. Security Interests

Though started following Anglo-French crisis, the naval competition appears neither to have been sustained by interstate political rivalry nor to have been connected to it. Arms racing did not retard improved diplomatic relations between the two countries. The two countries were allied in the Crimean War from 1852 to 1854, and in 1859 Cobden, a critic of the competition, negotiated a trade liberalization agreement with France on behalf of England.

The receptivity of British domestic opinion to panics about French invasion does not seem to have contributed to volatility in arms competition, as the size of the British fleet was not set by domestic opinion and the British public did not support extravagant naval expenditures. The most important source of arms restraint in the competition was the disutility of increased defense spending.

2. The Soviet-American Nuclear Competition, 1945–1991[53]

Superpower nuclear arms programs were sustained by deteriorating Soviet-American relations after the Second World War. The United States sought to keep military dominance by amassing a large strategic nuclear arsenal to compensate for Soviet superiority in standing armies. By the early 1960s it limited the number of missiles and bombers in favor of improving munitions and warhead technology. Though much weakened by the devastating impact of the Second World War, the Soviet Union aimed to blunt and undermine American dominance. It first sought parity in nuclear technology with the United States while accepting large inferiority in the number of deliverable nuclear weapons, but by the late 1960s it exceeded the United States in the number of long-range intercontinental and submarine-launched ballistic missiles (ICBMs and SLBMs).

Two-sided arms rivalry set in after the Soviet test of an atomic bomb in 1949. Thereafter, rapid technological changes in bomb technology and in the means of delivering atomic explosives fueled arms rivalry because of potential destruction, the speed with which nuclear attack could be inflicted, and the initial vulnerability of strategic forces to attack. The United States preceded the Soviets in developing atomic bombs, fusion bombs, more versatile atomic weaponry for battlefield purposes, long-range jet aircraft, submarine-launched ballistic missiles, and highly accurate multiple independently targeted warheads for ballistic missiles (MIRV). It elected to produce a "triad" of strategic forces (long-range aircraft, submarines, and ground-based long-range ballistic missiles) to ensure weapons survivability and a strike-back force in the event of a nuclear attack, a requirement for deterring war. The Soviets mostly imitated American technological advances to deter war, but they pioneered large ballistic missile rockets and the production of long-range ballistic missiles. Insecurities associated with projected Soviet production of long-range bombers, missiles, and orbital satellites in the 1950s stimulated accelerated American bomber and missile deployments.

Each side possessed strike-back forces with the advent of submarine- and underground- based ballistic missiles in the 1960s, but they continued to cultivate a counterforce capability (through the multiplication of warheads on long-range ballistic missiles and the improvement of missile accuracy), anticipating a nuclear war that arose not from surprise attack but from the escalation of superpower nonnuclear war in Europe.

Nuclear armaments were part of the superpower diplomatic agenda from the late 1940s, which aimed at reducing the danger of unlimited arms competition. At first, gamesmanship diplomacy focused on the unrealistic goal of general and complete disarmament, with the United States focusing on inspection of force cuts and the Soviets seeking cuts before inspection. Subsequent negotiations (in the mid-1950s) occurred on limiting long-range bombers and (beginning in the late 1950s) on a proposed nuclear weapons test ban. The superpowers agreed to a partial ban on nuclear weapons tests that did not require inspection (excluding underground testing) in 1963. The first superpower strategic arms limitation treaty (SALT I) in 1972 limited antiballistic missiles to very low levels while setting provisional, five-year unequal ceilings on Soviet and American ICBMs and SLBMs. The parties agreed in 1979 to permanent and equal force ceilings, along with limitations on long-range missiles equipped with multiple independently targeted warheads (SALT II). In 1987, the Soviet Union, giving priority to economic and political reform at home, signed with the United States a landmark treaty dismantling medium- and intermediate-range ballistic missiles in Europe, with the Soviets eliminating about three times as many launchers and twice as many missiles as did the United States.

In 1991, having agreed to end their cold war and arms race, the superpowers concluded the strategic arms reduction treaty (START I), cutting nuclear warhead levels by 4,000 for the United States and 5,000 for the Soviet Union, and began gradual agreed-upon reductions to Russian and American long-range nuclear forces. A follow-on START II treaty in 1993 cut START I levels by more than half, and in 2002 START II was superseded by the Strategic Offensive Reductions Treaty, providing for warhead levels of 1,700 to 2,200 on each side by 2012. The most recent New START treaty, concluded in March 2010, aims to reduce the number of deployed long-range ballistic missile warheads to 1,550 by 2017.

A. Force Equivalence

The political concept of parity, or rough equality in military force, legitimated the SALT negotiations, but rapid shifts in technology, differences in strategy, and asymmetries in the rivals' strategic forces impeded detailed comparisons of the forces and made reciprocated equivalence impossible.

First, rapid changes in weapons technology, which produced a condition in which, as Herman Kahn described it in 1960, "we are having a complete technological revolution in the art of war approximately every five years," inherently increased the uncertainty of force comparisons as weapons modifications were introduced.[54] Second, the rivals' force asymmetries were shaped in part by the fact that they adapted to technological changes in different ways. As indicated, the United States at first sought to be superior in all major weapons systems, irrespective of the rate of their obsolescence, while the Soviets avoided large weapon buildups. Later, the United States limited ballistic missile launchers in favor of warhead improvements, while the Soviet Union, behind in warhead technology, greatly increased the number of launchers.

Third, the two distinct superpower strategies that shaped their force goals—deterrence of direct attack and counterforce—each were affected by force vulnerability but presented different approaches to force comparison. Deterrence, in the form of strike-back forces, required mainly forces that were invulnerable rather than a large array of forces; numerical and even technological comparisons were of peripheral importance. Counterforce strategy was more conducive to detailed force comparisons because it depended on the relative potency of warhead lethality and weapons protection, but because military superiority depended on the counterforce mission, the rivals were not likely to agree on equivalence for that capability.

American force levels arguably owed more to domestic political considerations than to force equivalences. Sizing the American SLBM and ICBM forces in the early 1960s depended on accommodating congressional pressures at levels larger than needed for strike-back deterrence. Agreement to keep antiballistic missile (ABM) levels low in SALT I was dictated by the unpopularity of the ABM system in the United States.[55] SALT I, limiting American offensive missile forces not slated for quantitative expansion, was used politically by American military leaders to compensate for the then prevailing antidefense political climate. Those officials employed the treaty to highlight invidious quantitative comparisons of superpower forces and robust Soviet efforts to compete with the United States in making their case for force modernization.[56]

B. Intelligence Capabilities

Until the mid-1950s, American uncertainty over Soviet force plans was caused by the fact that the Soviet Union was effectively a closed society in which American intelligence assets were weak. Initial Soviet rejection of large quantitative buildups in nuclear weaponry contributed to its strategic vulnerability to the United States, enhancing the value of hiding the size and location of Soviet forces and thus the value of adding to American uncertainty about those forces. The uncertainty, in turn, contributed to American quantitative buildups, despite the rapidity of technological advances in weaponry; American panic episodes over Soviet bomber and later Soviet ICBM construction took place amid this considerable uncertainty. By contrast, Soviet intelligence of the United States was much better, permitting Soviet officials to know the American numerical force superiority relative to the Soviet forces in that period.

American intelligence weakness was corrected by the late 1950s through the American U-2 reconnaissance plane, controlled by the Central Intelligence Agency (CIA), which detected the small Soviet bomber and missile programs then underway. Highly guarded U-2 intelligence enabled the American government to conclude that earlier estimates of Soviet bomber and long-range missile construction were considerably exaggerated. In response, the Eisenhower administration practiced restraint in initial ICBM missile production, resisting domestic pressures to accelerate it.[57] Though overhead reconnaissance was initially an instrument of American superiority, by the late 1960s it provided reassurance of the defensive intentions of both sides, and beginning with the SALT I agreement it became the primary means of verifying the negotiated arms control. "It is no exaggeration to say," former CIA director Robert Gates writes, "that there would have been no SALT, no arms control at all, without CIA's active involvement."[58]

Improved intelligence ensured that the superpower rivals could compete more safely than in the past, as each was more aware of the other's intentions and capabilities, but it was by no means adequate to end arms competition. "Transparency," according to one analysis, "is certainly no recipe for dampening [arms] competition, as shown by the history of the Cold War."[59]

C. Security Interests

Downturns in superpower relations tended to intensify rivalry. For example, the North Korean attack against South Korea in 1950, which was interpreted as implemented in concert with Soviet intentions and heightened polarization of superpower relations, made possible a vast increase in American spending on fusion and fission weapons and on long-range bombers, all aimed at the Soviet Union. Prior to that time, American spending levels reflected little competition with the Soviet Union.[60] In the 1980s, as renewed cold war between the rivals set in following the Soviet invasion of Afghanistan, the American government—citing a larger threat from a major Soviet strategic weapons program—initiated a major force-building program of its own and declared it would no longer observe the force ceilings provided for in SALT II (which remained unratified because of the invasion), and the agreement lapsed.

Improved relations, on the other hand, did not slow the arms rivalry but made the rivals more willing to agree on arms controls. The Partial Test Ban treaty was negotiated in the wake of the Cuban missile crisis of 1962, in which the dangers of superpower confrontation were clear. It symbolized the public determination of Soviet and American leaders to work together to reduce the dangers of nuclear war. The SALT I accord of 1972 was the centerpiece of Soviet-American détente, which represented a wide-ranging effort to cooperate on military and diplomatic questions, even as the superpowers remained adversaries. Finally, the 1987 accord, and the START I and START

II agreements of 1991 and 1993, were made possible by radical improvement in superpower relations accompanying the end of the cold war. Soviet president Mikhail Gorbachev, looking to stimulate Soviet economic development, rejected further arms competition with the United States, and the American government, led by Presidents Ronald Reagan and George H. W. Bush, followed suit.

V. ANALYZING THE ROLE OF ARMS CONTROL IN RIVALRY

We now evaluate the importance of our variables—force equivalence, intelligence capabilities, and security interests—for the use or nonuse of diplomacy as arms management in our two cases. The significance of our independent variables depends in this analysis on how well they satisfy two requirements. First, our independent variables must significantly vary between our cases. They cannot have a causal impact on our dependent variable—the propensity of rivals to diplomatically manage their arms competition—unless they themselves vary.[61] Second, our independent variables must be causally linked to the dependent variable outcomes in our two cases. We must be able to demonstrate, in other words, that our independent variables impact the propensity of the states to cope diplomatically with rivalry in armaments—that is, why our cases tend to the extremes in the propensity of arms rivals to manage their rivalry.

A. Force Equivalence

The force equivalence variable shows little contrast between our two cases and therefore cannot explain the variance in the propensity to manage arms rivalry diplomatically.

First, no reciprocated equivalence, a logical basis for negotiated arms control, existed in either of our cases. This was partly because our arms races were technological in character. They raised uncertainties not only about attaining quantitative force goals but about the value of numerical goals as an indicator of relative strength. To be sure, the rivals did respond to each other's force deployment. For example, when one rival set the direction for a technological shift, the rival followed suit, and major quantitative buildups occurred despite the risk of obsolescence. But one rival could initially avoid heavy buildups in older weaponry to cultivate new weapons systems (France, the Soviet Union), while the other (England, the United States) could build heavily even in older weapons to preserve its lead. In the superpower case, the Soviet Union, which initially neglected large nuclear force buildups, stressed them later, while the United States, which built up heavily, limited its nuclear delivery systems to a preexisting number.

Second, if technological improvement in weaponry hampered the determination of weapons equivalence in both cases, it cannot explain the variance in our dependent variable. To be sure, protecting submarine-based and land-based long-range nuclear forces against attack provided stability in the form of strike-back forces that was lacking in the naval case. It invited the perception that technological arms competition was futile because any sustained effort to erode a superpower's ability to retaliate was likely to fail.

On the other hand, those emphasizing the tendency of superpowers to be cautious in utilizing nuclear weapons for war-making purposes because of strike-back forces maintained that the condition of mutual strike-back forces sufficed to make the rivals more objectively secure and rendered diplomatic efforts to negotiate arms agreement redundant or counterproductive.[62] They challenged the link between weapons stability and negotiation, and maintained that convergence was associated with objective conditions alone. Another challenge, applicable as well to the naval race, maintained that the strategic cultures of the superpowers were not convergent and that Soviet-American arms negotiations disguised that fact.[63] The superpowers persisted in seeking increasingly accurate weapons suitable for first-strike scenarios in which force superiority would be critical. Force superiority seems also to have been an objective of the British and French in their naval race. Technological developments in weaponry in each case made superiority more difficult to obtain but also made obtaining arms agreement between the rivals more difficult.

Third, unable to explain the variance in our dependent variable, technological competition in weaponry may deflate the significance of the variance in diplomatic arms management because the rivals may have competed in similar fashion regardless of whether they negotiated. Our cases suggest that while negotiation can, in principle, assist arms racers in attaining their force goals, the rivals may need to resist or confine negotiation to attain weaponry most significant for force superiority. Bernard Brodie, commenting on the naval case, observed, "The only manner in which Great Britain could assure herself of that continued superiority on the seas which she deemed indispensable to her security was to continue building, ceaselessly vigilant lest improvements abroad outdistance her own, and seeking always to build more units on each level of development than any two of her rivals."[64] The United States was similarly vigilant in relation to Soviet technological improvements. The problem Britain and the United States experienced in their two cases was, as Samuel Huntington notes, that new arms races in effect begin with each new weapons system, and "the more rapid the rate of [weapons] innovation, the more pronounced is the tendency toward equality" between the racers, regardless of whether they are intent on force superiority.[65]

B. Intelligence Capabilities

Intelligence capabilities vary significantly between our cases: the Anglo-French case dramatizes the condition of transparency, while the superpower case at first demonstrates the opposite extreme and later exhibits transparency in deployed delivery systems but not in warhead design. However, the logic by which these variances would contribute to self-help or negotiated arms restraint remains unclear, so intelligence capabilities therefore do not appear to explain variance in our dependent variable.

First, transparency does not necessarily contribute to arms negotiation. Rather, as illustrated in both our cases, it may discourage negotiation by accentuating how the rivals can compete safely and without the risk of highly exaggerating adversary programs. In the superpower case, overhead reconnaissance helped reassure the superpowers of each other's nonbelligerent intentions (though very imperfectly, given the scope of their arms competition), allowing the rivalry to proceed irrespective of the rivals' larger security relationship. Since they desired stability as protection against unwanted nuclear war, the superpowers were unlikely to have continued their rivalry so intensively if they were persuaded that it was dangerous. Their intelligence capabilities, allowing them to detect threatening behavior by their adversary, helped protect them against the possibility they underplayed the dangers of the rivalry.

Second, the early period of the superpower race shows how intelligence can be regarded as an instrument of strategic advantage, whether for the inferior or the superior side. If it is an advantage, the inferior side would wish to hide its forces, and the superior side would wish to reveal what its adversary seeks to hide. In that condition, intelligence capabilities can contribute to arms restraint by the superior side but not by the inferior, and diplomacy would not be a means for acquiring better intelligence.

Third, transparency, which underpinned self-help in the naval case, should be distinguished from the agreed use of reconnaissance to underpin arms control in the superpower case. The latter had value because intelligence was valued, but the value attached to intelligence was a function of other goals, including the desire for arms restraint. By contrast, transparency might not have value if agreement was not valued. In the naval case, two French invitations to the British government to monitor activity in the French dockyards, in 1853 and 1861, were rejected.

C. Security Interests

Security interests account significantly for the differences in negotiated arms restraint in our cases. Naval rivalry was largely disconnected from larger security relations between the rivals, being shaped instead by positional goals in a military hierarchy. Superpower competition, on the other hand, was at times directly affected by security interests, although at other times was disconnected from them. Linkage to larger conflict was an important motivator for negotiated arms restraint in the second instance, whereas the absence of the linkage accounts for the absence of agreed-upon restraint in the first.

First, while the disconnect between racing and larger security interests removes the arms racing from the diplomatic agenda, the reason for the disconnect remains unclear. The rivals may determine that a competing national interest overrides diplomatic requirements. Alternatively, certain behaviors, such as arms accumulation, may be regarded as outside the scope of diplomacy. Consistent with this second hypothesis is the possibility that changing diplomatic fashion or practice may affect the variance in our diplomacy variable.[66]

Second, the deep hostility between the United States and the Soviet Union in the cold war paradoxically underscored the importance of common superpower interests to prevent nuclear war; negotiated arms restraint symbolized the awareness of those common interests. A purely self-help competition, raising the perception of insecurity and danger under cold war conditions, would have been difficult to sustain, unlike the earlier naval competition. On the other hand, if what Robert Gates termed "hardball global competition" underscored the need for arms restraint, improved relations were required to implement it.[67] The durability of superpower competition is visible in its persistence from cold war to détente: arms negotiations, such as the Partial Test Ban and the SALT agreement, succeeded only as overall diplomatic relations improved.

But if it helps account for arms restraint, superpower détente also supported accelerated arms rivalry. As Gates observes, such American strategic force programs as the Trident submarine and missile, the B-1 bomber, the Minuteman III MIRVed ICBM, and the mobile ICBM were initially funded at low levels in an antidefense American climate and then saved in part by superpower détente and SALT.[68] When the larger security relationship between the rivals becomes the focus of analysis, the tension between arms restraint and self-help disappears. Détente, indispensable for negotiated arms restraint, was also indispensable for arms competition because it legitimated sustained competition in a way that protracted hostility between nuclear-equipped superpowers could not.

In the superpower case, shifts in superpower relations roughly coincided with shifts in the superpower force balance. During cold war in the 1950s, when the superpowers' nuclear forces were unequal, diplomacy offered an opportunity to the superior American side: bomber agreement in the 1950s might have prevented the Soviets from responding to American bomber deployments and gaining equality with the Americans. The Soviets were not likely to accept permanent negotiated bomber inferiority, and the opportunity was fleeting. By the late 1960s, with the widespread perception that the superpower relationship had become less dangerous, the primary superpower interest in arms restraint was no longer codifying force imbalance but instead ensuring flexibility in arms programs. Relative parity in superpower forces made it impossible for arms restraint to prevent a rival's reaction to its adversary's force program. As a result, each side could deploy what it wished and agree to restraint within that rubric. Easing the political pressure to agree, détente served the superpower interest in protecting self-help in armaments while providing politically attractive arms restraint.

These results are summarized in table 7.3.

Table 7.3.   Case Comparison Results

Variable	Variance between the cases?	Independent variable causally linked to dependent variable?
1. Force Equivalence	No. Primarily because technological rivalry in weaponry hampered the determination of force equivalence.	No. Technological developments in weaponry made agreement more difficult to obtain.
2. Intelligence Capabilities	Yes. Transparency prevailed in the Anglo-French case; asymmetry (initially) and agreed use of overhead reconnaissance to gather intelligence (later) in the superpower case.	Unclear. Openness to national intelligence-gathering does not necessarily contribute to negotiated force restraint; openness may discourage negotiations by defusing the dangers of racing.
3. Security and Political Interests	Yes. Naval rivalry was disconnected from Anglo-French security relations; superpower nuclear force rivalry was linked to Soviet-American relations.	Yes. Linkage to Soviet-American security motivated superpower arms control; détente supports arms agreement and self-help in force accumulation. Naval rivalry was not linked to broader Anglo-French relations; those relations did not motivate arms limitation.

VI. CONCLUSIONS: SECURITY RELATIONSHIPS AND ARMS CONTROL PROSPECTS

A limited empirical and conceptual focus can, if properly controlled, assist in developing empirically grounded generalizations about arms racing. Comparing only two arms race cases—even if unrepresentative—can usefully suggest hypotheses, refine concepts, and indicate directions for further research when such a comparison narrowly focuses on the clear-cut difference between the cases regarding the use of diplomacy to achieve arms restraint. We now recapitulate our key conclusions and apply them to two additional cases, the nuclear arms competitions now underway between Pakistan and India and between the United States and North Korea.

Both the prevalence and the absence of arms restraints are linked in our historical cases to the same independent variable: the overall security relationship of the arms rivals. That variable rules out or induces diplomatic arms control in arms competitions, depending on whether the competition is disconnected from or linked to the rivals' security relationship. When arms competition is disconnected from that larger relationship, as in the Anglo-French case, the rivals lack incentive to apply diplomatic management to the competition, and negotiated arms control will consequently not occur. But when the competition is linked to the rivals' security relationship, as in the superpower competition, incentives to the rivals to provide arms restraints are much larger, and consequently diplomacy is likely to provide them.

Because all arms rivalry is produced to some degree by the rivals' concern for military security, one might object that *every* arms competition should somehow be linked to the rivals' political and security relationship. However, while the security motive for competing in armaments is important, arms racing is essentially an issue of power hierarchy rather than security. When they compete in armaments, the competitors seek more favorable positions in the international hierarchy.[69]

Do the Pakistani-Indian and American–North Korean cases support the importance of the larger security relationship between the rivals in shaping arms restraint diplomacy?[70] An affirmative answer to this question highlights differences between our contemporary cases that seem to be explained by variance in the rivals' security relationship. The Pakistani-Indian competition has only very limited arms restraint diplomacy, while the rivalry between the United States and North Korea has featured it. A parallel difference is the absence of a security framework in one instance and its presence in the other; arms limitation can be plausibly linked to the security structure in the latter instance.

In the Pakistani-Indian case, formal restraint is ruled out by the absence of an agreed-upon security framework, which adds to the likelihood and danger of military confrontations. The rivals depend on outside states, principally the United States, to defuse confrontations over Kashmir. Tentative initiatives occasionally are made for diplomatic discussions; however, though they affirm the mutual need for peace and for symbolic economic and humanitarian ties, they lack substance. The American–North Korean rivalry does contain a security framework in the six-power talks and in the direct channels growing out of it. These frameworks are delicate and changeable, and they occasionally founder. It remains unclear whether they can help persuade North Korea to divest itself of its nuclear weapons program. However, the North Korean nuclear program and the American response appear to be linked to those frameworks.

Our second conclusion pertains to the arms control pathway mentioned above: the perception that the arms competition helps drive broader security competition between the rivals contributes to mutual efforts to reduce the dangers of security competition, even as the rivals retain strong competitive incentives and work to enhance their capabilities for self-help as well as self-restraint. Contrary to the working assumption guiding our analysis that self-help and arms restraint are in conflict, this conclusion suggests that relative advantage and mutual interest are interrelated when the overall security relationship and arms racing are linked: an intensified search for relative advantage then stimulates diplomatic cooperation, and the cooperation permits intensified competition.

This point has implications for neorealist logic and for recent critiques of arms control behavior. It suggests that neorealist logic explaining arms competition by the rivals' commitment to relative power is insufficient. And it argues for reevaluating the idea that arms limitation has been fatally overwedded to the need for restraint and insufficiently grounded in competitive values.

A puzzle emerges from our second conclusion: the stronger the link between the search for relative advantage and diplomatic cooperation, the more surprising and problematic becomes disconnection in the Anglo-French experience between arms rivalry and the larger Anglo-French relationship. Shouldn't *any* competition between arms rivals reflect an interaction between arms racing and the larger security relationship as is documented in the superpower case if, as has been argued here, preoccupations about relative power shape arms competition and arms restraint?

While additional case analysis is required to answer this question, a feature of both cases—the absence of effort to *shift* relative power between the rivals—provides a clue. Relative power is at stake in these cases, but the rivals are determined to neutralize their adversary's power rather than displace it. These two rivalries are primarily technological rather than quantitative: the parties respond to each other's technical achievements but not to shifts in the number of weapons and not with the aim of improving their relative force ratios. The Pakistani-Indian rivalry seems predicated on each side's determination to deny hegemony to the opponent rather than each side's efforts to gain advantage over the other. North Korea resists American hegemony on the Korean peninsula, even as the United States remains unquestionably the stronger power there.

This discussion points to a useful distinction between arms rivalries in which deadlock is sought from the outset by at least one competitor (such as France in the Anglo-French case) and competition in which both sides seek superiority and acknowledge deadlock only after subsequent indecisive force adjustments (as in the superpower case). The former, when power hierarchy is not at stake, may be the less *objectively* dangerous of the two and more difficult to stop. In such a case arms adjustments influence the rivals' security relationship less than when hierarchy is challenged. However, *subjective* security considerations may motivate even a clearly militarily superior rival to link its adversary's arms adjustments with diplomatic demands for arms restraint, as the United States has done in relation to North Korean nuclear weapons capability.

NOTES

1. Hans J. Morgenthau, *Politics among Nations*, 4th ed. (New York: Knopf, 1967), 394. On the importance of relative power in world politics, see John J. Mearsheimer, *The Tragedy of Great Power Politics* (New York: Norton, 2001), especially ch. 2. Well-known arms race writings include Samuel P. Huntington, "Arms Races: Prerequisites and Results," in *Public Policy*, ed. Carl J. Friedrich and Seymour E. Harris Cambridge, MA: Harvard University Graduate School of Public Administration, 1958), 41–58, included in *The Use of Force*, ed. Robert J. Art and Kenneth N. Waltz (Boston: Little, Brown, 1971), 365–401; Colin S. Gray, "The Arms Race Phenomenon," *World Politics* 24 (October 1971): 39–79; Colin S. Gray, "The Urge to Compete: Rationales for Arms Racing," *World Politics* 27 (January 1974): 208–33; Colin S. Gray, *The Soviet-American Arms Race* (Westmead, UK: Saxon House, 1978); Herman Kahn, "The Arms Race and Some of Its Hazards," in *Arms Control, Disarmament and National Security*, ed. Donald G. Brennan (New York: George Braziller, 1961), 89–121; Albert Wohlstetter, "Is There a Strategic Arms Race?," *Foreign Policy*, no. 15 (Summer 1974): 3–20; Albert Wohlstetter, "Rivals, but No Race," *Foreign Policy*, no. 16 (Fall 1974): 57–81; Matthew Evangelista, *Innovation and the Arms Race* (Ithaca, NY: Cornell University Press, 1998); George W. Downs, "Arms Races and War," in *Behavior, Society, and Nuclear War* , ed. Philip E. Tetlock et al. (New York: Oxford University Press, 1991), 73–109; Steve Weber, *Cooperation and*

Discord in US-Soviet Arms Control (Princeton: Princeton University Press, 1991); Charles L. Glaser, "When Are Arms Races Dangerous? Rational versus Suboptimal Arming," *International Security* 28 (Spring 2004): 44–84; Charles L. Glaser, "Political Consequences of Military Strategy: Expanding and Refining the Spiral and Deterrence Models," *World Politics* 44 (July 1992): 497–538; Andrew Kydd, "Arms Races and Arms Control: Modeling the Hawk Perspective," *American Journal of Political Science* 44 (April 2000): 222–38; and Alexander T. J. Lennon, ed., *Contemporary Nuclear Debates: Missile Defense, Arms Control and Arms Races in the Twenty-First Century* (Cambridge, MA: MIT Press, 2002).

2. Some have distinguished "arms races," on one hand, from "arms competition" and "arms rivalry," on the other, as metaphors to describe different intensities of competition. See, for example, Wohlstetter, "Rivals, but No Race." This chapter does not focus on the intensity of competition and uses the terms interchangeably.

3. A study of arms racing that stresses self-help is Weber, *Cooperation and Discord*. Other studies that focus on self-help are Morgenthau, *Politics among Nations*; Mearsheimer, *The Tragedy of Great Power Politics*; and Kenneth Waltz, *Theory of International Politics* (Reading, MA: Addison-Wesley, 1979).

4. On arms control problems more generally, see Robert O'Neill and David N. Schwartz, eds., *Hedley Bull on Arms Control* (New York: St. Martin's, 1987); Alexander L. George, Philip J. Farley, and Alexander Dallin, eds., *U.S.-Soviet Security Cooperation* (New York: Oxford University Press, 1988), part 3; McGeorge Bundy, *Danger and Survival* (New York: Random House, 1988); Colin S. Gray, *House of Cards: Why Arms Control Must Fail* (Ithaca, NY: Cornell University Press, 1992); Jeffrey A. Larsen and James J. Wirtz, eds., *Arms Control and Cooperative Security* (Boulder, CO: Lynne Rienner, 2009); Charles H. Fairbanks Jr. and Abram N. Shulsky, "From 'Arms Control' to Arms Reductions: The Historical Experience," *Washington Quarterly* 10 (Summer 1987): 59–73; "Arms Control: Thirty Years On," special issue of *Daedalus* 120, no. 1 (Winter 1991); and "Arms, Defense Policy, and Arms Control," special issue of *Daedalus* 104, no. 3 (Summer 1975).

5. Gray, *House of Cards*, 19–20. Gray's "Urge to Compete" fails to discuss arms control.

6. In *Soviet-American Arms Race*, 182, Colin Gray understands arms racing as "really only normal Great Power behavior somewhat accentuated." He has not compared arms competition cases to test his critical approach, but viewing arms racing as typical major power behavior does not seem to encourage comparisons.

7. Thomas C. Schelling and Morton A. Halperin, *Strategy and Arms Control* (New York: Twentieth Century Fund, 1961).

8. The idea that the causes of cooperation in arms races should be related to causes for the absence of cooperation is indebted to Geoffrey Blainey's argument that the causes of war are linked to the causes of peace. See Blainey, *The Causes of War*, 3rd ed. (New York: Free Press, 1988), ch. 3.

9. Gray, *House of Cards*, 21–22; Schelling and Halperin, *Strategy and Arms Control*.

10. See, on this approach, Alexander L. George, "Case Studies and Theory Development: The Method of Structured, Focused Comparison," in *Diplomacy: New Approaches in History, Theory, and Policy*, ed. Paul Gordon Lauren (New York: Free Press, 1979), 43–68. George writes in this essay that the choice of cases "*need not* be representative in

the statistical sampling sense in order to contribute to theory development" (60; emphasis in original).

11. This is a major point made in Gray, *House of Cards*.

12. For example, arms racing has been linked to domestic pressures for arms development. See, for example, Graham T. Allison and Frederic A. Morris, "Armaments and Arms Control: Exploring the Determinants of Military Weapons," *Daedalus* 104 (Summer 1975): 99–129.

13. For a pioneering effort to integrate these variables and others in an analytic framework, see Huntington, "Arms Races: Prerequisites and Results."

14. On the two-power naval standard, see Arthur Marder, *The Anatomy of British Sea Power: A History of British Naval Policy in the Pre-Dreadnought Era, 1880–1905* (New York: Knopf, 1940).

15. Thomas Schelling and Morton Halperin argue that "the arms race might be dampened if each side possessed better information about what the other is doing" (*Strategy and Arms Control*, 34). See also Thomas J. Hirschfeld, ed., *Intelligence and Arms Control* (Austin, TX: Lyndon B. Johnson School of Public Affairs, 1987); and J. Christian Kessler, *Verifying Nonproliferation Treaties* (Washington DC: National Defense University Press, 1995).

16. One text that examined arms competition and negotiation in terms of the competitors' broader security interests is George, Farley, and Dallin, *U.S.-Soviet Security Cooperation*.

17. On tacit arms control, see Schelling and Halperin, *Strategy and Arms Control*; and George W. Downs and David M. Rocke, *Tacit Bargaining, Arms Races, and Arms Control* (Ann Arbor: University of Michigan Press, 1990).

18. For gamesmanship in arms negotiations, see John J. Spanier and Joseph L. Nogee, *The Politics of Disarmament* (New York: Praeger, 1962).

19. Paul Kennedy, *Strategy and Diplomacy: 1870–1945* (Winchester, MA: George Allen & Unwin, 1983), 133.

20. Glaser, "Political Consequences of Military Strategy," 509, 511.

21. Mearsheimer, *Tragedy of Great Power Politics*, 36.

22. For superpower disarmament discussions in the period of relative American force superiority, see *Foreign Relations of the United States: 1955–1957*, vol. 20: *Regulation of Armaments: Atomic Energy* (Washington, DC: U.S. Government Printing Office, 1990). A bomber disarmament initiative is discussed in Jeremy J. Stone, *Containing the Arms Race* (Cambridge, MA: MIT Press, 1966), 75ff.

23. Weber, *Cooperation and Discord*, 54–55, spells out three "strategies of reciprocity." See also Thomas C. Schelling, *Arms and Influence* (New Haven, CT: Yale University Press, 1966), 270.

24. Gerard Smith, *Doubletalk* (Lanham, MD: University Press of America, 1985), 17. The distinction between quantitative and qualitative (technology-based) arms rivalry was first made by Huntington, "Arms Races: Prerequisites and Results."

25. Glaser, "Political Consequences of Military Strategy," 513–14. On the security dilemma, see John H. Herz, "Idealist Internationalism and the Security Dilemma," *World Politics* 2 (January 1950): 157–80; and Robert Jervis, "Cooperation under the Security Dilemma," *World Politics* 30 (January 1978): 167–214. For a detailed discussion of the logic and consequences of the security dilemma, see chapter 3 of this book.

26. Schelling and Halperin, *Strategy and Arms Control*, 34. For another study of arms races based on the racers' incomplete information of each other's capabilities and intent, see Kydd, "Arms Races and Arms Control."

27. Robert Jervis has argued that states, highlighting threats from adversaries, frequently underestimate the negative impact their own behavior has on those adversaries. "Hypotheses on Misperception," *World Politics* 20 (July 1968): 454–79.

28. Glaser, "Political Consequences of Military Strategy," 513.

29. Ibid.

30. While those distinguishing between offensive and defensive weapons primarily focus on the technical features of available weaponry for military purposes, perceptions of the offensive/defensive balance also contribute to this distinction. For example, Jack Levy points out that decisions are based on the psychological environment of leaders, and "the inherent difficulty of determining the offensive/defensive balance and the alleged tendency of the military to prepare for the last war rather than the next one may result in some profound misperceptions." "The Offensive/Defensive Balance of Military Technology: A Theoretical and Historical Analysis," *International Studies Quarterly* 28 (June 1984), reprinted in *Conflict after the Cold War*, 3rd ed., ed. Richard K. Betts (New York: Pearson, 2008), 428.

31. In practice, arms rivals enter negotiations partly to further understanding of their opposition's capabilities and intentions. For this negotiating motive, see Fred C. Iklé, *How Nations Negotiate* (New York: Columbia University Press, 1964), 48–50.

32. Glaser, "Political Consequences of Military Strategy," 528–29.

33. Robert Jervis, *Perception and Misperception in International Politics* (Princeton, NJ: Princeton University Press, 1976), 64.

34. Ibid., 66.

35. On crisis prevention as a major power concern, see Alexander L. George, ed., *Managing U.S.-Soviet Rivalry* (Boulder, CO: Westview, 1983), especially the essay by Paul Gordon Lauren, "Crisis Prevention in Nineteenth-Century Diplomacy," 31–64. The Soviet-American interest in crisis prevention is well documented in George, Farley, and Dallin, *U.S.-Soviet Security Cooperation*.

36. Alexander L. George, "Incentives for U.S.-Soviet Security Cooperation and Mutual Adjustments," in George, Farley, and Dallin, *U.S.-Soviet Security Cooperation*, 644.

37. For examples of the importance of relative advantage in this connection, see Alexander L. George, "The Arab-Israeli War of October 1973: Origins and Impact," in *Managing U.S.-Soviet Rivalry* (Boulder, CO: Westview, 1983), 139–54; and, in the same volume, Larry C. Napper, "The African Terrain and U.S.-Soviet Conflict in Angola and Rhodesia: Some Implications for Crisis Prevention," 155–86.

38. Philip J. Farley explains that arms negotiations are not adequate in themselves as "an independent or alternate route to common security. If stability is unlikely without arms control, arms control by itself will not do the job. Arms control policy and programs cannot be any better than foreign and defense policy and programs. . . . When overall foreign security policy seeks a cooperative component [in the superpower era] in the US relationship with the Soviet Union, arms control is an important route and element, but one which supplements and moderates, rather than replaces, defense measures." Philip J. Farley, "Arms Control and U.S.-Soviet Security Cooperation," in George, Farley, and Dallin, *U.S.-Soviet Security Cooperation*, 638.

39. On diplomatic linkage, see Alexander L. George, "Strategies for Facilitating Cooperation," in George, Farley, and Dallin, *U.S.-Soviet Security Cooperation*, 693ff.

40. Michael Krepon, *Strategic Stalemate: Nuclear Weapons and Arms Control in American Politics* (New York: St. Martin's, 1984), 128. See also Morgenthau, *Politics among Nations*, 392ff.; and William A. Schwartz and Charles Derber, "Arms Control: Misplaced Focus," *Bulletin of the Atomic Scientists* 62 (March 1986): 39–44.

41. This argument was made by a panel of consultants led by Robert Oppenheimer that in 1952 addressed problems of Soviet-American competition, when superpower understandings were weak or nonexistent. See Bundy, *Danger and Survival*, 288–89.

42. Barry H. Steiner, *Arms Races, Diplomacy, and Recurring Behavior: Lessons from Two Cases* (Beverly Hills, CA:: Sage, 1973).

43. Adam Watson, *Diplomacy* (Philadelphia: ISHI Publications, 1986), 33.

44. Paul Gordon Lauren, Gordon A. Craig, and Alexander L. George, *Force and Statecraft*, 4th ed. (New York: Oxford University Press, 2007), 154; emphasis in original.

45. For the idea that convergent interests are a benchmark of diplomacy that is shaped by nondiplomatic developments, see Barry H. Steiner, "Diplomacy as Independent and Dependent Variable," *International Negotiation* 6 (2001): 79–104, which argues that the inability of states with convergent interests to act on them had to be explained by nondiplomatic causal factors, such as domestic public opinion and widely held political ideologies. But the ability of states to act on convergent interests may also be ascribed to nondiplomatic developments, such as a heightened threat of war, necessitating quick diplomatic agreement.

46. The practice of insulating relations between great powers from differences over less vital or less consequential international issues (such as defusing small-power civil strife) is developed in Barry H. Steiner, *Collective Preventive Diplomacy* (Albany: State University of New York Press, 2004).

47. The distinction between "bargaining" and "negotiation" is a central preoccupation of chapter 4.

48. Glaser, "Political Consequences of Military Strategy," 509. Arms agreement may, moreover, increase tensions as the rivals question whether their adversary has conformed to the agreement's terms and whether the adversary's violation of the agreement reflects malevolent intent.

49. In his essay, "When Are Arms Races Dangerous? Rational versus Suboptimal Arming," Charles L. Glaser contends that "if a state's security environment necessitates an arms buildup, then arming, as well as the competition that ensues if its adversary responds, is rational," and any dangers of war in that scenario must be attributed to the anarchic international environment and not to the arms race (45). This is also the approach taken by Colin S. Gray, "Urge to Compete."

50. One careful recent diplomatic overview of great power diplomacy in the early nineteenth century failed to acknowledge that the competition was underway and instead observed that "there was a virtual absence of any serious arms race" in the period in question. Lauren, Craig, and George, *Force and Statecraft*, 30.

51. Sources for this case include Richard Cobden, "The Three Panics," in *Political Writings*, vol. 2 (London: Ridgway, 1867), 214–435; Bernard Brodie, *Sea Power in the Machine Age* (Princeton: Princeton University Press, 1941), chs. 3–5; and Huntington, "Arms Races: Prerequisites and Results."

52. Cobden, "Three Panics," 219–20.

53. Sources for this case include: Ernest R. May, John D. Steinbruner, and Thomas W. Wolfe, "History of the Strategic Arms Competition, 1945–1972," 2 vols., unpublished study prepared for the Historical Office, Office of the Secretary of Defense, March 1981, accessed from the U.S. Department of Defense FOIA Reading Room, 1993; Albert Carnesale and Richard N. Haas, eds., *Superpower Arms Control: Setting the Record Straight* (Cambridge, MA: Ballinger, 1987); and a file of newspaper clippings taken from the *New York Times*.

54. Kahn, "Arms Race and Some of Its Hazards," 109.

55. Smith, *Doubletalk*, 30.

56. Robert M. Gates, *From the Shadows* (New York: Simon & Schuster, 2002), 46–47.

57. President Eisenhower's personal concern for the U-2 program (Operation "Clean Up") is indicated in *Foreign Relations of the United States (1958–1960)*, vol. 10, part 1: *Eastern Europe Region: Soviet Union; Cyprus* (Washington, DC: United States Government Printing Office, 1993), 260–62, 264–65; 306–7.

58. Gates, *From the Shadows*, 44.

59. Bruno Tertrais, "Do Arms Races Matter?," in Lennon, *Contemporary Nuclear Debates*, 217.

60. One major study described superpower arms rivalry prior to 1948 as "almost exclusively political." May, Steinbruner, and Wolfe, "History of the Strategic Arms Competition," 280.

61. In practice, the case material reflected not only variance in the independent variables between cases but also variations within one of our two cases: the superpower rivalry. The latter finding suggests that fully developed theory should allow for changeability within cases, and conceptualizations in our independent variables need to be sharpened further. Given the preliminary state of the work reported on here, this point is neglected in the analysis that follows.

62. Weber, *Cooperation and Discord*, 39.

63. For an argument against convergent cultures, see Gray, *House of Cards*.

64. Brodie, *Sea Power in the Machine Age*, 253.

65. Huntington, "Arms Races: Prerequisites and Results," 109.

66. As an example of diplomatic fashion, Anglo-French tensions in the New World were largely excluded from the diplomatic agenda because the British and French governments were seeking maximum flexibility until war finally made negotiation necessary. Patrice Louis-René Higonnet, "The Origins of the Seven Years' War," *Journal of Modern History* 40 (March 1968): 78.

67. Gates, *From the Shadows*, 41.

68. Ibid., 47.

69. Neorealists especially stress the importance of position in the international hierarchy of states; see Waltz, *Theory of International Politics*; and Mearsheimer, *Tragedy of Great Power Politics*. An example of an arms competition in which competitor concern with security was much less important than concern with hierarchy is the Anglo-American naval competition following the First World War.

70. On the Pakistan-India competition, see Sumit Ganguly and S. Paul Kapur, eds., *Nuclear Proliferation in South Asia: Crisis Behavior and the Bomb* (New York: Routledge, 2009); and Scott D. Sagan, ed., *Inside Nuclear South Asia* (Stanford, CA:

Stanford University Press, 2009). On the competition between the United States and North Korea, see Leon V. Sigal, *Disarming Strangers* (Princeton: Princeton University Press, 1998); Joel S. Wit, Daniel B. Poneman, and Robert L. Gallucci, *Going Critical* (Washington, DC: Brookings Institution Press, 2004); and Michael O'Hanlon and Mike Mochizuki, *Crisis on the Korean Peninsula* (New York: McGraw-Hill, 2003).

8

Diplomacy as Effect

Public Opinion as Constraint and Pressure

This chapter studies diplomatic statecraft as effect, responsive to or dependent on nondiplomatic sources of influence. As noted earlier, these sources narrow or challenge the ability of diplomats to act on their preferences.[1] To understand their impact, it is necessary to probe how the causal influences are brought to bear on diplomats and how diplomats would act when left to themselves. The focus for diplomatic effect must be on the diplomatic choice of how to react to oppositional opinion—whether to defer to it and modify the diplomatic program or to resist opposition and pursue diplomatic priorities.[2] The ability of diplomats to adapt diplomatically to nondiplomatic influences must also be considered.

The source of influence on diplomats to be studied here, the independent variable, is domestic public opinion, defined as "opinions held by private persons which governments find it prudent to heed."[3] Marshaling popular opposition to foreign policies is commonly motivated by political as well as substantive differences. Foreign policies have external (international) and internal (domestic) determinants, and factions and advocates pushing for preferred policies use externally generated action to enhance their own domestic agendas. To explain foreign policy, Robert Putnam argues, "we must aim . . . for 'general equilibrium' theories that account simultaneously for the interaction of domestic and international factors."[4]

The concern here, however, is not with mutual accommodation between domestic and internal influences on policy but with the one-sided result when they clash to such a degree that no accommodation between them is possible.[5]

Political realists, who maintain that foreign policy requirements should receive a higher priority than their domestic counterparts, have focused on such situations. They have concluded that oppositional public opinion in democratic countries curtailed diplomats' flexibility and independence to meet foreign policy needs because the diplomats, concerned about voter support and retribution, accommodated to public demands and thereby weakened classical diplomatic norms and their own effectiveness.[6] While many developments weakened classical statecraft norms, establishing the impact of oppositional public opinion would be a first step to understand shifting diplomatic conduct.

This chapter uses conflict between war and peace preferences to examine a condition in which arguments and demands on diplomats from a domestic political system conflict with those from externally directed interests based on state relationships. It explores instances in which public opinion in a democratic polity, focused on some perceived injustice at the hands of a foreign power, clamors for war at the same time that government diplomacy is committed to peace with that power. Given such conflict, diplomats must choose between acquiescing in domestic belligerent opinion and deciding on war, or resisting the belligerence and remaining committed to peace. Joe Hagan, supporting an inquiry into this condition, writes that "although much is made of analyzing how domestic politics contribute to war, explaining when strong domestic pressure does not provoke the use of force would also seem of critical theoretical value."[7]

Because government often affects popular attitudes, the latter are difficult to study as an independent element. Moreover, foreign policy specialists have traditionally viewed public opinion as policy support rather than as opposition. For example, John Spanier and Eric M. Uslaner, studying the process of making foreign policy, argue that the public's most important foreign policy role is to respond to executive officials, and that these officials, interested in "reinforc[ing] the 'we' in domestic politics," have an advantage in influencing the public.[8] "In truth," Morgenthau writes, "public opinion is not a static thing to be ascertained and quantified by polls as legal precedents are by the science of law and as that data of nature are by the natural sciences. Rather it is a dynamic thing to be created and continuously re-created by . . . political leadership which also creates the foreign policy to be supported by public opinion."[9]

Others question this perspective. Continuing differences between elected officials and the public highlighted by American opinion polls suggest that mobilizing public support for foreign policies is of limited utility. Benjamin I. Page and Marshall M. Bouton, providing an empirical case for examining public opinion as an independent political element, write that "most public officials say they want to go in the *opposite direction* from what most members of the public want, on so many important foreign policy issues—including major issues of war and peace and economic relations."[10]

To examine public opinion's impact on diplomacy, we limit analysis to instances in which government is unable to manipulate popular attitudes. This condition applies when oppositional opinion is strong enough to rule out short-term governmental counterefforts to affect it. When political leaders' preferences and the demands of their domestic opposition conflict *and compete* for official approval, the two provide a window for probing diplomacy as effect.

Understanding oppositional public opinion as an independent variable also requires allowing for different intensities of oppositional opinion. This is facilitated here by distinguishing constraint and pressure as manifestations of oppositional public opinion. *Constraint* is defined as an obstacle to or veto of specific executive foreign policy behavior. A passive form of influence, it generally does not impinge on diplomatic priorities or prevent policy autonomy.[11] Leaders may anticipate and defuse constraints. Bruce Russett and Harvey Starr write that public opinion affects policy by "setting broad limits of constraint and identifying a range of policies within which decision makers must choose if they are not to face retaliation in competitive elections."[12] Realists, whose understanding of the conflict between governments and publics is the starting point of this chapter, cite opinion constraints as the main source of the impact of public opinion. *Political pressure* is active effort to gain a specific foreign policy decision. It inherently threatens diplomats by limiting their flexibility on an issue in which they cannot sidestep substantive political conflict. Opinion pressures are therefore more challenging for diplomats than are constraints.

A review of the literature on public opinion in relation to foreign policy uses the realist outlook as a starting point but also critiques it and elaborates on the idea, missing in realist writings, that oppositional opinion can focus on concern with a political system's balance of political power and not only on differences over policy.[13] The distinction between constraint and pressure, when applied to this literature, draws attention to the gap between the realists, who emphasize constraints, and their critics, who discuss pressures.

Taking opinion pressures as more important for generating opposition between governments and publics, the chapter employs the focused comparison method to compare four cases, each reflecting such political turbulence that government cannot affect public attitudes.[14] The case comparisons take account of the preoccupation by government officials and oppositional opinion with the balance of political power and with policy issues. The most important finding from the perspective of diplomacy as effect is that governments defending peace requirements can adapt to belligerent opinion by collaborating with the state targeted by domestic belligerence, insulating diplomacy against popular belligerence.

I. THE LITERATURE

Political realists concede oppositional opinion's impact on policy but reject it as independently shaping policy for two reasons: first, they maintain that democratic countries' statecraft should be preoccupied with objective state needs and not with the conflicts and compromises usually made on domestic questions, and, second, they believe that the public's appreciation of foreign policy is deficient because it is uninformed by an understanding of the challenges of world politics. We will deal with these in turn.

According to the realists, public opinion can be influential only when weak leaders allow it to be, accommodating to the public because of their concerns about voter support and voter retribution should they act independently. Realists cite repeated instances in which leaders knowingly impair objective national needs and concede to oppositional opinion. "In order to win Congress over and to placate public opinion," Morgenthau argues when addressing postwar American politics, "[the president] may well be tempted to throw overboard the more controversial elements of . . . policy [and] win the support of Congress and of public opinion for policies that are hardly worth supporting," and to "gamble away the interests and perhaps the very existence of the nation for a fleeting triumph in the next elections."[15]

Gordon Craig and Alexander George, addressing the same problem in twentieth-century British history, make a strikingly similar appraisal. "The retribution that [British] public feeling could wreak upon statesmen and diplomats seeking to deal with complicated international problems in accordance with the rules of *raison d'etat* or national interest was real," they wrote, "and this was intimidating. It tended to make the people who were charged with the conduct of foreign policy more cautious than their nineteenth-century predecessors had been. It induced them to alter the way they did their business. And in several ways, it made them less effective than their predecessors."[16]

The deficiency in public attitudes—realists' second point—is visible, according to Morgenthau, in the gap "between a good foreign policy and a bad one that public opinion demands."[17] "The popular mind," Morgenthau writes, "unaware of the fine distinctions of the statesman's thinking, reasons more often than not in the simple moralistic and legalistic terms of absolute good and absolute evil."[18] Writing about interwar British opinion, Harold Nicolson notes, "The difficulty of inducing the people to think rapidly and correctly—the danger that their initial emotion may, although rapid, be incorrect—tempt the modern negotiator to avoid those problems which are likely to prove unpopular and to concentrate on secondary issues which will be more comprehensible, and therefore more welcome, to the popular mind."[19]

Public opinion analysts, appraising the impact of public opinion on empirical rather than normative grounds, deflated that impact, emphasizing the difficulty of translating oppositional opinion into policy impact. V. O. Key, in his classic portrait of American public opinion, highlights how the American political system depressed the impact of oppositional public opinion. He maintains that in foreign as well as domestic policy arenas, "the ultimate weapon of public opinion is the minority party . . . a crowd of outs who can be elevated to power—and the capacity to boot the ins from office. The mechanism is cumbersome."[20] Party influence, Key goes on, suffered from the low influence of popular attitudes more generally, as domestic issue alignments have not coincided with those on foreign policy. "When popular cleavages do not coincide," he writes, "party groups within the electorate may encounter the most serious difficulty in the maintenance of sufficient unity for effective action. Within the representative body party groups may be converted into a congeries of factions, no one of which possesses the power to govern."[21]

Large-scale interparty cooperation on foreign affairs in Congress further weakened postwar political opposition to the president's foreign policy. The bipartisanship was intended, according to an assistant secretary of state in 1949, "to make it virtually impossible for 'momentous divisions' to occur in our foreign affairs."[22] In Great Britain, interwar party competition was similarly contained. "There was no profound cleavage between [British] parties," the historian A. J. P. Taylor writes of that period, "despite much synthetic bitterness. They offered [after the First World War] old policies which had been their stock-in-trade before the war." Taylor characterized British foreign policy as "largely an agreed matter between the parties after the fall of Lloyd George [in 1922], except in regard to Soviet Russia, and even here the differences were smaller than they seemed."[23]

Morgenthau's observation about the deficiency in the public's foreign policy attitudes was challenged by American polling results, which suggested, according to Page and Bouton, that the public's foreign policy attitudes "have generally been sensible, coherent, and logically related to a reasonable set of foreign policy goals," and they question whether leaders can do better by affecting public attitudes.[24] "Our detailed look at Americans' foreign policy preferences," they conclude, "indicates that they could indeed generally serve as a useful guide to decision makers."[25]

Beyond these normative issues is a question of conceptualization: realists focus on issue differences and election dynamics to define the gap between governmental officials and public attitudes, but the gap at times extends to the preoccupation held by policymakers and the opposition with the balance of political power. Jack Levy and William Mabe, defining "political opposition as a group or collection of groups that often engages in the activity of opposing the government's policies or leadership," distinguish its oppositional nature from its opposition to policies, "one of many choices open to an opposition group."[26] For example, a group may be motivated to oppose war-making because it believes that the war's result could affect the balance of political power between the government elite and the opposition.

Whereas leaders faced with choosing between acting on their own peace preferences and responding to public belligerence might well decide in favor of the former if opposition was limited to policy differences, an unstable or volatile balance of domestic power might lead them in a different direction. "Wars of primarily partisan and internal dynamic," the historian Arno Mayer writes, "are decided by political actors and classes whose political tenure and social position tend to be insecure and whose latitude for foreign policy decisions tends to be circumscribed."[27] Domestic and external needs of the regime fuse together through the regime's need to legitimate its leadership. "Even though opposition may stem from domestic issues quite unrelated to international affairs," Joe Hagan writes of this approach, "foreign policy becomes engulfed by domestic considerations because leaders manipulate themes of nationalism and foreign threats as a way of diverting attention away from domestic problems and enhancing the legitimacy of the regime." After diverting their people by blaming foreign states for domestic problems, leaders may find it difficult to back down in crisis. The consequence "is a bias for confrontation, if not war, in foreign policy."[28]

Mayer documented class-based agitation in late nineteenth-and early twentieth-century Europe that led many governments to highlight an external enemy to foster domestic unity. Counterrevolutionary agitation rather than elections became the primary governmental concern in many European countries, when, according to Mayer, a counterelite sought to mobilize against progressive parties' "crisis strata"—enfranchised groups such as small and middle farmers, shopkeepers, white-collar employees, professionals, civil service employees, laborers, and ambitious academics—who were "insecure in both income and status, [and] harbor[ed] latent resentments, fears, and anxieties." Oppositional leaders could relate to these groups because, "more likely than not they have family, geographic, status, professional, and economic roots in the poor gentry, *petite bourgeoisie*, or new middle classes." Creating a unified political movement in opposition to then-ruling socialist elites, they manipulated "psychic discomforts" of these sectors of the population toward groups higher and lower in the socioeconomic hierarchy. Aiming at "power from above," they sought the rulers' cooperation to protect national traditions while blaming them for a diminished ability to do so on their own.[29]

Although Mayer makes a strong case for leaders being guided by *domestic* pressures to define foreign policy needs, an alternative possibility is that vital foreign policy considerations may shape leaders' management of domestic pressures. Resistance can be motivated by the defense of vital foreign policy interests or by the defense of stakes in the balance of political power, a motive that might incline leaders to prevent a foreign policy issue from serving as a wedge for political challenge against them later.

II. CONSTRAINTS AND PRESSURES

Our distinction between constraints and pressures reveals another division between the realists and their critics. Realists, who argue that public opinion was more influential on foreign policy than was appropriate for diplomatic needs, tend to concentrate on opinion *constraints*, the passive form of public attitude. This emphasis, which is apparent from the examples of leader accommodation that they cite, underpins their critique of leaders and diplomats who *avoided* conflicts with public viewpoints. Those who evaluate public attitudes through empirical analysis tend instead to concentrate on opinion *pressures*, which, as has been indicated, provide a potentially stronger opinion impact than do constraints because they directly conflict with governmental priorities. Belligerent pressures, for example, tend to be more problematic than belligerant constraints for peace-committed diplomats. Deflating the influence of public opinion pressures therefore require more extensive argument than that put forward by the realists. To do so, public opinion itself—and not merely how it is managed—requires attention.

A. Constraints

Morgenthau urges government to avoid "sacrifice[ing] what it considers good policy upon the altar of public opinion," and to abstain from "widening the unavoidable gap between the requirements of good foreign policy and the preferences of public opinion."[30] Finding policy leaders more concerned about the second of these prescriptions than about the first, he faults them for fearing public opinion, accommodating to public attitudes "for the apparent primary purpose of gaining popularity at home."[31] The issues he cites to illustrate conflict avoidance reflect opinion constraints rather than pressures. One example is the Truman administration's decision to "shy away from realistic negotiations with the Soviet Union," in spite of appearing to believe they were necessary. "Frightened by a public opinion that is in good measure but a figment of a politician's imagination," Morgenthau observes, "the Administration has suspended diplomacy altogether [with the Soviet Union] rather than face with courage and determination the accusation of appeasement, or of worse, by demagogues who represent only a small minority of the American people."[32]

Morgenthau also criticized a Republican congressional proposal to overthrow by aerial bombardment the Communist regime in China that had taken power in 1949 and to restore Chiang Kai-shek's rule in that country. "The Eisenhower administration," he writes, "frightened like its predecessor by this specter of public opinion, at least appeared to have accepted the objectives and expectations of the opposition and thus allowed its own policies to be judged by the standards of the opposition. . . . The executive branch had thus become the prisoner of the opposition, [t]oo responsible to do what the opposition wanted it to do and prevented by its fear of public opinion from substituting a positive policy of its own for that of the opposition, [and] was reduced to having no positive policy at all."[33]

Realist commentators similarly fault interwar British government's accommodation to public attitudes. "The Bonar Law-Baldwin government of 1922–1924, the MacDonald government of 1924, and the Baldwin government of 1924–1929," Gordon A. Craig contends, "all tended to follow rather than to lead public opinion in foreign affairs, to satisfy the immediate desires of the electorate rather than the ultimate interests of the nation, to make foreign policy the prisoner of domestic politics rather than to seek to pursue a farsighted independent course and to carry the public with them step by step."[34] Illustrating this deference, Craig singles out the Ramsay McDonald cabinet negotiation of the Anglo-Russian agreement of 1924, which dealt with compensation for Tsarist debts repudiated and British property confiscated by the Communist government after the Russian Revolution. The negotiations were deadlocked, and about to be broken up by the British Foreign Office, whereupon a delegation of Labour Party members, who had been holding parallel talks with the Russian delegation, argued that the breakdown of talks would fatally impair the Labour Party's reputation. The members submitted a vague formula to save the talks that bridged no differences yet was accepted by the British government.[35]

Harold Nicolson, providing another illustration of the British leadership's fear of public opinion in the interwar period, notes how its choice of diplomatic issues was designed to avoid overexciting the public. He recalls that twenty-three separate, highly publicized international conferences were held between January 1920 and December 1922 in the midst of "intense popular expectancy." The conferences were staffed by politicians rather than professional diplomatists or experts, and "the negotiators . . . again and again . . . evaded the central problem and dealt only with subsidiary manifestations of that problem."[36]

Realists do not probe the limits of deference to public opinion constraints, two of which have been noted in this chapter. One is the perceived importance of foreign policy interests. Leaders would be expected to override foreign policy constraints when they believe the interests at stake are vital. Kenneth Waltz has argued that "a President who does what the moment seems to require can then often expect that he and his party will have to pay the domestic political bill, however unjustly it may be drawn. Here . . . foreign policy is not so very different from domestic policy."[37] The classic case in which perceptions of vital interest overrode opinion constraints is President Franklin Roosevelt's secret decision, contrary to the will and legislation of an isolationist Congress, to contest the German economic blockade of England in 1940 and to authorize American naval forces to "shoot on sight" German submarines standing in the way.[38]

A second incentive to override oppositional opinion is a leader's perception that the balance of political power is at stake. Rising oppositional pressures may increase the incentives for policymakers to resist popular pressures when they understand their political position to be in jeopardy. However, opinion constraints, which leaders can sidestep, do not place the power balance between leaders and oppositional publics at risk. Realists, who have not conceptualized opinion pressure as a problem for national leaders, would not be expected to identify this override possibility. But because oppositional opinion potentially exercises a greater impact on policy by pressure than by constraints, as we have noted, the override option is explicitly considered in this chapter's cases and comparisons, all of which focus on opinion pressures.

B. Pressures

Students of American and British politics play down the impact of oppositional opinion on policy by addressing opinion pressures. V. O. Key had opinion pressures in mind when he wrote in his classic study of American public opinion that "the generality of public preferences [and] the low intensity of the opinions of many people . . . point to the existence of a wide latitude for the exercise of creative leadership."[39] He also portrays American politics and party competition as subdued, citing the difficulty for the opposition party to mobilize public opinion to challenge policy elites.

Similarly, Waltz, comparing American and British political cultures, points out that while democratic opinion often diverged from governmental policy, it allowed for considerable leadership autonomy.[40] In England, "fusion of powers and the concentration of responsibility encourage governments to avoid problems while broad accommodations are sought," whereas "in the United States, where it is publicly unclear just who has done what, everyone can try to do something. The fragmentation of power and the confusion of responsibility encourage competitive political habits and in the twentieth century have more often than not produced governments of innovative zeal and vigorous leadership."[41]

This gap between the realists and their critics generates a puzzle. If the critics are correct to maintain that public opinion does not generally threaten foreign policy priorities, it is difficult to understand why policymakers should be so insecure about the public's attitudes, as the realists maintain. The priority attached by realists to foreign policy is not a satisfactory answer to this question because it logically discourages concessions to public opinion. A second answer is that leaders have an interest in avoiding conflict with nongovernmental groups on less important questions to enhance their legitimacy and capability to pursue vital diplomatic initiatives outside the public arena unhindered by public criticism or complaint. Legitimacy, a measure of policy control and leadership potential, diminishes officials' vulnerability to direct, and perhaps irresponsible, oppositional public opinion. Gaining it, however, requires avoiding conflict on the domestic front.[42]

III. CASES OF OPPOSITIONAL PRESSURE

We now implement a focused comparison of four cases to develop answers to the main issues identified in this chapter. Our cases are (1) the Genêt affair (1793), (2) the Jay Treaty episode (1793–1794), (3) American entry into the Spanish-American War (1897–1898), and (4) Italy and postwar peacemaking (1918).[43] Our very small case sample incorporates a very large temporal range.

Our main interest is in the *consequences* of that intrusion for diplomatic behavior rather than in its causes. Diplomats in each of our cases were placed in a position in which, because of the pressures of belligerent domestic opinion, they were required to choose between a peace policy supported by their understanding of the national interest, on the one hand, and war initiation supported by public opinion, on the other. To display the greatest challenge to governmental officials in making this choice, each of our cases illustrates oppositional pressures. The pressures create two possible independent incentives for policy officials to resist public opinion opposition: (1) the high importance attached by government officials to the pursuit of peace, and (2) the large concern of those officials, in accord with the logic of Levy and Mabe, that the balance of political power between government and its domestic opponents might shift against the government, possibly through the use of foreign policy as a political wedge concern.

In accord with the focused comparison method, each of our cases is treated as deviant and is studied with the same list of questions. The common questions are detailed in table 8.1.

1. The Genêt Affair (1793)[44]

Following the successful American revolt against English rule, decisively assisted by alliance with France, the Washington administration defined a policy of neutrality in relation to ongoing Anglo-French naval warfare. The French alliance remained popular following the war, however, among Americans who remained hostile to Great Britain during the Anglo-French War in the 1790s. "Washington was aggravated," according to Richard van Alstyne, "by the internal division of opinion, which was traceable to a smouldering resentment against Britain on the one hand and a foolish attachment to French republicanism on the other."[45] The issue was framed as promoting support for France. Pro-French sentiment increased during a visit to the United States in 1793 by Citizen Genêt, an official French representative seeking American "benevolent" neutrality.[46] Genêt, carrying an " 'appeal to the people' over Washington's head," sought to influence the public to elect a Congress that favored the French cause.[47] Benevolent neutrality was said to "ha[ve] weight, and was unquestionably supported by a large number, if not a majority, of the American *people* and by numerous important public officials."[48] Thomas Jefferson, divesting himself temporarily of his position as secretary of state, actively concerted with Genêt.

Table 8.1.   Questions for Oppositional Pressure Cases

1. How did diplomats understand the interests of their country? What was the basis for their preference for peace?
2. What was the source of belligerent public opinion?
3. How was oppositional opinion brought to bear on diplomats?
4. How was the choice between peace and war framed for diplomats?
5. How did the diplomats decide, and why?

The administration held firm to its prior neutrality. According to Alexis de Tocqueville, "the sympathies of the [American] people declared themselves with so much violence in favor of France that nothing but the inflexible character of Washington and the immense popularity which he enjoyed could have prevented the Americans from declaring war against England."[49] Anti-English hostility could not be effective until grassroots sentiment activated Congress to rewrite American neutrality law, but Congress was not in session in the summer of 1793, when Genêt sought support. The alliance was left in the form that it took during the Revolutionary War, a guarantee of each state's territory in North America and the West Indies.

2. The Jay Treaty (1793–1795)[50]

Official American neutrality and peace-mindedness in the Anglo-French War was challenged by seizures of American merchant vessels by the British fleet and lingering British support of Indian tribes in poorly demarcated territory in the American West, both of which provoked popular hostility to England. The issue divided the two major American political parties. James Madison and Thomas Jefferson, advocating economic retaliation against England for its abuses, divided openly from Alexander Hamilton, who argued for defusing disputes with England to encourage British investment in the United States. Madison and Jefferson viewed foreign policy as a reflection of domestic policy, in particular the need for popular control of government and economic independence, while Hamilton believed domestic policy priorities should be subordinated to foreign policy, especially commercial alliance with England.

The Federalist administration appointed John Jay in April 1794 as special envoy to deal with outstanding British-American issues, reflecting, according to Paul Varg, "that the governing group at home desperately needed some kind of treaty that would put an end to the dangerous tendency to take hostile measures toward England."[51] The resulting treaty compensated Americans for losses to the British on the high seas and provided for arbitral commissions to determine boundaries in the West.

House debate on the Jay Treaty, which came about when the House was required to initiate a bill paying for arbitral commissions created by the treaty, rested on foreign policy assumptions but was highly partisan. Madison, the leader of the opposition to the treaty in the House, hesitated at first to campaign against it because of his inability to unite his party with a single course of action. However, after the first caucus of his Republican Party occurred on this issue and enough votes were registered to defeat the treaty, Madison advocated outright defeat. The Federalists fought back, using the fear of war with Britain and the ruin of merchant voyages that would ensue; Madison's faction denied that rejection of the treaty would mean war with England, the main question in House debate. In the Senate, treaty advocates were prepared to virtually shut down the government if the Jay Treaty were defeated. In the end, peace was ensured when the treaty prevailed in the House by one vote.

3. American Entry into the Spanish-American War (1897–1898)[52]

Responding to harsh Spanish suppression of rebellion against Spanish rule in Cuba, the administration of President William McKinley at first followed the least aggressive stance and sought diplomatic flexibility. Public alarm about atrocities growing out Spain's forcible Cuban pacification program led to a concurrent resolution from the Republican-controlled Congress recognizing Cuban belligerency, but the administration rejected the resolution while prodding Spain to accept Cuban autonomy and bring an end to forcible pacification and violence.

Late in October 1897, a new Spanish government recalled its army chief from Cuba, ended pacification, instituted some reforms, and promised home rule to the island. These proved inadequate, and the Cuban rebels rejected home rule. In December 1897 the administration gave Spain more time to pacify the island but held out the possibility American action if the rebellion were not ended in the "near future."

Following the explosion sinking the American battleship *Maine* in Havana Harbor in February 1898, American economic elites shifted from resisting to acquiescing in war, and there ensued for two months "a tug of war . . . [that] would pit the people against William McKinley."[53] Late in March, McKinley issued an ultimatum to Spain insisting on a Cuban armistice until October 1898 and, if peace negotiation failed during that time, Spanish acceptance of the United States as the final arbiter between Spain and the insurgents. Spain on April 10 proclaimed a temporary armistice, but a day later McKinley, accommodating to the aroused public's demands for war with Spain—including strong sentiment in his own party—asked Congress for authority to intervene militarily in Cuba.

4. Italian Peacemaking after World War I (1918–1920)[54]

Italian war-making in the First World War had been predicated on territorial gains at the expense of the Triple Alliance adversary; these gains were conceded to Italy by Britain, France, and Russia in the secret 1915 Treaty of

London. The gains included Trentino, the Dalmatian coast of the Adriatic, and territory in Turkey. In postwar peacemaking at Versailles, Italy strongly sought not only this territory but also Fiume, which Italian forces had captured from the Austro-Hungarians just before the end of the war. These demands were viewed by Italy as compensation for its war costs; Woodrow Wilson opposed Italy's claim to Fiume and the Dalmatian coast.

The "sacred" character of the Treaty of London and the Fiume demand united Italians,[55] but jingoism was enhanced further by intense conflicts between Italian political parties. As a result, new territory was sought by the government to dampen party divisions. According to Mayer, "The Left denounced the smoldering horrors and uneven sacrifices of war in its campaign to discredit the political forces, symbols, and institutions which were blocking wide-ranging constitutional, economic, and social reforms. In turn, the Right pointed up the disloyalty, the defeatism, and the *renunciarismo* of the Left with a view to discrediting the political carriers of basic change."[56] Benito Mussolini, a counterrevolutionary, led demands for a victor's peace. The Italian foreign minister, Sidney Sonnino, said to have "ignored the rest of the world while pursuing Italy's territorial interests with parochial and unbending single-mindedness," maintained that unless Italian territorial demands were accepted, Italy's internal crisis between leftist and rightist parties would worsen, and its government might no longer be able to keep order.[57]

With action by the Versailles conference on Italy's demands imminent and Wilson's possible opposition to the demands, Italy experienced in April 1919 a "week of simmering civil war," as "the ongoing radicalization of the Left merely reinforced the Right in its resolve to hold the government to an intransigent foreign policy course."[58] Wilson encouraged Italian moderates to influence the Italian prime minister to make territorial concessions, but the moderates were not strong enough to do so, illustrating that Wilson's efforts to reform the international system were "fatally emasculat[ed]" by counterrevolution.[59] In 1919, Italian forces landed at Adalia, in southwestern Anatolia, adding to the Dodecanese and Rhodes that Italy received under the Treaty of Sèvres. Three years later, a Fascist coup overthrew the Fiume government and Italian troops occupied the town.

IV. ANALYZING THE CASES

The willingness and motive of peace-minded diplomats to resist belligerent opinion varied in our cases. The cases also varied in the importance of foreign policy and political motives in stimulating resistance. The two motives had independent sources; they could work together to reinforce the choice to resist opinion pressures, or they could be in tension, making choice more difficult.

Political motives combined with the perception of vital interest in the Jay Treaty case to bring resistance to oppositional opinion. While American policy officials might well have resisted if only the party conflict or only the aspect of vital interest were present, the probability of resistance increased with the presence of both factors. At the opposite extreme, political and less-than-vital national interest considerations together strengthened the case for accommodating domestic pressures. In the case of the Spanish-American War, expression of public opinion was not due to party conflict, so the wedge issue did not arise; although McKinley had doubts about American preparedness for war with Spain, his administration, interested in maximizing diplomatic flexibility, does not appear to have regarded preventing such war with Spain as vital.

In between these cases are the Genêt and Italian cases, in which only one pressure factor is present. The Genêt case was not one of political party conflict, yet the administration held back from revising the French alliance in order to protect American neutrality in the ongoing Anglo-French War, something it saw as vital. In the Italian case, virulent domestic party conflict dictated territorial acquisition irrespective of interstate relationships. In that example, diplomats' understanding of national interests was based on domestic considerations. Intense Italian party conflict not only brought accommodation to belligerent party pressures but also led Italian diplomatists to view their country's territorial objectives as vital.

V. CONCLUSIONS: DIPLOMACY AS EFFECT

This chapter demonstrated the feasibility of studying diplomacy as effect—that is, diplomacy responding to a nondiplomatic influence. Some prerequisites for doing so are evident in the foregoing analysis. First, nondiplomatic alternatives must be conceptualized as competing for support with action linked to diplomats' own understanding of policy conditions and needs. The analyst must provide a framework in which the choice can logically vary; while many types of choices might be appropriate for such a framework, the interest in theory would encourage selecting cases with a very clear-cut choice, such as between peace and war.

Second, studying diplomacy as effect requires a focus on the strongest imperatives of the independent variable that enable it to compete with diplomatic imperatives generated by international politics. Indeed, the usefulness of diplomacy as effect seems increased to the degree that diplomats are faced with major challenges and severe decision-making tests, as in the cases considered in this chapter. In these cases, the necessary active public opinion ingredient providing that competition was oppositional pressure; a more formidable test for diplomats than constraint, oppositional pressure sharply conflicted with diplomatic imperatives generated by state relationships. Political realist writings centered on opinion constraints were deemed inadequate in this respect. However, the theorist seeking to bolster the nondiplomatic independent variable by distinguishing the domestic political process (highlighting public opinion) from the international system (highlighting diplomatic imperatives) is supported by the political realist, who also makes this distinction.

Third, the theorist must allow that diplomatic choices may be conditioned by domestic politics, as in the McKinley and Italian cases discussed here. The potential for this result is bolstered by the Levy-Mabe idea that leaders accommodate to opinion pressure not only on the basis of differences over policy with their public opposition but also because they perceive power relationships with the opposition to be at stake. Alternatively, diplomats faced with a two-sided choice between peace and war may resist their opposition for domestic political reasons as much as for national interest considerations. Domestic party politics can dictate diplomats' definition of foreign policy priorities, as in the Italian case; at the other extreme, perception of vital foreign interests, coupled with concern about the domestic balance of power, may provoke resistance to opinion pressures, as in the Jay Treaty case.

Finally, even when peace-minded foreign policy priorities are challenged by strong belligerent opinion, policy officials can use statecraft to defend their priorities, especially when they perceive them to be vitally important. Such action, reflected in John Jay's successful mission to preempt the hostile American action toward England then contemplated by Congress, illustrates diplomatic adaptation to causal developments challenging statecraft. Adaptation must be considered before it can be established that specific nondiplomatic developments weaken or permanently alter the character of statecraft.

Diplomatic adaptation, which remains unappreciated by realists, has implications for diplomatic theory. Realists have argued that diplomatic accommodation to public opinion weakens norms and procedures associated with classical diplomacy. However, diplomatic adaptation to oppositional opinion defends existing norms, procedures, and patterns of statecraft questioned by public opinion and does not relax them. Such adaptation must be taken into account by diplomatic theorists before older norms, procedures, and patterns are treated as obsolete. The larger this adaptive ability, the larger the diplomatic potential to mitigate influences brought to bear against diplomatists' preferences.

NOTES

1. On the distinction between independent and dependent variable, see chapter 5.

2. On this point, see Brian C. Rathbun, *Diplomacy's Value* (Ithaca, NY: Cornell University Press, 2014), 2.

3. V. O. Key Jr., *Public Opinion and American Democracy* (New York: Knopf, 1964). On public opinion as it affects foreign policy see James N. Rosenau, *Public Opinion and Foreign Policy: An Operational Formulation* (New York: Random House, 1961); John Mueller, *War, Presidents, and Public Opinion* (New York: Wiley, 1973); Benjamin I. Page and Robert Shapiro, "Effects of Public Opinion on Policy," *American Political Science Review* 77 (March 1983): 175–90; Benjamin I. Page and Jason Barabas, "Foreign Policy Gaps between Citizens and Leaders," *International Studies Quarterly* 44 (September 2000): 339–64; John W. Spanier and Eric M. Uslaner, *American Foreign Policy Making and the Democratic Dilemmas*, 6th ed. (New York: Macmillan, 1994), 208–36; Benjamin I. Page and Robert Y. Shapiro, *The Rational Public: Fifty Years of Trends in Americans' Policy Preferences* (Chicago: University of Chicago Press, 1992); Benjamin I. Page with Marshall M. Bouton, *The Foreign Policy Disconnect* (Chicago: University of Chicago Press, 2006); Jack S. Levy and William F. Mabe Jr., "Politically Motivated Opposition to War," *International Studies Review* 6 (March 2004): 65–83; Thomas Risse-Kappen, "Public Opinion, Domestic Structure, and Foreign Policy in Liberal Democracies," *World Politics* 43 (July 1991): 479–512; Ole R. Holsti, "Public Opinion and Foreign Policy: Challenges to the Almond-Lippmann Consensus," *International Studies Quarterly* 36 (December 1992): 439–66; Bruce W. Jentleson and Rebecca L. Britton, "Still Pretty Prudent: Post-Cold War American Opinion on the Use of Military Force," *Journal of Conflict Resolution* 42 (August 1998): 395–417; and Richard C. Eichenberg, "Victory Has Many Friends: U.S. Public Opinion and the Use of Military Force," *International Security* 30 (Summer 2005): 140–77.

4. Robert D. Putnam, "Diplomacy and Domestic Politics: The Logic of Two-Level Games," *International Organization* 42 (Summer 1988): 430.

5. Discussions of the impact of domestic politics on foreign policy behavior include Jack S. Levy, "Domestic Politics and War," in *The Origin and Prevention of Major Wars*, ed. Robert I. Rotberg and Theodore K. Rabb (New York: Cambridge University Press, 1989), 79–100; Barry B. Hughes, *The Domestic Context of American Foreign Policy* (San Francisco: W. H. Freeman, 1978); Natsuko H. Nicholls, Paul K. Huth, and Benjamin J. Appel, "When Is Domestic Political Unrest Related to International Conflict? Diversionary Theory and Japanese Foreign Policy, 1890–1941," *International Studies Quarterly* 46 (December 2010): 916–37; Susan Peterson, *Crisis Bargaining and the State* (Ann Arbor: University of Michigan Press, 1999); Joe D. Hagan, "Domestic Political Systems and War Proneness," *Mershon International Studies Review* 38 (October 1994): 183–207; Kenneth N. Waltz, *Foreign Policy and Democratic Politics: The American and British Experience*

(London: Longmans, 1968); Robert Keohane, *After Hegemony: Cooperation and Discord in the World Political Economy* (Princeton: Princeton University Press, 1984), Robert Keohane, *International Institutions and State Power* (Boulder, CO: Westview, 1989); Michael W. Doyle, "Liberalism and World Politics," *American Political Science Review* 80 (December 1986): 1151–69; and Arno J. Mayer, *Dynamics of Counterrevolution in Europe, 1870–1956* (New York: Harper & Row, 1971).

6. Gordon A. Craig and Alexander L. George, *Force and Statecraft*, 3rd ed. (New York: Oxford University Press, 1995), 286. Craig and George claim that the prominence of public opinion as an independent political factor "erod[ing] both the conditions and the norms that supported the classical European [diplomatic] system" was brought about by the great popular sacrifice experienced by the British public in the First World War (53, 286), but the phenomenon was reflected a century earlier in the United States. Selection of cases to be compared in this chapter takes account of this earlier experience.

7. Hagan, "Domestic Political Systems," 189.

8. John Spanier and Eric M. Uslaner, *How American Foreign Policy Is Made* (New York: Praeger, 1974), 93. See also Spanier and Uslaner, *Democratic Dilemmas*, 229, 233. The "rally 'round the flag" attitude can be used by governments to bolster support for their behavior in crisis periods. See Bruce W. Jentleson, *American Foreign Policy*, 4th ed. (New York: Norton, 2010), 63.

9. Hans J. Morgenthau, "The Subversion of Foreign Policy," *Year Book of World Affairs*, 1955, reproduced in Hans J. Morgenthau, *Politics in the 20th Century*, vol. 1: *The Decline of Democratic Politics* (Chicago: University of Chicago Press, 1962), 417.

10. Page and Bouton, *Foreign Policy Disconnect*, 210–11; emphasis in original.

11. The most difficult constraint for government to handle consists of demands for action *under particular conditions.* For example, American military involvement in Vietnam was shaped by the anticommunist American climate; American leaders intervened in Vietnam to preempt public opposition they anticipated if communist adversaries overran Vietnam. See Leslie H. Gelb with Richard K. Betts, *The Irony of Vietnam* (Washington, DC: Brookings Institution Press, 1979), 354. For another such case, which occurred in the so-called Trent Affair in 1861, see David F. Krein, *The Last Palmerston Government* (Ames: Iowa State University Press, 1978), 45, 47. Space limitations prevent further discussion of this type of constraint here.

12. Bruce Russett and Harvey Starr, *World Politics: The Menu for Choice*, 5th ed. (New York: W. H. Freeman, 1996), 207. Bruce Jentleson notes that elites ordinarily define opinion constraints. "Public opinion," he writes, "imposes limits on the range of the president's policy options via assessments made by presidential advisers of which options have any chance of being made to 'fly' with the public and which are 'nonstarters.'" *American Foreign Policy* 65. Joe Hagan has noted that "political leaders can deflect or reduce constraints on their foreign policy choices." Hagan, "Domestic Political Systems and War Proneness," 196. The much-discussed "democratic peace" theory, which asserts that democratic countries do not fight each other because they are less prone to war involvement, focuses on opinion constraints. On the democratic peace theory, see, for example, Michael E. Brown et al., *Debating the Democratic Peace* (Cambridge, MA: MIT Press, 1996); and James L. Ray, *Democracy and International Conflict: An Evaluation of the Democratic Peace Proposition* (Columbia: University of South Carolina Press, 1995).

13. Levy and Mabe, "Politically Motivated Opposition to War."

14. The literature on public opinion discusses the gap between government (leaders, policymakers) and the oppositional public. Although the primary interest in that chapter is diplomacy as effect—that is, the impact of oppositional politics on *diplomats*—it accepts discussions of "leaders" and "policymakers" in the literature as equivalent to "diplomats" because of their common responsibility to choose between foreign policy peace imperatives and opposition-favored belligerence.

15. Hans J. Morgenthau, *In Defense of the National Interest* (New York: Knopf, 1951), 229–30. Morgenthau maintained that "fear of Congress has become a veritable obsession of many members of the executive departments" (231).

16. Craig and George, *Force and Statecraft*, 54.

17. Hans J. Morgenthau, *Politics among Nations*, 4th ed. (New York: Knopf, 1967), 142.

18. Ibid. Morgenthau reproduced Alexis de Toqueville's statement, from *Democracy in America*, that "democracies [obeyed] impulse rather than prudence, and . . . abandon[ed] mature design for the gratification of momentary passion" (141).

19. Harold Nicolson, *Curzon: The Last Phase, 1919–1925* (London: Constable, 1937), 185.

20. Key, *Public Opinion and American Democracy*, 556.

21. Ibid., 154.

22. Spanier and Uslaner, *How American Foreign Policy Is Made*, 79. On bipartisanship, see also Waltz, *Foreign Policy and Democratic Politics*, 92–95. According to a study by Eric Uslaner, "not a single roll call on a straightforward foreign policy vote during the twenty-four years from 1947 to 1970 found 80 per cent of House Democrats opposing 80 per cent of House Republicans." Cited in Spanier and Uslaner, *How American Foreign Policy Is Made*, 79.

23. A. J. P. Taylor, *English History: 1914–1945* (New York: Oxford University Press, 1965), 195, 359.

24. Page and Bouton, *Foreign Policy Disconnect*, 224.

25. Ibid., 228.

26. Levy and Mabe, "Politically Motivated Opposition," 66–67.

27. Mayer, *Dynamics of Counterrevolution in Europe*, 138.

28. Hagan, "Domestic Political Systems," 188.

29. Mayer, *Dynamics of Counterrevolution*, 60–61.

30. Morgenthau, *Politics among Nations*, 142.

31. Morgenthau, *Decline of Democratic Politics*, 417. Part of his critique was that officials were too preoccupied with public opinion: "The mistaken identification of press, radio, polls, and Congress with public opinion has had a distorting as well as paralyzing influence upon American foreign policy," he wrote in 1951. Morgenthau, *In Defense of the National Interest*, 222. Senator Hubert Humphrey made the same point when he faulted many Senate colleagues for being "POPPs," "public opinion poll politicians" on foreign policy. Jentleson, *American Foreign Policy*, 66.

32. Morgenthau, *In Defense of the National Interest*, 233.

33. Morgenthau, *Decline of Democratic Politics*, 417–18.

34. Gordon A. Craig, "The British Foreign Office from Grey to Austen Chamberlain," in *The Diplomats: 1919–1939*, ed. Gordon A. Craig and Felix Gilbert, vol. 1: *The Twenties* (New York: Atheneum, 1968), 36. The one example of political retribution Craig and

George discussed when they detailed the impact of public opinion on diplomacy was outside the 1922–1929 period: the well-known forced resignation in 1935 of Sir Samuel Hoare, the British foreign secretary, following Hoare's efforts with French foreign minister Pierre Laval to negotiate a face-saving agreement over Ethiopia that favored Italy after the Italian invasion of that country. Craig and George, *Force and Statecraft*, 53–54. A. J. P. Taylor wrote that protest of the Hoare-Laval plan, "perhaps the greatest since the campaign against the 'Bulgarian horrors' in 1876," came from within the ruling Conservative party. Taylor, *English History*, 385.

35. Craig, "British Foreign Office from Grey to Austen Chamberlain," 38.

36. Nicolson, *Curzon*, 187–88.

37. Waltz, *Foreign Policy and Democratic Politics*, 281, 283.

38. Henry Kissinger, *Diplomacy* (New York: Simon & Schuster, 1994), 389–93.

39. Key, *Public Opinion and American Democracy*, 555.

40. Waltz, *Foreign Policy and Democratic Politics*, 270ff.

41. Ibid., 304.

42. This idea seems compatible with Morgenthau's idea that leaders should manage public opinion by "tak[ing] the long view, proceeding slowly and by detours, paying with small losses for great advantage, [being] . . . able to temporize, to compromise, to bide . . . time." *Politics among Nations*, 142.

Leaders can also concede to oppositional demands once policy opposition has been overcome on the more important issue. In the wake of the failure of Congress in 2015 to derail the Joint Comprehensive Plan of Action on the Iranian nuclear program, the United States responded to Iranian ballistic missile tests (which were not prohibited by the Plan of Action) by imposing sanctions that it was not likely to have imposed in the absence of the agreement. The sanctions were said to be "a carefully calibrated answer to critics" who argued that President Barack Obama was prepared "to overlook almost any Iranian transgression in order to avoid derailing the [Iran] nuclear deal." Helene Cooper and David E. Sanger, "Iran's Missile Tests Remind the U.S. that Tensions Have Not Ended," *New York Times*, 31 December 2015. (For another reference to this article, see chapter 5.)

43. On the focused case comparison method, see Alexander L. George, "Case Studies and Theory Development: The Method of Structured, Focused Comparison," in *Diplomacy: New Approaches in History, Theory, and Policy*, ed. Paul Gordon Lauren (New York: Free Press, 1979), 43–68; and Alexander L. George and Andrew Bennett, *Case Studies and Theory Development in the Social Sciences* (Cambridge, MA: MIT Press, 2005).

44. The source for this case is Richard W. Van Alstyne, *American Diplomacy in Action*, rev. ed. (Stanford, CA: Stanford University Press, 1947), 707–14.

45. Ibid., 689.

46. Ibid., 712.

47. Ibid., 714.

48. Ibid., 712; emphasis in original.

49. Alexis de Tocqueville, *Democracy in America* (New York: Knopf, 1945), 1:234–35, cited in Morgenthau, *Politics among Nations*, 141, and in Morgenthau, *In Defense of the National Interest*, 222–23.

50. On this episode, see Jerald A. Combs, *The Jay Treaty* (Berkeley: University of California Press, 1970; and Paul A. Varg, *Foreign Policies of the Founding Fathers* (Baltimore, MD: Penguin, 1970).

51. Varg, *Foreign Policies*, 103.

52. On this case, see David A. Trask, *The War with Spain in 1898* (New York: Macmillan, 1981); David Traxel, *1898: The Birth of the American Century* (New York: Knopf, 1998); Walter LaFeber, *The New Empire: An Interpretation of American Expansion: 1860–1898* (Ithaca, NY: Cornell University Press, 1963); Ernest R. May, *American Imperialism: A Speculative Essay* (New York: Atheneum, 1968); and Edward P. Crapol and Howard Schonberger, "The Shift to Global Expansion, 1865–1900," in *From Colony to Empire*, ed. William A. Williams (New York: Wiley, 1972), 135–202.

53. Trask, *War with Spain*, 31.

54. The source for this case is Arno J. Mayer, *Politics and Diplomacy of Peacemaking: Containment and Counterrevolution at Versailles, 1918–1919* (New York: Knopf, 1967), 194–226, 673–715.

55. Ibid., 216.

56. Ibid., 675.

57. Ibid., 680–81.

58. Ibid., 687.

59. Ibid., 15, 715.

9

Seeking Diplomatic Theory

An Interim Report

Diplomatic statecraft is perhaps the last frontier for theorizing in international relations. This study, a prospectus for generalizing about a subject long-neglected as an object of theory, has located diplomatic theory-building within the wider theoretical concerns in the discipline of international relations.[1] It has done so to legitimate the search for generalizations about statecraft and to build on other theoretical work for this purpose. Its main point, however, is to argue that the protean character of diplomacy is no barrier to empirically grounded theory.

This study centers around an inductive method for identifying and investigating empirically verifiable patterns in diplomatic conflict resolution. However, deductive insights are by no means neglected; they assist diplomatic theory-building because they contribute generalizations. As Alexander L. George and Andrew Bennett note, "Deductive methods can usefully develop entirely new theories or fill the gaps in existing theories."[2] Most analysts in practice contribute to theory through their attachment to paradigmatic thought. "Ordinarily," James N. Rosenau and Mary Durfee write, "one is locked into the paradigm comprising those underlying presumptions with which one is most comfortable."[3]

Diplomatic theorists share with other theoretically minded persons a desire to spell out and solve researchable puzzles. "If," write Rosenau and Durfee, "one is genuinely puzzled by why events unfold as they do, one is committed to always asking why they occur in one way rather than another and, in so doing, pressing one's theoretical impulses as far as possible."[4] By this standard, designing and implementing empirically grounded theory of diplomatic conflict management and resolution is no more difficult than doing so for any other international problem area.

Accepting this standard, this book has distinguished diplomacy as cause and as effect. As a cause, diplomacy is an alternative to warfare, and the plentiful literature on crisis management, mediation, and negotiation helps ascertain its causal impact. Choices made by governments impact policy outcomes. This book explores choices between contestation and negotiation, between making war or making peace, and between a decision to negotiate and a decision not to do so.

Diplomacy as effect is less well established and documented. To study it, analysts must link independent variables to diplomatic statecraft using a literature largely unstimulated by such a concern. They must also isolate the impact that their independent variable has on diplomatic behavior. We have asked whether diplomats are independent from or accommodative to nondiplomatic pressures, and have pointed out that adaptation to nondiplomatic influences affects diplomatic outcomes. Several recent studies that accentuate newer forms of diplomatic interaction appear to understand diplomacy primarily as effect.[5]

This chapter considers how deductive insights, borrowed from standard paradigms used by international relations analysts, have an important role in theory-building. Openness to these ideas is defended in two ways. First, there is no one way to conceptualize diplomatic statecraft as policy instrument. Second, the clash among these ideas is a key to theory-building. It provides useful critiques of initial working assumptions and, by encouraging alternate understandings of relationships between key variables, suggests new questions and answers deserving of analysis. It also helps define a diplomatic point of view.

The chapter's second purpose is to recapitulate this study's substantive questions addressed to diplomatic issues; these take the form of puzzles animating case comparison analyses. As with paradigms, they aim to understand underlying historical patterns, but because the study is primarily inductive, questions and answers are more limited and specific than those found in specific paradigms.

Finally, the chapter discusses methodological issues raised by studying diplomatic statecraft inductively. Focused case comparison grounds theory-building in historical cases considered in terms of general variables, despite their unique character. The book concludes with a review of prior chapters to show how case study contributes to theory in different ways.

I. AN ECLECTIC FOCUS

We have defined diplomacy as "technique and strategy that, pursuant to national objectives, facilitate interaction of states to deal with their common problems."[6] This definition, understanding diplomatic statecraft as means-serving, supporting bargaining between states, and enhancing bargaining results, depends heavily on insights from the realist paradigm. Nevertheless, I have sought to avoid overdependence on realist thought. Rather, pursuing diplomatic theory should take account of many understandings of statecraft and conflict resolution and should question analytical assumptions. It does not, and cannot, affirm the superiority of any one deductive framework over others.

We begin a review of our stock of paradigmatic ideas with political realism. First, realists understand diplomacy to be a key for determining whether disputes are managed peacefully.[7] Second, as realists emphasize, technique and strategy enable diplomatic statecraft to enhance state interests when interstate conflict arises. Bargaining in turn bridges foreign policy concerns with the character of the international system.[8] Focusing on diplomatic techniques and strategy, an analyst can probe means-ends relationships. Holding objectives constant, she can test how variable techniques and strategies were effective in implementing those objectives; holding means constant, she can test for their ability to implement varying objectives. Another type of study tests for the technique and strategy chosen in a specified policy context, using context as a constraint on choice. The distinction between diplomacy as cause and diplomacy as effect also is much indebted to the realists.

Yet some of this study's analyses begin where realism is ambivalent or weak. One example is whether to use contestation or negotiation as a diplomatic strategy.[9] A realist case can be made that contestation, aiming at a superior result, most fits an anarchical, self-help state system, yet an equally strong realist argument can be made that negotiation, focusing on a common problem, fits the realist priority to avoid war. A second example is whether states should prioritize the seeking of interstate agreement, on the one hand, or autonomy, on the other.[10]

Regarding diplomacy of effect, a third problem area, the diplomatic theorist insists on the equal importance of diplomatic cause and effect, whereas the realist emphasis on causal diplomacy detracts from the study of diplomacy as effect.[11] In addition, the realist association of diplomacy as effect with passivity neglects opportunities for diplomatic adaptation that do not require policy changes.

Liberal internationalism, applied diplomacy, and the Galtung and security community approaches have complemented political realism as theoretical conceptions. First, in response to questions motivated by the realist paradigm, other frameworks suggest legitimate hypotheses or tests of significance appropriate for comparative case study. They also sensitize the analyst to different answers.

Controversy can generate a focus for analysis in which elements of different paradigms are tested against each other. For example, while the consequences of the absence of diplomatic communication are logically very large
for the realist, the liberal internationalist paradigm, attaching less significance
to the loss of such communication, insists that international order can prevail
even in its absence.[12] An applied diplomacy paradigm highlights how secure,
reliable diplomatic communication can contribute to overoptimistic assumptions about cooperation potential, encouraging risky behavior.

Second, just as our paradigms taken together demonstrate that there is no
one way to understand diplomatic statecraft, they also suggest new questions.
For example, the realist preoccupation with diplomacy as the primary means
for coping with an anarchical international system can suggest the hypothesis
that war is more likely in the absence of interstate diplomacy. The Galtung
and security community literatures bring contrasting assumptions about the
character of diplomacy in world politics. Galtung cites a "war system faultline" characterized by highly competitive diplomacy, whereas a security
community approach highlights diplomatic convergence based on similar
transnational elite interests in a security community.[13]

Another source of new questions is Galtung's portrait of how negative
peace pressures in world politics can collide with the positive peace pressures
in some countries' domestic politics. Diplomatic statecraft is then buffeted
from two sides, and the two influences are difficult or impossible to reconcile.
Given those pressures, how does diplomatic statecraft function? Does it aim
to reconcile the influences, or does it work to strengthen one against the
other? How does it adapt when political influences make adaptation difficult?

Deductive insights can highlight the distinctive character of diplomatic
statecraft as a subject of theoretical study. As points of view they can serve
as a basis for critiquing deductive ideas that do not focus on diplomacy yet
have diplomatic implications. They can also ground an understanding of the
independent significance of diplomacy on other variables.[14]

II. LIMITING THE SCOPE OF
RESEARCH QUESTIONS

This study has sought empirically verified, recurrent diplomatic patterns and
outcomes. It has anticipated and explained variable patterns prior to comparing cases. "Genuine puzzles," write Rosenau and Durfee, "encompass specified dependent variables for which adequate explanations are lacking. We do
not see how to think theoretically without discerning recurrent outcomes that
evoke curiosity and puzzlement."[15] As a result, we move inductively from

the particular to the general rather than deductively from the general to the particular.[16]

The study distinguishes between employing paradigmatic insights and depending on models based on paradigms. The latter assumes that certain regularities must exist, closing off the variety of paradigmatic insights employed in this study. More comprehensive in scope than their inductive counterparts, models based on paradigms identify a priori relationships between key variables, often in elegant fashion, assuming that neglected variables are unimportant. They have been criticized for discouraging detailed, empirically grounded case analysis. "Broad generalizations," George and Bennett write, "often end up as probabilistic in character, with little indication of the conditions under which they hold. They are pitched at a level of abstraction that fails to give insightful explanation of foreign policy decisions or of interactions between states that lead to specific outcomes. Middle-range theories . . . are deliberately limited in their scope; they . . . attempt to formulate well-specific conditional generalizations of more limited scope. These features make them more useful for policymaking."[17]

George and Bennett's critique can be illustrated, for example, by Hans Morgenthau's classical political realist theory.[18] Arguing for the autonomy of the political process and claiming that the actual rather than the ideal, facts rather than obligations, should be understood by the diplomatic analyst prior to explaining how states behave, Morgenthau's theory explains diplomacy in terms of what Rosenau has termed "rational reconstruction," the coherence between means and ends.[19] It formed a "rational outline" based on interest defined in terms of power, "link[ing] . . . reason trying to understand international politics and the facts to be understood." The analyst using this outline would be placed "in the position of a statesman who must meet a certain problem of foreign policy under certain circumstances, and . . . ask . . . what the rational alternatives are from which a statesman may choose who must meet this problem under these circumstances (presuming always that he acts in a rational manner), and which of these rational alternatives this particular statesman, acting under these circumstances, is likely to choose."[20] The rationality concept, Morgenthau argues, enabled the analyst who studied the statesman to understand him better than the statesman understood himself.[21]

This approach can be questioned, as Rosenau and Durfee note, because "a wide range of behaviors are available to states that are rationally consistent with their perceived interests."[22] Theoretical benefit from empirical study remains unclear if rationality becomes the standard for generalizations. The approach also overlooks that diplomatic strategy can be explored in terms of choice, irrespective of objectives.

Some formal models omit diplomatic statecraft entirely. For example, the structural realist paradigm dwells on how the anarchy of the international system constrains the ability of states to satisfy their objectives and how states accept a diminished range of choice as the price for system membership.[23] Freedom of choice depends in turn not only on the type of international system—that is, whether the system is multipolar or bipolar—but also on the intensity of great power competition. "The game of power politics," writes Kenneth Waltz about a multipolar international system, "*if really played hard*, presses the [state] players into two rival camps, though so complicated is the business of making and maintaining alliances that the game may be played hard enough to produce that result only under the pressure of war."[24] Maintaining that states primarily act defensively in multipolar or bipolar systems, Waltz used the "play hard" logic, reflected for him in the alliance polarity of the pre–World War I period, to argue that multipolarity was less stable than bipolarity. But John Mearsheimer, agreeing with Waltz that multipolarity was less stable than bipolarity, maintained that states intensively competed and "played hard" for relative advantage even under bipolar conditions.[25] Diplomatic statecraft could help explain whether "playing hard" is more associated with one specific international system or is generally significant. But neither Waltz nor Mearsheimer studied diplomatic statecraft.

Omission of diplomatic analysis is a theoretical choice but not a necessity. It is not justified, as previously argued, by the protean character of diplomatic behavior. But, because of the need for detailed information about nation-state plans and calculations to understand causes and results, limiting the scope of analysis is a key to tackling any diplomatic puzzle. "The black boxes of decision-making and strategic interaction," George and Bennett write, referring to the case comparison method, "were opened up and efforts were made to study actual processes of decision-making and of strategic interaction insofar as available data permitted."[26]

For example, if the focus is on statecraft strategy, one puzzle is why governments choose one strategy over another, and how diplomatic context affects their choice. Such a puzzle understands policy choices in such areas as negotiation, crisis management, and coercive diplomacy to be contingent on circumstances that themselves need examination. Alternatively, the puzzle may be the *consequence* of specific diplomatic strategies, a problem that is particularly important for policy planners. George, viewing diplomacy as an alternative to war, was highly interested in improved policy-making.[27] But inductive analysis of cases need not be designed for policy purposes, as George and Bennett concede.[28] For example, such an analysis can test whether states have a stronger propensity to negotiate on security questions when they are relatively equal in military strength than when they are highly unequal.

We now recapitulate the contingent, differentiated midrange theory-building efforts about diplomatic behavior made in this study:

1. Communication

Analysis in chapter 3 probed the significance of the "givens" of the diplomatic environment—the ordinary ability of states to exchange views and to bargain in formal channels set aside for that purpose. It tested the realist view that states unable to communicate formally would be more likely to confront each other, less flexible in their relationship, and more likely to defect from previously undertaken commitments and from existing norms of behavior than would states capitalizing on diplomatic channels. The analysis depended on counterfactual study of whether communication *might* have made for a difference in conflict, flexibility, and defection when interstate conflict was intense and when it was dampened and stabilized.[29]

Case analysis deflated the importance of diplomatic communication. It suggested that states in inflamed conflict that do not communicate do not *desire* to make use of diplomatic channels in order to better manage their relationship, while noncommunicating states whose relations were not inflamed and were already subject to controls do not *need* to employ diplomatic instruments to preserve those controls. The cases underscore how complacence seems to fuel neglect of diplomatic channels, despite its risks. They suggest that, in the absence of immediate payoffs from communication, states may lack incentive to prepare for diplomatic communication by formulating objectives for *improved* relations and bargaining tactics in support of improvement. But as "snapshots" of existing relations and nondiplomatic activity, our cases cannot testify to the value of diplomatic channels when incentives for utilizing them are higher—that is, for *changing* relations for the better or protecting them from worsening. When such changes have higher priority, considerable diplomatic preparation and effort would be expected.

2. Alliance Strategy

In chapter 4, the analysis tested the hypothesis that two countries whose interests converge against a common enemy are more likely to employ a diplomacy of collaboration than of contestation. It discussed the contestation strategy as a potential threat to the alliance relationship but also distinguished alliances in which the fear of a common enemy was very strong, as in wartime collaboration, from those in which third-power concerns were much weaker. The analysis was preoccupied with the motivation for convergent alignment, the allies' ability to cooperate to implement their shared interests, and the possibly disruptive impact of contestation on common interests and on the alliance itself.

Although in no case did contestation lead to the termination of an alliance, there was considerable variability about its effects, and the efforts at generalization focused on the largest contrast in the case sample—between cases in which contestation did not detract from the effectiveness of the alliance or threaten common interests, on the one hand, and cases in which it did seem to imperil the allies' common interests, on the other. In the latter, diplomatic crisis management was important for alliance solidarity, whereas in the former cases, the commonality of allies' interests rather than diplomatic effort was primarily responsible for the efficiency of the alliance. Here again, the limits of the analysis are evident. The case sample, lacking examples prior to the eighteenth century, is biased in favor of longer-lasting alliance associations than those in earlier periods, which were shorter in duration; the analysis would need to be extended to collaboration and contestation in alliances of earlier eras. Another problem is that crisis management efforts were exceptionally strong beginning in the nineteenth century, which suggests that alliance protection against contestation strategies was weaker prior to that time.

3. Diplomatic Effort as a Causal Factor

Causes are defined by context and by exceptional activity. Analysis in chapter 5 distinguished diplomatic statecraft as a cause of behavior in three different contexts—as intention or purpose, as impact or consequence, and as policy success—and displayed the analytic choices in examining these contexts. Exceptional activity depends on one of these contexts to produce causal effects. Coupled with intention, such activity endeavors to neutralize opposed forces; combined with impact, it brings effects disproportional to the effort exerted; and linked with success, exceptional activity leverages undesired stalemate and deadlock. Chapter 6 studied the first and third of these contexts in regard to mediation in intractable interstate and intrastate disputes, testing the common belief that defusing internal conflict diplomatically is much more difficult than defusing interstate conflict. Limited to mediation success, the case sample focused on obstacles to be overcome (reflecting intentionality) and the ability to capitalize on the adversity of primary antagonists (the policy success aspect).

Some but not all differences between intrastate and interstate conflict were found to account for the greater difficulty of mediating civil strife. In the former, intractability was mostly caused by war; in the latter, by diplomacy.

In the former, mediation is ordinarily not invited; in the latter, it is. And in the former, cease-fires depend on agreement on other issues; in the latter, they enhance the chances of political agreement. The analysis concluded that the more inflamed and difficult the mediating situation, the more important the mediator's manipulation of the conflict became for the success of the mediation. Other differences between the intrastate and interstate cases, including mediator motives and mediator agendas, did not seem to explain the difference in mediating difficulty.

4. Diplomacy as Effect

One focal point of dependent diplomacy analysis is the potential for adaptation when diplomacy is constrained or influenced by nondiplomatic developments. Diplomats in such an instance must decide between deferring to constraints and pressures and adhering to objectives and norms in spite of them. Analysis of diplomacy as effect in chapter 8 probed the impact of public opinion, whose growing political impact on government is widely believed to have weakened state-centered diplomatic initiatives. The impact was studied using cases in which domestic belligerence opposed governmental determination to avoid war, based on perceptions of national interest, and the conflicts were so severe that governments were unable to affect popular attitudes. Diplomatic effect was defined by whether diplomats accommodated to domestic pressures opposing their peace preferences or resisted them. Cases profiled how belligerent opposition was brought to bear on governments and how diplomats decided between domestic war pressures and their own preferences for peace. Case analysis concluded that diplomatic officials use statecraft to defend peace priorities against oppositional pressure when they perceive those priorities to be vital and that they can use diplomacy for this purpose to adapt to the opposition. A second motive to resist oppositional pressures in this way was also identified: namely, policymakers' defense of their political power in relation to that of the opposition.

A second focal point of diplomacy as effect is the diplomatic operational milieu, reflecting consequences of changes in diplomatic norms and procedures. Problematic outcomes in diplomatic mediation were shown in chapter 5 to be linked to a series of changes in the diplomatic environment that weakened diplomatic norms, as did more assertive public opinion, as described above. Defining the operational environment as a dependent variable in terms of negotiating success or failure, analysis revealed that decisions that failed to anticipate changes in the diplomatic environment impaired negotiating potential.

5. Variance in Diplomacy as Effect

The analyst selects a specific case type and a small case sample distinguished by one key source of variation. Her objective is to explain the case variability in terms of a single nondiplomatic feature or development. Chapter 7 highlighted two interstate arms competitions, one containing a high degree of diplomatic management in the form of arms control negotiations, and the other lacking such diplomacy. Questions about these cases (the cold war Soviet-American arms race and the nineteenth-century Anglo-French naval competition) dealt with the search for relative military advantage, problems in estimating force advances of the opponent, the security relationship between the adversaries, and the reasons for arms restraint. The objective was to explain the difference in propensity of arms competitors to cooperate in the two instances. Three explanatory candidates, each widely significant for arms racing, were distinguished as independent variables.

Only one of these accounted for the variance in this instance: the differing willingness of the arms competitors to improve their diplomatic relationship, and specifically to use arms agreement as a means of doing so. In the cold war case, the superpowers accepted that unrestricted competition for force advantage would potentially endanger their security and imperil cooperation on other issues. In the naval case, the competitors did not link their competition to security issues more generally.

III. USING STRUCTURED, FOCUSED COMPARISON

This study has shown the inductive focused case method to be not only well suited but also essential to building and testing diplomatic theory. It facilitated comparing divergent forms of diplomatic behavior, probing alternative explanations for that behavior, and using detailed historical cases to test these explanations. No fewer than four of the six theory-building modes distinguished by George and Bennett in their discussion of the case method were employed in prior chapters.[30]

This fruitful result was expected, given the focused case method's adaptability to a variety of other theoretical pursuits.[31] But the conditional generalizations reached here are incremental and not revolutionary additions to theory. They are preliminary results of focused comparison that can and should be followed up. This section summarizes this study's indebtedness to the case comparison method. It first addresses how the method fits the present state of diplomatic theory and then lists varied ways in which that method has been employed here.

George and Bennett allow for more and less elaborate variants of the focused case method. In its modest version, which is evidently the more popular of the two, the analyst is challenged to limit the scope and aims of theoretical study. As George and Bennett note, "Case study researchers *usually* limit themselves to narrow and well-specified contingent generalizations about a type."[32] The main reason for this concern, they inform us, is the inherent risk of overgeneralization. Analysts seeking to generalize from cases that "differ in the value of variables that have been already identified as causally related to the outcome" must be concerned about the risk of attributing too much explanatory power from using a relatively small number of cases. The risk is especially significant when the analyst's fund of explanations is meager.

The ambitious form of the focused case method introduces complexity in the number of variables and relationships, and probes links between independent and dependent variables (in what is known as "process tracing"). This type of case study, characterized by George and Bennett as "typological theory," entails conditional generalizations in which each specified relationship has an assigned place in a general framework.[33] George is especially known for such study; he coauthored, for example, a complex and highly differentiated study of deterrence, which added variables, such as the relative importance of the deterrence effort and the utility calculations of the target state, to permit study of different types of deterrence failure.[34]

George and Bennett note that the focused comparison method's potential depends on the interests of the theorist. "Study of cases," they argue, must "be 'focused' . . . undertaken with a specific research objective in mind and a theoretical focus appropriate for that objective."[35] This supports the choice made in this volume to employ focused comparison in modest and uncomplicated fashion, forgoing process tracing, complexity, and typological theory. Diplomatic theory is at present relatively weak and underdeveloped, as has been noted; theory-building for diplomatic statecraft is therefore better pursued by controlling complexity and striving for simplification where possible. By contrast, complexity is more useful when theory is elaborate; for example, George's study of deterrence used a sizable and influential deductive theory of deterrence to develop a framework for inductive study.[36] A second argument for choosing the modest version of the case method is that subjecting theory to empirical tests is easier when there are fewer variables,[37] and testing less developed theory is more important than testing more elaborate and integrated theoretical frameworks.

The four modes of case comparison cited by George and Bennett employed here include (1) "heuristic" case study, identifying new hypotheses and causal relationships; (2) "theory testing," evaluating the validity and scope of a given theory or competing theories; (3) "plausibility probes," preliminary studies to determine whether more intensive tests are justified; and (4) "disciplined configurative studies," applying specific theories to explain new cases. We now summarize the use that has been made here of these modes.

1. Heuristic Study

George and Bennett note that study of "deviant" or "outlier" cases, unlikely to be anticipated by existing theories, can test the foundations of theory. Chapter 2 provided a heuristic challenge to the assumed importance of diplomatic communication by considering a series of "deviant" cases in which such communication was missing.[38] The cases could not challenge the central importance of interstate communication but were intended to refine an understanding of it through study of its absence, asking whether the absence of communication brought unfavorable consequences for states that failed to communicate or whether those states might coexist even in the absence of communication. Guided by three different theoretical perspectives, counterfactuals were employed to consider the impact of communication in these cases.

The finding that communication would not have made much difference for state relationships in these instances affirmed, with the realist perspective, that states can deliberately reject communication. It upheld liberal internationalist views that interstate stability did not require diplomatic communication and could depend instead on compliance with international norms. And, in accord with the applied diplomatic perspective, it suggested that communication could be outweighed by state opportunism and miscalculation, on the one hand, and cautious behavior, on the other. These results argued for studying these variables by controlling for the communication factor.

2. Theory Testing

Two types of theory testing are contained in the present study, both using inductive analysis to control for differences in case types. Chapter 6 tested a theory articulated in the literature in the expectation that differences between mediation in intrastate and interstate wars would validate the theory. By contrast, chapter 7 framed new theory to explain diplomatic variance in two very different types of arms competition.

Chapter 6 tested the theory that mediation of intrastate wars is more difficult than mediating interstate armed conflict. Logical supports for this theory, which does not appear to have been tested elsewhere, include the higher

proportion of interstate wars settled by negotiation, the less accepted intervention of a mediator in intrastate conflicts, and the usual asymmetry in the
military strength of intrastate belligerents, which reduces the chances of hurting stalemate. Three successful mediation cases of each type were studied, in
the belief that differences between intrastate and interstate mediation could
most effectively be probed in instances of successful mediation. Six objective
indicators were used to compare the two case types.

Analysis upheld the theory, but by a smaller margin than anticipated. Distinctive intrastate war features in only three of the six indicators accounted
for the greater difficulty of mediating intrastate wars. These intrastate war
features—the regularized condition of war, the unwelcome role of mediators,
and the need for the mediator to arrange a cease-fire—require study in additional cases and justify planning for mediation in advance of the outbreak of
intrastate war. The failure of the three other indicators to reflect a difference
in mediating difficulty requires further attention. Intrastate cases did not show
greater difficulty in gaining mediation collaboration or in handling a larger
number of mediating issues or military asymmetries between the primary
antagonists; these negative findings need to be further tested in other cases.

In chapter 7, a historically validated difference between arms racing
with and without arms negotiation stimulated an effort to explain the
difference—to ask, that is, why diplomacy intervened in one competition but
not in the other, a question that does not seem to have been asked elsewhere.
The difference in cooperative tendencies, which the analysis sought to
explain, constituted the dependent variable in this exercise, while three logical explanatory candidates were treated as independent variables. The intent
was to find out whether these candidates presented differences in the two
cases that not only coincided with the difference in diplomatic intervention
but could have had causal importance for the diplomatic dynamic. According
to one theory, agreed-upon standards of force equivalence facilitated arms
agreement and the absence of such standards undermined it. A second theory
proposed that agreement was promoted by intelligence of the rival's force
plans and improvements and was hindered by its absence. And a third theory
maintained that arms agreement was facilitated by the integration of arms
programs with broader diplomatic objectives and hindered by the absence of
that integration.

Analysis questioned the first two of these theories but upheld the third.
Naval rivalry in which arms negotiation was absent was disconnected from
security relations between the rivals and was limited to a search for favorable
force goals. Nuclear arms competition featuring substantial arms negotiation
was linked more generally to the political relationship between the arms

rivals. This difference was strong enough to explain the absence of agreed-upon arms restraint in the former case and the extensive arms cooperation in the latter instance. Further study is needed to understand the logic tying the security disconnect and linkage, on the one hand, with the diplomatic variance, on the other. The security integration theory also needs to be tested on other cases. However, as a preliminary exercise, the analysis provides empirically grounded insight to inform a largely prescriptive and normative dispute in the contemporary period about the value of cooperation between arms competitors.

3. Plausibility Probes

Whether a diplomatic relationship affects the choice of diplomatic technique by states in that relationship is an issue of theoretical interest. Chapter 4 investigated the idea that states whose security interests converge to ally against a common enemy emphasize collaborative problem-solving diplomacy (a strategy of negotiation) rather than the self-interested pursuit of diplomatic advantage (contestation).

This plausibility probe posits the alliance relationship as a significant causal factor and the choice of technique as the dependent variable. It builds on ambivalence in the realist perspective on this question. The case for linkage is bolstered by Morgenthau's view that states as allies ordinarily demonstrate shared interests through practical cooperative actions. But realists, emphasizing self-interested diplomatic motivations, must also allow that even in alliances the effort to maximize national advantage can remain ascendant and that collective action may be impeded by historical suspicions or complacence. Analysis of six contemporary alliance cases, treating each case as unique, could not establish the existence of alliance norms, but by tracking problem-solving and self-interested diplomatic techniques, and especially the effect of contestation on alliance collaboration, it clarified whether the diplomatic relationship and the problem-solving diplomacy were linked. Methodologically, an effective inductive focus on problem-solving diplomacy presupposes an equally strong focus on the rival strategy of contestation.

Contestation was employed in all our cases, confirming that, consistent with the realist emphasis on self-interest and self-help, alliances are subject to challenge. In the most difficult contestation cases, allies employed crisis management to maintain alliance solidarity. The stronger ally then tended to give way to the weaker. In cases when contestation was less challenging, problem-solving diplomacy was strongest, and the alliance sustained itself by its cooperative potential. These findings would need to be further tested by focusing more narrowly on alliances with high contestation and, more widely, by taking account of complementary as well as convergent alliance associations.

4. Disciplined Figurative Studies

Realists argue that the emergence of public opinion in democratic countries contributed to weakening classical diplomatic norms emphasizing flexible behavior and support for the balance of power. Chapter 8 questioned whether the political motive was strong enough to explain the willingness of leaders to accommodate to public oppositional attitudes, and it critiqued the realist view for failing to distinguish opinion constraint, a passive form of influence that does not prevent independent policy behavior, from opinion pressure that challenges policy independence. The realist view was limited to the impact of opinion constraint, but a stronger test of the impact of public opinion necessitated an emphasis on opinion pressure.

Analysis concluded that diplomats determined to sustain peace had a diplomatic counter to domestic pressure: they could approach the target of domestic belligerence and seek to defuse tensions that might otherwise lead to war. Analysts should consider the potential for such action before concluding that diplomatic statecraft acquiesces to oppositional political pressures.

NOTES

1. Writings rarely address diplomatic theory, but see Paul Sharp, *Diplomatic Theory of International Relations* (Cambridge: Cambridge University Press, 2009); Brian C. Rathbun, *Diplomacy's Value* (Ithaca, NY: Cornell University Press, 2014); and Costas M. Constantinou, Pauline Kerr, and Paul Sharp (eds.), *The SAGE Handbook of Diplomacy* (Los Angeles, CA: Sage, 2016).

2. Alexander L. George and Andrew Bennett, *Case Studies and Theory Development in the Social Sciences* (Cambridge, MA: MIT Press, 2005), 111.

3. James N. Rosenau and Mary Durfee, *Thinking Theory Thoroughly*, 2nd ed. (Boulder, CO: Westview, 2000), 8.

4. Ibid., 235.

5. One broad account of changes in diplomatic practice highlights "new diplomacy, newer diplomacy, newest diplomacy." Halvard Leira, "A Conceptual History of Diplomacy," in *SAGE Handbook of Diplomacy,* 34ff. See also Pauline Kerr and Geoffrey Wiseman, eds., *Diplomacy in a Globalizing World* (New York: Oxford University Press, 2013).

6. See chapter 1.

7. Recall the views of Hans Morgenthau and Martin Wight in chapter 1.

8. Recall Richard Rosecrance's definition of diplomacy as "modes or techniques of foreign policy affecting the international system," cited in chapter 1, from *International Encyclopedia of the Social Sciences*, vol. 4, edited by David L. Sills, 187–91 (New York: Macmillan and Free Press, 1968), s.v. "Diplomacy."

9. See chapter 4.

10. See chapter 7.

11. See chapter 8.

12. See chapter 3.

13. See chapter 2.

14. The issue of developing a diplomatic point of view was first raised in Barry H. Steiner, "Diplomacy and International Theory," *Review of International Studies* 30 (2004): 507.

15. Rosenau and Durfee, *Thinking Theory*, 236.

16. A discussion of the relative merits of deductive and inductive methods is found in "Methodological Foundation of the Study of International Conflict," a symposium published in *International Studies Quarterly* 29 (June 1985): 119–54.

17. George and Bennett, *Case Studies and Theory Development*, 266.

18. Hans J. Morgenthau, *Politics among Nations*, 4th ed. (New York: Knopf, 1967), ch. 1.

19. Rosenau and Durfee, *Thinking Theory*, 16. For the realist's concern about political autonomy and self-sufficiency, see also Martin Wight, *International Theory*, ed. Gabriele Wight and Brian Porter (New York: Holmes & Meier, 1992), 17 and 144.

20. Morgenthau, *Politics among Nations*, 5.

21. Ibid.

22. Rosenau and Durfee, *Thinking Theory*, 14.

23. Kenneth N. Waltz, *Theory of International Politics* (Reading, MA: Addison-Wesley, 1979); and John J. Mearsheimer, *The Tragedy of Great Power Politics* (New York: Norton, 2001). George and Bennett observe that Waltz studied the international system as a constraint on states (*Case Studies and Theory Development*, 7, 268).

24. Waltz, *Theory of International Politics*, 167; emphasis added.

25. Mearsheimer, *Tragedy of Great Power Politics*, 32ff.

26. George and Bennett, *Case Studies and Theory Development*, xi.

27. See especially, Alexander L. George, *Bridging the Gap* (Washington, DC: United States Institute of Peace Press, 1993).

28. The last chapter of George and Bennett's study, *Case Studies and Theory Development*, is devoted to "Policy-Relevant Theory."

29. On using the deviant case, see George and Bennett, *Case Studies and Theory Development*, 112–15.

30. Ibid., 74–75.

31. See ibid., appendix.

32. George and Bennett, *Case Studies and Theory Development*, 110; emphasis added.

33. Ibid., 233ff.

34. Alexander L. George and Richard Smoke, *Deterrence in American Foreign Policy* (New York: Columbia University Press, 1974). See also Alexander L. George and William E. Simons, *The Limits of Coercive Diplomacy* (Boulder, CO: Westview, 1994).

35. George and Bennett, *Case Studies and Theory Development*, 70.

36. George and Smoke, *Deterrence*, 66ff. Although George and Bennett give considerable attention (including an entire chapter) to more ambitious focused case comparison in *Case Studies and Theory Development* (247), they acknowledge that the case study analyst must ultimately compare the potential of the two choices. "The more general trade-off for the case study researcher," they write, "is whether the problem at hand requires

added theoretical complexity, whether process-tracing evidence is available to deal with this complexity, and whether the problem is important enough to merit a complex theory. . . . Parsimony and simplicity are always preferable, but they should be sacrificed when complexity is necessary for adequate explanatory theory." As an example of complexity's theoretical value, a differentiated theory of deterrence failures is likely to be more useful than a theory that explains all deterrence failures in the same way (ibid., 241).

George's first major outline of the focused case method, published after his ground-breaking *Deterrence* study, did not discuss the complexity option. See Alexander George, "Case Studies and Theory Development: The Method of Structured, Focused Comparison," in *Diplomacy: New Approaches in History, Theory, and Policy*, ed. Paul Gordon Lauren (New York: Free Press, 1979), 43–68.

37. George and Bennett, *Case Studies and Theory Development*, 116.

38. It could be argued that chapter 6, comparing crisis diplomacy in interstate and intrastate wars, was also heuristic because, holding results constant, the cases highlighted diverse pathways to that result.

Bibliography

Acharya, Amitav. "Collective Identity and Conflict Management in Southeast Asia." In *Security Communities*, edited by Emanuel Adler and Michael Barnett, 198–227. Cambridge: Cambridge University Press, 1998.

Adler, Emanuel. "The Emergence of Cooperation: National Epistemic Communities and the International Evolution of the Idea of Nuclear Arms Control." In *Knowledge, Power, and International Policy Coordination*, edited by Peter M. Haas, 101–46. Columbia: University of South Carolina Press, 1992.

———. "Seeds of Peaceful Change: The OSCE's Security Community-Building Model." In *Security Communities*, edited by Emanuel Adler and Michael Barnett, 119–60. Cambridge: Cambridge University Press, 1998.

Adler, Emanuel, and Michael Barnett. "A Framework for the Study of Security Communities." In *Security Communities*, edited by Emanuel Adler and Michael Barnett, 29–65. Cambridge: Cambridge University Press, 1998.

Adler, Emanuel, and Michael Barnett, eds. *Security Communities*. Cambridge: Cambridge University Press, 1998.

Allison, Graham T. *Essence of Decision*. Boston, MA: Little Brown, 1971.

Allison, Graham T., and Frederic A. Morris. "Armaments and Arms Control: Exploring the Determinants of Military Weapons." *Daedalus* 104 (Summer 1975): 99–129.

"Arms Control: Thirty Years On." Special issue of *Daedalus* 120, no. 1 (Winter 1991).

"Arms, Defense Policy, and Arms Control." Special issue of *Daedalus* 104, no. 3 (Summer 1975).

Bartos, Otomar J., and Paul Wehr. *Using Conflict Theory*. Cambridge: Cambridge University Press, 2002.

Beer, Francis A., ed. *Alliances: Latent War Communities in the Contemporary World*. New York: Holt, Rinehart & Winston, 1970.

Bell, Coral. *Conventions of Crisis: A Study in Diplomatic Management*. London: Oxford University Press, 1971.

Bercovitch, Jacob. "Mediation in the Most Resistant Cases." In *Grasping the Nettle*, edited by Chester A. Crocker, Fen Osler Hampson, and Pamela Aall, 99–121. Washington, DC: United States Institute of Peace Press, 2005.

———, ed. *Resolving International Conflicts: The Theory and Practice of Mediation.* Boulder, CO: Lynne Rienner, 1996.

———. *Social Conflicts and Third Parties.* Boulder, CO: Westview, 1984.

Bercovitch, Jacob, and Jeffrey Z. Rubin, eds. *Mediation in International Relations: Multiple Approaches.* New York: St Martin's, 1992.

Bjola, Corneliu, and Markus Kornprobst. *Understanding International Diplomacy.* New York: Routledge, 2013.

Blainey, Geoffrey. *The Causes of War.* 3rd ed. New York: Free Press, 1988.

Bose, Sumantra. *Kashmir.* Cambridge, MA: Harvard University Press, 2003.

Brand-Jacobsen, Kai Frithjof, with Carl G. Jacobsen, "Beyond Mediation: Towards More Holistic Approaches to Peacebuilding and Peace Actor Empowerment." In *Searching for Peace*, edited by Johan Galtung and Carl G. Jacobsen, 231–67. London: Pluto, 2000.

Brandon, Henry. *Special Relationships.* New York: Atheneum, 1988.

Brodie, Bernard. *Sea Power in the Machine Age.* Princeton, NJ: Princeton University Press, 1941.

———. *War and Politics.* New York: Macmillan, 1973.

Brown, David. *Palmerston.* New Haven, CT: Yale University Press, 2010.

Brown, Michael E., Owen R. Coté Jr., Sean M. Lynn-Jones, and Steven E. Miller, eds. *Debating the Democratic Peace.* Cambridge, MA: MIT Press, 1996.

———. *Rational Choice and Security Studies: Stephen Walt and His Critics.* Cambridge, MA: MIT Press, 2000.

Bull, Hedley. *The Anarchical Society.* New York: Columbia University Press, 1977.

Bundy, McGeorge. *Danger and Survival.* New York: Random House, 1988.

Burgess, Philip M. "Commentary." In *Instruction in Diplomacy: The Liberal Arts Approach*, edited by Smith Simpson, 152–75. Philadelphia, PA: American Academy of Political and Social Science, 1972.

Burke, Edmund. "Three Letters . . . on the Proposals for Peace with the Regicide Directory of France." In *The Works of the Right Honourable Edmund Burke*, vol. 4, 331–554. London: Henry G. Bohn, 1845.

Carnesale, Albert, and Richard N. Haas, eds. *Superpower Arms Control: Setting the Record Straight.* Cambridge, MA: Ballinger, 1987.

Carrington, Peter Lord. *Reflecting on Things Past.* New York: Harper & Row, 1988.

Clemens, Walter C., Jr. *Dynamics of International Relations.* 2nd ed. Lanham, MD: Roman & Littlefield, 2004.

Cobden, Richard. "The Three Panics." In *Political Writings*, by Richard Cobden, vol. 2, 214–435. London: Ridgway, 1867.

Cohen, Herman J. *Intervening in Africa.* New York: St. Martin's, 2000.

Combs, Jerald A. *The Jay Treaty.* Berkeley: University of California Press, 1970.

Constantinou, Costas, Pauline Kerr, and Paul Sharp, eds. *The SAGE Handbook of Diplomacy.* Los Angeles, CA: Sage, 2013.

Cooper, Helene, and David E. Sanger. "Iran's Missile Tests Remind the U.S. That Tensions Have Not Ended." *New York Times*, 31 December 2015.

Craig, Gordon A. "The British Foreign Office from Grey to Austen Chamberlain." In *The Diplomats: 1919–1939*, edited by Gordon A. Craig and Felix Gilbert, vol. 1, 15–48. New York: Atheneum, 1968.

Craig, Gordon A., and Alexander L. George. *Force and Statecraft*. 3rd ed. New York: Oxford University Press, 1995.

Crapol, Edward P., and Howard Schonberger. "The Shift to Global Expansion, 1865–1900." In *From Colony to Empire*, edited by William A. Williams, 135–202. New York: Wiley, 1972.

Crocker, Chester A. *High Noon in Southern Africa*. New York: Norton, 1992.

———. "The Varieties of Intervention: Conditions for Success." In *Managing Global Chaos* edited by Chester A. Crocker, Fen Osler Hampson, and Pamela Aall, 183–96. Washington, DC: United States Institute of Peace Press, 2006.

Crocker, Chester A., Fen Osler Hampson, and Pamela Aall, eds. *Grasping the Nettle*. Washington, DC: United States Institute of Peace Press, 2006.

———. *Managing Global Chaos*. Washington, DC: United States Institute of Peace Press, 1996.

Daalder, Ivo H. "The United States and Military Intervention in Internal Conflict." In *The International Dimensions of Internal Conflict*, edited by Michael E. Brown, 461–88. Cambridge, MA: MIT Press, 1996.

Danto, Arthur C. *Analytical Philosophy of History*. Cambridge: Cambridge University Press, 1965.

Deane, John R. *Strange Alliance*. New York: Viking, 1947.

Deutsch, Karl W. *The Analysis of International Relations*. Englewood Cliffs, NJ: Prentice-Hall, 1968.

———. *Nationalism and its Alternatives*. New York: Knopf, 1969.

Deutsch, Karl W., Sidney A. Burrell, Robert A. Kann, Maurice Lee Jr., Martin Lichterman, Raymond E. Lindgren, Francis L. Loewenheim, and Richard W. Van Wagenen. "Political Community and the North Atlantic Area." In *International Political Communities: An Anthology*, 1–91. Garden City, NY: Anchor Books, 1966.

Downs, George W. "Arms Races and War." In *Behavior, Society, and Nuclear War*, edited by Philip E. Tetlock, Jo L. Husbands, Robert Jervis, Paul C. Stern, and Charles Tilly, 73–109. New York: Oxford University Press, 1991.

Downs, George W., and David M. Rocke. *Tacit Bargaining, Arms Races, and Arms Control*. Ann Arbor: University of Michigan Press, 1990.

Doyle, Michael W. "Liberalism and World Politics." *American Political Science Review* 80 (December 1986): 1151–69.

Druckman, Daniel, and Robert Mahoney. "Processes and Consequences of International Negotiations." *Journal of Social Issues* 33 (1977): 60–87.

Druckman, Daniel, and Christopher Mitchell, eds. "Flexibility in International Negotiation and Mediation." Special volume of the *Annals of the American Academy of Political and Social Science* 542 (November 1995).

Eichenberg, Richard C., "Victory Has Many Friends: U.S. Public Opinion and the Use of Military Force." *International Security* 30 (Summer 2005): 140–77.

Etheridge, Mark, and Cyril Black. "Negotiating on the Balkans, 1945–1947." In *Negotiating with the Russians*, edited by Raymond Dennett and Joseph E. Johnson, 171–206. Boston, MA: World Peace Foundation, 1951.

Evangelista, Matthew. *Innovation and the Arms Race*. Ithaca, NY: Cornell University Press, 1998.

Evans, Peter, Harold Karan Jacobson, and Robert D. Putnam, eds. *Double-Edged Diplomacy: International Bargaining and Domestic Politics*. Berkeley: University of California Press, 1993.

Fairbanks, Charles H., Jr., and Abram N. Shulsky. "From 'Arms Control' to Arms Reductions: The Historical Experience." *Washington Quarterly* 10 (Summer 1987): 59–73.

Fisher, Roger, Andrea Kupfer Schneider, Elizabeth Borgwardt, and Brian Ganson. *Coping with International Conflict*. Upper Saddle River, NJ: Prentice-Hall, 1997.

Fisher, Roger, Elizabeth Kopelman, and Andrea Kupfer Schneider. *Beyond Machiavelli*. Cambridge, MA: Harvard University Press, 1994.

Fletcher, Tom. *The Naked Diplomat*. London: William Collins, 2016.

Foreign Relations of the United States (1958–1960). Vol. 10, part 1: *Eastern Europe Region: Soviet Union; Cyprus*. Washington, DC: United States Government Printing Office, 1993.

Fox, Annette Baker. *The Politics of Attraction: Four Middle Powers and the United States*. New York: Columbia University Press, 1976.

Friedman, Thomas L. "Diplomacy Is Minding Other Nations' Business." *New York Times*, 30 January 1994.

Gaddis, John Lewis. *The Landscape of History*. New York: Oxford University Press, 2002.

Galtung, Johan. *Solving Conflicts*. Honolulu: University of Hawaii Institute for Peace, 1989.

———. *A Theory of Peace: Building Direct Structural Cultural Peace*. Bergen, Norway: Kolofon, 2013.

Galtung, Johan, and Carl G. Jacobsen, eds. *Searching for Peace*. London: Pluto, 2000.

Galtung, Johan, and Mari Holmboe Ruge. "Patterns in Diplomacy." *Journal of Peace Research* 2 (1965): 101–35.

Ganguly, Sumit. *Conflict Unending*. New York: Columbia University Press, 2001.

Ganguly, Sumit, and S. Paul Kapur, eds. *Nuclear Proliferation in South Asia: Crisis Behavior and the Bomb*. New York: Routledge, 2009.

Garthoff, Raymond. *Reflections on the Cuban Missile Crisis*. Rev. ed. Washington, DC: Brookings Institution Press, 1989.

Gates, Robert M. *From the Shadows*. New York: Simon & Schuster, 2002.

Gelb, Leslie H., with Richard K. Betts. *The Irony of Vietnam*. Washington, DC: Brookings Institution Press, 1979.

George, Alexander L. *Bridging the Gap*. Washington, DC: United States Institute of Peace Press, 1993.

———. "Case Studies and Theory Development: The Method of Structured, Focused Comparison." In *Diplomacy: New Approaches in History, Theory, and Policy*, edited by Paul Gordon Lauren, 43–68. New York: Free Press, 1979.

———, ed. *Managing U.S.-Soviet Rivalry*. Boulder, CO: Westview, 1983.

———. "U.S.-Soviet Efforts to Cooperate in Crisis Management and Crisis Avoidance." In *U.S.-Soviet Security Cooperation*, edited by Alexander L. George, Philip J. Farley, and Alexander Dallin, 581–99. New York: Oxford University Press, 1988.

George, Alexander L., and Andrew Bennett. *Case Studies and Theory Development in the Social Sciences*. Cambridge, MA: MIT Press, 2005.

George, Alexander L., and William E. Simons. *The Limits of Coercive Diplomacy*. Boulder, CO: Westview, 1994.

George, Alexander L., and Richard Smoke. *Deterrence in American Foreign Policy: Theory and Practice.* New York: Columbia University Press, 1974.

George, Alexander L., Philip J. Farley, and Alexander Dallin, eds. *U.S.-Soviet Security Cooperation.* New York: Oxford University Press, 1988.

Gibler, Douglas M., and John A. Vasquez. "Uncovering the Dangerous Alliances, 1495–1980." *International Studies Quarterly* 42 (December 1998): 785–807.

Glaser, Charles L. "Political Consequences of Military Strategy." *World Politics* 44 (July 1992): 497–538.

———. "When Are Arms Races Dangerous? Rational versus Suboptimal Arming." *International Security* 28 (Spring 2004): 44–84.

Goldstein, Joshua A. *Winning the War on War.* New York: Dutton, 2011.

Gray, Colin S. "The Arms Race Phenomenon." *World Politics* 24 (October 1971): 39–79.

———. *House of Cards: Why Arms Control Must Fail.* Ithaca, NY: Cornell University Press, 1992.

———. *The Soviet-American Arms Race.* Westmead, UK: Saxon House, 1978.

———. "The Urge to Compete: Rationales for Arms Racing." *World Politics* 27 (January 1974): 208–33.

Haas, Ernst B. "International Integration: The European and the Universal Process," *International Organization* 15 (Autumn 1961): 366–92. Reprinted in *International Political Communities: An Anthology*, 1–91. Garden City, NY: Anchor Books, 1966.

Haas, Peter M., ed. *Knowledge, Power, and International Policy Coordination.* Columbia: University of South Carolina Press, 1997.

Hagan, Joe D. "Domestic Political Systems and War Proneness." *Mershon International Studies Review* 38 (October 1994): 183–207.

Hampson, Fen Osler. *Multilateral Negotiations.* Baltimore, MD: Johns Hopkins University Press, 1995.

Handel, Michael I. *The Diplomacy of Surprise: Hitler, Nixon, Sadat.* Cambridge, MA: Harvard University Center for International Affairs, 1981.

Hastedt, Glenn P., and Kay M. Knickrehm. *International Politics in a Changing World.* New York: Longman, 2003.

Henrikson, Alan K. "Diplomatic Method." In *Encyclopedia of U.S. Foreign Relations*, edited by Bruce W. Jentleson and Thomas G. Paterson, vol. 2. New York: Oxford University Press, 1997.

Herz, John H. "Idealist Internationalism and the Security Dilemma." *World Politics* 2 (January 1950): 157–80.

Higonnet, Patrice Louis-René. "The Origins of the Seven Years' War." *Journal of Modern History* 40 (March 1968): 57–90.

Hinsley, Frank H. *Power and the Pursuit of Peace.* Cambridge, UK: University Press, 1963.

Hirschfeld, Thomas J., ed. *Intelligence and Arms Control.* Austin, TX: Lyndon B. Johnson School of Public Affairs, 1987.

Holbrooke, Richard. *To End a War.* New York: Random House, 1998.

Holsti, Ole R. "Public Opinion and Foreign Policy: Challenges to the Almond-Lippman Consensus." *International Studies Quarterly* 36 (December 1992): 439–66.

Hughes, Barry B. *The Domestic Context of American Foreign Policy.* San Francisco, CA: W. H. Freeman, 1978.

Huntington, Samuel P. "Arms Races: Prerequisites and Results." In *Public Policy*, edited by Carl J. Friedrich and Seymour E. Harris, 41–58. Cambridge, MA: Harvard University Graduate School of Public Administration, 1958. Reprinted in *The Use of Force*, edited by Robert J. Art and Kenneth N. Waltz, 365–401. Boston, MA: Little, Brown, 1971.

Iklé, Fred C. *How Nations Negotiate*. New York: Praeger, 1964.

Jackson, Galen. "The Showdown that Wasn't: U.S.-Israeli Relations and American Domestic Politics, 1973–75." *International Security* 40 (Spring 2015): 130–69.

Jaster, Robert S. "The 1988 Peace Accords and the Future of Southwestern Africa." *Adelphi Paper*, no. 253. London: International Institute for Strategic Studies, 1990.

Jentleson, Bruce W. *American Foreign Policy*. 4th ed. New York: Norton, 2010.

Jentleson, Bruce W., and Rebecca L. Britton. "Still Pretty Prudent: Post-Cold War American Opinion on the Use of Military Force." *Journal of Conflict Resolution* 42 (August 1998): 395–417.

Jervis, Robert. "Cooperation under the Security Dilemma." *World Politics* 30 (January 1978): 167–214.

———. "Hypotheses on Misperception," *World Politics* 20 (July 1968): 454–79.

———. *The Logic of Images in International Relations*. Princeton, NJ: Princeton University Press, 1970.

———. *Perception and Misperception in International Politics*. Princeton, NJ: Princeton University Press, 1976.

———. "Realism, Game Theory, and Cooperation." *World Politics* 40 (April 1988): 317–49.

———. "Security Regimes." In *International Regimes*, edited by Stephen D. Krasner, 173–94. Ithaca, NY: Cornell University Press, 1983.

Kahn, Herman. "The Arms Race and Some of its Hazards." In *Arms Control, Disarmament and National Security*, edited by Donald Brennan, 89–121. New York: George Braziller, 1961.

———. *On Escalation*. New York: Praeger, 1965.

Kapstein, Ethan B. "Two Dismal Sciences Are Better than One—Economics and the Study of National Security." *International Security* 27 (Winter 2002–2003): 158–87.

Kennan, George F. *Memoirs: 1950–1963*. New York: Bantam, 1969.

Kennedy, Paul. *Strategy and Diplomacy: 1870–1945*. Winchester, MA: George Allen & Unwin, 1983.

Keohane, Robert O. *After Hegemony: Cooperation and Discord in the World Political Economy*. Princeton, NJ: Princeton University Press, 1984.

Keohane, Robert O., and Joseph S. Nye Jr. *Power and Interdependence*. Boston, MA: Little, Brown, 1977.

Kent, Sherman. "A Crucial Estimate Relived." In *Sherman Kent and the Board of National Estimates: Collected Essays*, edited by Donald P. Steury, 173–88. Washington, DC: Center for the Study of Intelligence, Central Intelligence Agency, 1994.

Kerr, Pauline, and Geoffrey Wiseman, eds. *Diplomacy in a Globalizing World*. New York: Oxford University Press, 2013.

Kershner, Isabel. "A Compromise at the Western Wall, but a Wider Divide among Jews." *New York Times*, 3 February 2016.

Kerry, John, John McCain, and Bob Kerrey. "Lessons and Hopes in Vietnam." *New York Times*, 24 May 2016.

Kertesz, Stephen. "Commentary." In *Instruction in Diplomacy: The Liberal Arts Approach*, edited by Smith Simpson, 26–39. Philadelphia: American Academy of Political and Social Science, 1972.

Kessler, J. Christian. *Verifying Nonproliferation Treaties*. Washington, DC: National Defense University Press, 1995.

Key, V. O., Jr. *Public Opinion and American Democracy*. New York: Knopf, 1964.

King, Gary, Robert O. Keohane, and Sidney Verba. *Designing Social Inquiry*. Princeton, NJ: Princeton University Press, 1994.

Kissinger, Henry. *Diplomacy*. New York: Simon & Schuster, 1994.

———. *White House Years*. Boston, MA: Little, Brown, 1979.

———. *World Restored*. New York: Grosset & Dunlap, 1964 .

Kirkpatrick, David D. "Strife in Libya Could Presage a Long Civil War." *New York Times*, 25 August 2014.

Krasner, Stephen D., ed. *International Regimes*. Ithaca, NY: Cornell University Press, 1983.

Krein, David F. *The Last Palmerston Government*. Ames, IA: Iowa State University Press, 1978.

Kremenyuk, Victor A. "The Emerging System of International Negotiation." In *International Negotiation: Analysis, Approaches, Issues*, edited by Victor A. Kremenyuk, 22–39. San Francisco, CA: Jossey-Bass, 1991.

Krepon, Michael. *Strategic Stalemate: Nuclear Weapons and Arms Control in American Politics*. New York: St. Martin's, 1984.

Kydd, Andrew. "Arms Races and Arms Control: Modeling the Hawk Perspective." *American Journal of Political Science* 34 (April 2000): 222–38.

Lamy, Steven L., John Baylis, Steve Smith, and Patricia Owens. *Introduction to Global Politics*. New York: Oxford University Press, 2011.

Larson, Jeffrey A., and James J. Wirtz, eds. *Arms Control and Cooperative Security*. Boulder, CO: Lynne Rienner, 2009.

Lauren, Paul Gordon, Gordon A. Craig, and Alexander L. George. *Force and Statecraft: Diplomatic Challenges of Our Time*. 4th ed. New York: Oxford University Press, 2007.

Leffler, Melvyn P. "Adherence to Agreements: Yalta and the Experiences of the Early Cold War." *International Security* 11 (Summer 1986): 88–123.

LaFeber, Walter. *The New Empire: An Interpretation of American Expansion: 1860–1898*. Ithaca, NY: Cornell University Press, 1963.

Lederer, Ivo J., ed. *Russian Foreign Policy: Essays in Historical Perspective*. New Haven, CT: Yale University Press, 1962.

Leguey-Feilleux, Jean-Robert. *The Dynamics of Diplomacy*. Boulder, CO: Lynne Rienner, 2009.

Leira, Halvard, "A Conceptual History of Diplomacy." In *The SAGE Handbook of Diplomacy*, edited by Costas M. Constantinou, Pauline Kerr, and Paul Sharp. Los Angeles, CA: Sage, 2016.

Lennon, Alexander T. J., ed. *Contemporary Nuclear Debates: Missile Defense, Arms Control and Arms Races in the Twenty-First Century*. Cambridge, MA: MIT Press, 2002.

Levy, Jack S. "Alliance Formation and War Behavior: An Analysis of the Great Powers, 1495–1975." *Journal of Conflict Resolution* 25 (1981): 581–613.

———. "Domestic Politics and War." In *The Origin and Prevention of Major Wars*, edited by Robert I. Rotberg and Theodore K. Rabb, 79–100. New York: Cambridge University Press, 1989.

———. "The Offensive-Defensive Balance of Military Technology: A Theoretical and Historical Analysis." *International Studies Quarterly* 28 (June 1984): 219–38.

Levy, Jack S., and William F. Mabe, Jr. "Politically Motivated Opposition to War." *International Studies Review* 6 (March 2004): 65–83.

Low, Stephen. "The Zimbabwe Settlement, 1976–1979." In *International Mediation in Theory and Practice*, edited by Saadia Touval and I. William Zartman, 94–109. Boulder, CO: Westview, 1985.

MacFarquhar, Neil. "American Envoy to Hold Talks with Russians on Peace Deal for Ukraine." *New York Times*, 18 May 2015.

Marder, Arthur. *The Anatomy of British Sea Power: A History of British Naval Policy in the Pre-Dreadnought Era, 1880–1905*. New York: Knopf, 1940.

Mattingly, Garrett. *Renaissance Diplomacy*. New York: Penguin, 1964.

May, Ernest R. *American Imperialism: A Speculative Essay*. New York: Atheneum, 1968.

———. *Lessons of the Past: The Use and Misuse of History in American Foreign Policy*. New York: Oxford University Press, 1973.

May, Ernest R., John D. Steinbruner, and Thomas W. Wolfe. "History of the Strategic Arms Competition, 1945–1972." 2 vols. Unpublished study prepared for the Historical Office, Office of the Secretary of Defense, March 1981. Accessed from the U.S. Department of Defense FOIA Reading Room, July 1993.

Mayer, Arno J. *Dynamics of Counterrevolution in Europe, 1870–1956*. New York: Harper & Row, 1971.

———. *Politics and Diplomacy of Peacemaking: Containment and Counterrevolution at Versailles, 1918–1919*. New York: Knopf, 1967.

McGowan, Patrick J. "Coups and Conflict in West Africa." *Armed Forces & Society* 32 (October 2005): 5–23.

Mearsheimer, John J. "Disorder Restored." In *Rethinking America's Security*, edited by Graham Allison and Gregory F. Treverton, 213–37. New York: Norton, 1992.

———. *The Tragedy of Great Power Politics*. New York: Norton, 2001.

Mingst, Karen A., and Ivan M. Arreguín-Toft. *Essentials of International Relations*. 5th ed. New York: Norton, 2011.

Modelski, George. "A Study of Alliances: A Review." In *Alliance in International Politics*, edited by Julian R. Friedman, Christopher Bladen, and Steven Rosen, 63–73. Boston, MA: Allyn and Bacon, 1970.

Morgenthau, Hans J. *In Defense of the National Interest*. New York: Knopf, 1952.

———. *Politics among Nations*. 4th ed. New York: Knopf, 1967.

———. *Politics in the 20th Century*. Vol. 1, *The Decline of Democratic Politics*. Chicago: University of Chicago Press, 1962.

Morse, Edward. *Modernization and Transformation in International Relations*. New York: Free Press, 1976.

Mosely, Philip E. "Some Soviet Techniques of Negotiation." In *The Kremlin and World Politics*, by Philip E. Mosley, 3–41. New York: Vintage, 1960.

Moskowitz, Eric, and Jeffrey S. Lantis. "Conflict in the Balkans." In *Fateful Decisions: Inside the National Security Council*, edited by Karl F. Inderfurth and Loch K. Johnson, 253–67. New York: Oxford University Press, 2004.

Mueller, John. *War, Presidents, and Public Opinion.* New York: Wiley, 1973.

Napper, Larry C. "The African Terrain and U.S.-Soviet Conflict in Angola and Rhodesia: Some Implications for Crisis Prevention." In *Managing U.S.-Soviet Rivalry*, edited by Alexander L. George, 155–86. Boulder, CO: Westview, 1983.

Neustadt, Richard E. *Alliance Politics.* New York: Columbia University Press, 1970.

Neustadt, Richard, and Ernest R. May. *Thinking in Time: The Uses of History for Decision Makers.* New York: Free Press, 1986.

Nicholls, Natsuko H., Paul K. Huth, and Benjamin J. Appel. "When Is Domestic Political Unrest Related to International Conflict? Diversionary Theory and Japanese Foreign Policy, 1890–1941." *International Studies Quarterly* 46 (December 2010): 916–37.

Nicolson, Harold. *Curzon: The Last Phase, 1919–1925.* London: Constable, 1937.

———. *Diplomacy.* London: Harcourt Brace, 1939.

———. *Peacemaking: 1919.* New York: Grosset & Dunlap, 1965 [1933].

Nish, Ian. *The Origins of the Russo-Japanese War.* London: Longman, 1985.

O'Hanlon, Michael, and Mike Mochizuki. *Crisis on the Korean Peninsula.* New York: McGraw-Hill, 2003.

O'Neill, Robert, and David N. Schwartz, eds. *Hedley Bull on Arms Control.* New York: St. Martin's, 1987.

Ostrower, Alexander. *Language, Law, and Diplomacy: A Study of Linguistic Diversity in Official International Relations and International Law.* 2 vols. Philadelphia, PA: University of Pennsylvania Press, 1965.

Owen, David. *Balkan Odyssey.* New York: Harcourt Brace, 1995.

Page, Benjamin I., with Marshall Bouton. *The Foreign Policy Disconnect.* Chicago: University of Chicago Press, 2006.

Page, Benjamin I., and Jason Barabas. "Foreign Policy Gaps between Citizens and Leaders." *International Studies Quarterly* 44 (September 2000): 339–64.

Page, Benjamin I., and Robert Shapiro. "Effects of Public Opinion on Policy." *American Political Science Review* 77 (March 1983): 175–90.

———. *The Rational Public: Fifty Years of Trends in Americans' Policy Preferences.* Chicago: University of Chicago Press, 1992.

Paige, Glenn D. *The Korean Decision.* New York: Free Press, 1968.

Parker, Ian. "The Greek Warrior." *New Yorker*, 3 August 2015, 44–57.

Pearson, Frederic S., and J. Martin Rochester. *International Relations: The Global Condition in the Late Twentieth Century.* 3rd ed. New York: McGraw-Hill, 1992.

Perlmutter, Amos. "Crisis Management: Kissinger's Middle-East Negotiations (October 1973-June 1974)." *International Studies Quarterly* 19 (September 1974). Reprinted in *The Theory and Practice of International Relations*, edited by Fred A. Sondermann, David S. McLellan, and William C. Olson, 5th ed., 209–18. Englewood Cliffs, NJ: Prentice-Hall, 1979.

Peterson, Susan. *Crisis Bargaining and the State.* Ann Arbor: University of Michigan Press, 1999.

Pigman, Geoffrey A. "Debates about Contemporary and Future Diplomacy." In *Diplomacy in a Globalizing World*, ed. Pauline Kerr and Geoffrey Wiseman, 68–84. New York: Oxford University Press, 2013.

Pogue, Forrest C. "The Struggle for a New Order." In *The Meaning of Yalta*, edited by John L. Snell, 3–36. Baton Rouge: Louisiana State University Press, 1956.

Posen, Barry R. "The Security Dilemma and Ethnic Conflict." In *Ethnic Conflict and International Security*, edited by Michael E. Brown, 103–24. Princeton, NJ: Princeton University Press, 1993.

Princen, Thomas. *Intermediaries in International Conflict*. Princeton, NJ: Princeton University Press, 1992.

Pruitt, Dean G. "Strategy in Negotiation." In *International Negotiation: Analysis, Approaches, Issues*, edited by Victor A. Kremenyuk, 78–89. San Francisco, CA: Jossey-Bass, 1991.

Putnam, Robert D. "Diplomacy and Domestic Politics: The Logic of Two-Level Games." *International Organization* 42 (Summer 1988): 427–60.

Quandt, William B. *Peace Process*. 3rd ed. Washington, DC: Brookings Institution Press; and Berkeley, CA: University of California Press, 2005.

Rathbun, Brian C. *Diplomacy's Value*. Ithaca, NY: Cornell University Press, 2014.

Rosecrance, Richard N. "Diplomacy." In *International Encyclopedia of the Social Sciences*, vol. 4, edited by David L. Sills, 187–91. New York: Macmillan and Free Press, 1968.

Rosegrant, Susan, and Michael D. Watkins. "Getting to Dayton: Negotiating an End to the War in Bosnia." In *Perspectives on American Foreign Policy*, edited by Bruce W. Jentleson, 204–25. New York: Norton, 2000.

Rosenau, James N. "Comparative Foreign Policy: Fad, Fantasy, or Field?" In *The Scientific Study of Foreign Policy*, by James Rosenau, 67–94. New York: Free Press, 1971.

———. *Public Opinion and Foreign Policy: An Operational Formulation*. New York: Random House, 1961.

Rosenau, James N., and Mary Durfee. *Thinking Theory Thoroughly*. 2nd ed. Boulder, CO: Westview, 2001.

Rostow, W. W. *The Division of Europe after World War II: 1946*. Austin: University of Texas Press, 1981.

———. *The United States in the World Arena*. New York: Harper & Row, 1960.

Rothchild, Donald. "The United States and Africa: Power with Limited Influence." In *Eagle Rules? Foreign Policy and American Primacy in the Twenty-First Century*, edited by Robert J. Lieber, 214–40. Upper Saddle River, NJ: Prentice Hall, 2002.

———. "Successful Mediation: Lord Carrington and the Rhodesian Settlement." In *Managing Global Chaos*, edited by Chester A. Crocker, Fen Osler Hampson, and Pamela Aall, 475–86. Washington, DC: United States Institute of Peace Press, 2006.

Rourke, John T., and Mark A. Boyer. *International Politics on the World Stage, Brief*. 8th ed. New York: McGraw Hill, 2010.

Rusk, Dean. *As I Saw It*. Edited by Daniel S. Papp. New York: Penguin, 1990.

Russett, Bruce, and Harvey Starr. *World Politics: The Menu for Choice*. 5th ed. New York: W. H. Freeman, 1996.

Sagan, Scott D., ed. *Inside Nuclear South Asia*. Stanford, CA: Stanford University Press, 2009.

Saunders, Harold H. "Prenegotiation and Circum-negotiation: Arenas of the Peace Process." In *Managing Global Chaos*, edited by Chester A. Crocker, Fen Osler Hampson, and Pamela Aall, 419–32. Washington, DC: United States Institute of Peace Press, 2006.

———. "Regulating Soviet-U.S. Competition and Cooperation in the Arab-Israeli Arena,

1967–86." In *U.S.-Soviet Security Cooperation*, edited by Alexander L. George, Philip J. Farley, and Alexander Dallin, 540–80. New York: Oxford University Press, 1988.

Saunders, Harold H., and Cecilia Albin. *Sinai II: The Politics of International Mediation.* Pew Case Studies in International Affairs, no. 421. Washington, DC: Institute for the Study of Diplomacy, Georgetown University, 1991.

Sawyer, Jack, and Harold Guetzkow. "Bargaining and Negotiation in International Relations." In *International Behavior: A Social-Psychological Analysis*, edited by Herbert C. Kelman, 464–520. New York: Holt, Rinehart and Winston, 1965.

Schelling, Thomas C. *Arms and Influence*. New Haven, CT: Yale University Press, 1966.

———. *The Strategy of Conflict*. Cambridge, MA: Harvard University Press, 1960.

Schelling, Thomas C., and Morton A. Halperin. *Strategy and Arms Control*. New York: Twentieth Century Fund, 1961.

Schoenbaum, David. "The World War II Allied Agreement on Occupation and Administration." In *U.S.-Soviet Security Cooperation*, edited by Alexander L. George, Philip J. Farley, and Alexander Dallin, 21–45. New York: Oxford University Press, 1988.

Schwartz, William A., and Charles Derber. "Arms Control: Misplaced Focus." *Bulletin of the Atomic Scientists* 62 (March 1986): 39–44.

Sciolino, Elaine. "Records Dispute Kissinger on His '71 Visit to China." *New York Times*, 28 February 2002.

Sengupta, Somini. "Dispute over Opposition's Seat at Table Threatens to Push Back Syria Peace Talks." *New York Times*, 19 January 2016.

Sharp, Paul. "Diplomacy in International Relations Theory and Other Disciplinary Perspectives." In *Diplomacy in a Globalizing World*, edited by Pauline Kerr and Geoffrey Wiseman, 51–67. New York: Oxford University Press, 2013.

———. *Diplomatic Theory of International Relations*. Cambridge: Cambridge University Press, 2009.

———. "Practitioners, Scholars and the Study of Diplomacy." *Foreign Service Journal*, January/February 2015, 39–41.

Sheehan, Edward R. F. "Step by Step in the Middle East." *Foreign Policy*, no. 22 (Spring 1976): 3–70.

Sigal, Leon V. *Disarming Strangers*. Princeton, NJ: Princeton University Press, 1998.

Simpson, Smith, ed. *Instruction in Diplomacy: The Liberal Arts Approach*. Philadelphia, PA: American Academy of Political and Social Science, 1972.

Slaughter, Anne-Marie. "The Real New World Order." *Foreign Affairs* 75 (September/ October 1997): 183–97.

Smith, Alastair. "Alliance Formation and War." *International Studies Quarterly* 39 (December 1995): 405–25.

Smith, Gerard. *Doubletalk*. Lanham, MD: University Press of America, 1985.

Snyder, Glenn, and Paul Diesing. *Conflict among Nations*. Princeton, NJ: Princeton University Press, 1977.

Sofer, Sasson, "Debate Revisited: Practice over Theory?" *Review of international Studies* 14 (July 1988): 195–208.

Spanier, John J., and Joseph L. Nogee. *The Politics of Disarmament*. New York: Praeger, 1962.

Spanier, John L., and Eric M. Uslaner. *American Foreign Policy Making and the Democratic Dilemmas*. 6th ed. New York: Macmillan, 1994.

———. *How American Foreign Policy Is Made*. New York: Praeger, 1974.

Sofer, Sasson. "Debate Persisted: Practice Over Theory?" *Review of International Studies* 14 (July 1988): 195–208.

Sprout, Harold, and Margaret Sprout. *The Ecological Perspective on Human Affairs*. Princeton, NJ: Princeton University Press, 1965.

———. *Toward a Politics of the Planet Earth*. New York: Van Nostrand Reinhold, 1971.

Stedman, Stephen John. *The Lancaster House Constitutional Conference on Rhodesia*. Pew Case Study in International Affairs, no. 341. Washington, DC: Institute for the Study of Diplomacy, Georgetown University, 1993.

———. *Peacemaking in Civil War: International Mediation in Zimbabwe, 1974–1980*. Boulder, CO: Lynne Rienner, 1991.

Steiner, Barry H. *Arms Races, Diplomacy, and Recurring Behavior: Lessons from Two Cases*. Sage Professional Paper in International Studies 02–013. Beverly Hills, CA: Sage, 1973.

———. *Collective Preventive Diplomacy*. Albany, NY: State University of New York Press, 2004.

———. "Diplomacy and International Theory." *Review of International Studies* 30 (2004): 493–509.

———. "Diplomacy as Independent and Dependent Variable." *International Negotiation* 6 (2001): 79–104.

———. "When Images and Alarm Collide: The Significance of Information Disparity." *International Journal of Intelligence and CounterIntelligence* 28 (2015): 319–46.

Stern, Sheldon M. *The Week the World Stood Still*. Stanford, CA: Stanford University Press, 2005.

"Symposium: Methodological Foundations of the Study of International Conflict." Special issue of *International Studies Quarterly* 29 (June 1985): 119–54.

Taylor, A. J. P. *English History: 1914–1945*. New York: Oxford University Press, 1965.

———. *Europe: Grandeur and Decline*. Harmondsworth, UK: Penguin, 1967.

———. *The Origins of the Second World War*. New York: Atheneum, 1985.

———. *The Struggle for Mastery in Europe: 1848–1918*. Oxford: Clarendon, 1957.

Tetlock, Philip, and Aaron Belkin. *Counterfactual Thought Experiments in World Politics*. Princeton, NJ: Princeton University Press, 1996.

Tertrais, Bruno. "Do Arms Races Matter?" In *Contemporary Nuclear Debates: Missile Defense, Arms Control and Arms Races in the Twenty-First Century*, edited by Alexander T. J. Lennon, 213–25. Cambridge, MA: MIT Press, 2002.

Thornberry, Cedric. "Namibia." In *The UN Security Council*, edited by David M. Malone, 407–22. Boulder, CO: Lynne Rienner, 2004.

Thornton, Thomas P. "The Indo-Pakistani Conflict: Soviet Mediation at Tashkent, 1966." In *International Mediation in Theory and Practice*, edited by Saadia Touval and I. William Zartman, 141–65. Boulder, CO: Westview, 1985.

Thornton, Thomas P., and Maxim Bratersky. "India and Pakistan: The Roots of Conflict." In *Cooperative Security*, edited by I. William Zartman and Victor A. Kremenyuk, 179–203. Syracuse, NY: Syracuse University Press, 1995.

Touval, Saadia, and I. William Zartman, eds. *International Mediation in Theory and Practice*. Boulder, CO: Westview, 1985.

Trask, David A. *The War with Spain in 1898*. New York: Macmillan, 1981.

Traxel, David. *1898: The Birth of the American Century*. New York: Knopf, 1998.

Van Alstyne, Richard W. *American Diplomacy in Action*. Rev. ed. Stanford, CA: Stanford University Press, 1947.

Varg, Paul A. *Foreign Policies of the Founding Fathers*. Baltimore, MD: Penguin, 1970.

Varoufakis, Yanis. *Adults in the Room: My Battle with the European and American Deep Establishment*. New York: Farrar, Straus and Giroux, 2017.

Waever, Ole. "Insecurity, Security, and Asecurity in the West European Non-war Community." In *Security Communities*, edited by Emanuel Adler and Michael Barnett, 69–118. Cambridge: Cambridge University Press, 1998.

Waltz, Kenneth N. *Foreign Policy and Democratic Politics: The American and British Experience*. London: Longmans, 1968.

———. *Theory of International Politics*. Reading, MA: Addison-Wesley, 1979.

Watson, Adam. *Diplomacy*. Philadelphia, PA: ISHI Publications, 1986.

Weber, Steve. *Cooperation and Discord in US-Soviet Arms Control*. Princeton, NJ: Princeton University Press, 1991.

Whelan, Joseph G. *Soviet Diplomacy and Negotiating Behavior: Emerging New Context for U.S. Diplomacy*, vol. 1. Prepared for the Committee on Foreign Affairs, U.S. House of Representatives, House Document 96–238. Washington, DC: U.S. Government Printing Office, 1978.

White, John Albert. *The Diplomacy of the Russo-Japanese War*. Princeton, NJ: Princeton University Press, 1964.

Wight, Martin. *International Theory*. Edited by Gabriele Wight and Brian Porter. New York: Holmes & Meier, 1991.

———. *Power Politics*. Edited by Hedley Bull and Carsten Holbraad. New York: Holmes & Meier, 1978.

———. "Why Is There No International Theory?" In *Diplomatic Investigations*, edited by Herbert Butterfield and Martin Wight, 17–34. London: George Allen & Unwin, 1969.

Wit, Joel S., Daniel B. Poneman, and Robert L. Gallucci. *Going Critical*. Washington, DC: Brookings Institution Press, 2004.

Wolfers, Arnold. "The Actors in International Politics." In *Discord and Collaboration*, by Arnold Wolfers, 3–24. Baltimore: Johns Hopkins University Press, 1962.

Wohlstetter, Albert. "Is There a Strategic Arms Race?" *Foreign Policy*, no. 15 (Summer 1974): 3–20.

———. "Rivals but No Race." *Foreign Policy*, no. 16 (Fall 1974): 57–81.

Wohlstetter, Albert, and Roberta Wohlstetter. "Controlling the Risks in Cuba." *Adelphi Paper*, no. 17. London: Institute of Strategic Studies, April 1965.

Woodward, E. L. "The Old and the New Diplomacy." *Yale Review* 36 (Spring 1947): 405–22.

Wriggins, Howard. "Up for Auction: Malta Bargains with Great Britain, 1971." In *The 50% Solution*, edited by I. William Zartman, 208–34. New York: Anchor, 1976.

Wright, Quincy. *A Study of War*. Chicago: University of Chicago Press, 1965 [1942].

Yardley, Jim. "Pushing for a Place at Europe's Power Table." *New York Times*, 29 January 2016.

Zartman, I. William. "Alternative Attempts at Crisis Management: Concept and Processes." In *New Issues in International Crisis Management*, edited by Gilbert Winham, 199–223. Boulder, CO: Westview, 1998.

———. "The Analysis of Negotiation." In *The 50% Solution*, edited by I. William Zartman, 1–41. New York: Anchor, 1976.

———. *Cowardly Lions*. Boulder, CO: Lynne Rienner, 2005.

———. "Dynamics and Constraints in Negotiations in Internal Conflicts." In *Elusive Peace*, edited by I. William Zartman, 3–29. Washington: Brookings Institution Press, 1995.

———, ed. *The 50% Solution*. New York: Anchor, 1976.

———. "Negotiations and Prenegotiations in Ethnic Conflict: The Beginning, The Middle, and the Ends." In *Conflict and Peacemaking in Multiethnic Societies*, edited by Joseph V. Montville, 511–34. New York: Lexington, 1991.

———. "The Political Analysis of Negotiation: How Who Gets What and When." *World Politics* 26 (April 1974): 385–99.

———. *Ripe for Resolution*. New York: Oxford University Press, 1985.

———. "Ripeness: The Hurting Stalemate and Beyond." In *International Conflict Resolution After the Cold War*, edited by Paul C. Stern and Daniel Druckman, 225–50. Washington, DC: National Academy Press, 2000.

———. "The Structure of Negotiation." In *International Negotiation: Analysis, Approaches, Issues*, edited by Victor A. Kremenyuk, 65–77. San Francisco, CA: Jossey-Bass, 1991.

Zartman, I. William, and Maureen R. Berman. *The Practical Negotiator*. New Haven: Yale University Press, 1982.

Zartman, I. William, and Jeffrey Z. Rubin, eds. *Power and Negotiation*. Ann Arbor: University of Michigan Press, 2000.

Index

Page numbers in *italic* indicate tables.

247

CSCE. *See* Commission on Security and Cooperation in Europe
Cuban missile crisis, 29–30, 62, 65n29, 107–8, 111, 122n51, 122n54, 179

Danto, Arthur, 101
Danzig negotiations. See German-Polish relations (1939)
Declaration of Liberation in Europe, at Yalta, 81, 88, 97n59; Leahy on ambiguity of, 97n60; Leffler on, 97n56, 97n59;
deductive theory, 4, 14–16, 215, 218
defection: alliance-building and, 13; in Anglo-French arms competition (1840–1866), 60–61; in Anglo-French relations (1750s), 60; from commitments and norms, communication and, 22n64, 53–54, 62; communication influence on, 59–60, 62; in German-Polish relations (1939), 60; liberal internationalists on, 54; in Libya (2011–2014), 59–60; realists on, 54; in Soviet-American relations (1952), 60
democratic peace theory, 211n12
dependent diplomacy, 23–24, 26, 40; as conflict management, 99–123; in Galtung peace approach, 28–29, 31; security community and, 36–37, 39. See also diplomacy as effect
dependent variable, 114; for arms control, 170–73; diplomacy as, 99–123; diplomatic statecraft as, 23, 24; operational results as, 110–13. See also dependent diplomacy
de Tocqueville, Alexis, 205
Deutsch, Karl, 24, 32
Diesing, Paul, 122n69
diplomacy: affected by political change, 8; Nicolson definition of, 20n21; Rosecrance definition of, 229n8; texts, 7–9; Watson definition of, 170
diplomatic action, 106; nonvital interests and, 108–9; vital interests and, 107–8
diplomacy as effect, 105–9 194–214, 216, 217, 223–24; operational milieu, 110–12. *See also* dependent diplomacy

diplomatic process: Bull on absence of, 65n26; convergent interests simplify, 72; for France-Russia (1894), 73; for United States-China (1969), 74–75; Schelling on, 50, 65n26. *See also* applied diplomacy
diplomatic revolution: Craig and George on, 106, 111.
diplomatic safety net, 50–51
diplomatic statecraft, 11, 27, 217, 219–20; bilateral practice and, 30; Burke on, 17; as dependent variable, 23, 24; domestic public opinion and, 18; as independent variable, 23; peace weakened by, 30; as war tool, 13, 29
diplomatic strategy, 25, 40; of Galtung peace approach, 29–31, 31; policy objectives link with, 11–14; of security community, 37–39, 39. *See also* contestation; negotiation
diplomatic study, 5–9
diplomatic viewpoint, 17, 23–24, 40; Galtung peace approach, 25–31; security communities, 31–39
Dobrynin, Anatoly, 107, 108
Durfee, Mary, 120n4; on theory, 100, 215, 218

Economic Community of West African States (ECOWAS), 116
Eisenhower, Dwight D., 83
ethnic conflict, 27; in Yugoslavia, 113–16
European Union (EU), 139

Fisher, Roger, 89, 100
focused comparison method, 19n16; 224; communication and, 17; disciplined figurative studies, 229; of George, 16; George and Bennett on, 224–26, 230n36; heuristic study, 226; use for inductive theory, 16–17; plausibility probes of, 228–29; theory testing, 226–28; use to probe cause-and-effect, 100
force equivalence, in arms control, 163,

(2015); Pakistan-India nuclear competition; Soviet-American nuclear
competition; United States-North Korea
nuclear competition
Nye, Joseph E., 75

Obama, Barack, 10, 35, 123n89, 213n42
offensive weapons, 190n30
"old" diplomacy, 9, 10
operational milieu: source of dependent
variable, 110–3; Sprout, H., and Sprout,
M., on, 106.
opportunity, Zartman on, 104, 112–18
oppositional pressures: Levy and Mabe on,
199, 209; Mayer on, 199–200; from
public opinion, 196, 202–3; questions
for, *204*
oppositional public opinion, 194, 198,
212n14, 213n44; as independent
variable, 196; political realism on, 195,
197
Organization for Security and Cooperation
in Europe (OSCE), 32, 36–38
Oslo Accords, 26; negative peace and,
28–29
Owen, David, 115

Pakistan-India nuclear competition (1974
to the present), 185–87
Pakistan-India (1964–1965): Soviet mediation, 133–35
paradigm pluralism, 23, 219
Patriotic Front: in Rhodesia, 136, 149
PD. *See* preventive diplomacy; prisoners'
dilemma
peace: through accommodation,
Morgenthau on, 1; action, dialogue and,
26; democratic peace theory, 211n12;
as diplomatic objective, 6, 8, 11, 12, 49;
praxis, 26; from social solidarity, 24;
strategy, diplomacy texts on, 7; theory,
26. *See also* Galtung peace approach;
negative peace; positive peace
Pearson, Frederic, 68
people-factor diplomatic conduct, 10

Poland, 56; Yalta conference on, 82, 88.
See also German-Polish relations
policy: elites, 34–35; failures, Craig and
George on, 110
policy improvement theory, 100
policy success: cause and, 101, 104–5,
105, 222–23; Wight on, 104
political change, diplomacy and, 8
political leadership, security community
role of, 32
political realism, 6, 21n51, 217; bargaining
and, 75–76, *78*, 90–91; on British
government and public opinion, 201–2;
on cause-and-effect, 99–100; communication and, 48–49, *52*, 61, 63, 218;
contestation and, 75–76; crisis
management and, 61; of Morgenthau,
11, 219; on defection, 54; on diplomatic
constraints, 106; on oppositional public
opinion, 195, 197
Posen, Barry, 59
positive images, in France-Russia (1894),
73
positive peace: in Galtung peace approach,
26; independent of state involvement,
28
positivism, 15
power: effectiveness brought about by
diplomacy, 6; major states' use of, 28.
preventive diplomacy (PD), of US, 112–18
prisoners' dilemma (PD) metaphor, 46, 54;
in Libya (2011–2014), 59–60
protean diplomatic experience, Nicolson
on, 2–4, 25
public diplomacy, 6
public opinion, 223; in American Entry
into the Spanish American War (1897–
1898), 203, 206; as constraint and
pressure, 194–214; Craig and George
on, 197, 201, 211n6, 212n34; diplomatic statecraft and, 18; in The Genêt
Affair (1793), 203, 204–5, 208; in
Great Britain, 197–98, 201–2; impact
of, 25, 121n41, 196; in Italy and
postwar peacemaking (1918), 203,
206–7; in Jay Treaty approval (1793–

About the Author

Barry H. Steiner is professor emeritus of political science at California State University, Long Beach (CSULB), specializing in war and peace studies. He was a member of the teaching faculty of the CSULB political science department from 1968 until his retirement in 2017. He published an intellectual history about a pioneer nuclear strategist, *Bernard Brodie and the Foundations of American Nuclear Strategy* (1991) and subsequently, supported by a grant from the United States Institute of Peace, completed a monograph, *Collective Preventive Diplomacy: A Study of International Conflict Management* (2004). He has also published articles on arms racing and arms control, diplomacy, Israel-Palestine conflict, and national intelligence estimation. His latest book-length study, advocating inductive, focused case comparisons to generate diplomatic theory, reports on a project begun in 1988.

Professor Steiner lives in Los Angeles with his wife JoAnn Victor. They have twin children, Mitzi and Benjamin.